Quick Guide to
CAREER TRAINING
IN TWO YEARS
OR LESS

Laurence Shatkin, Ph.D.

jist
Works

Quick Guide to Career Training in Two Years or Less

© 2004 by JIST Publishing, Inc.

Published by JIST Works, an imprint of JIST Publishing, Inc.
8902 Otis Avenue
Indianapolis, IN 46216-1033
Phone: 1-800-648-JIST   Fax: 1-800-JIST-FAX   E-mail: info@jist.com

---

Visit our Web site at www.jist.com for information on JIST, free job search information, book excerpts, and ordering information on our many products. For free information on 14,000 job titles, visit www.careeroink.com.

Quantity discounts are available for JIST books. Please call our Sales Department at 1-800-648-5478 for a free catalog and more information.

Acquisitions and Development Editor: Lori Cates Hand
Associate Development Editor: Stephanie Koutek
Proofreader: Dave Faust
Interior and Cover Designer: Aleata Howard
Page Layout: Carolyn Newland and Trudy Coler
Indexer: Tina Trettin

Printed in Canada
08 07 06 05 04 03   9 8 7 6 5 4 3 2 1

Library of Congress Cataloging-in-Publication data is on file with the Library of Congress.

ISBN 1-56370-981-3

Why You're Going to Love This Book

Every day, thousands of people enter interesting and rewarding careers *without* having completed four years of college. If you're looking at this book, you probably are thinking about doing the same. Perhaps you will eventually obtain a four-year degree, but for now you want to spend two years or less in education or training before entering the work force. That can be a very good strategy for starting a career.

But one consequence of this strategy is that you can no longer postpone the task of targeting a career goal. Most programs requiring two years or less are very career-oriented, so choosing a program is essentially the same thing as choosing the career you intend to enter.

The reason this book is so special is that it lets you choose an educational/training program and a career goal *simultaneously* instead of considering just one or the other. It links 104 programs to 358 careers. It informs you about what the careers are like and tells you about what you study in the program. It tells you which careers are commonly associated with the program and the amount of education or training that is usually required for each of these careers.

So the choice is yours: You can sign up for an expensive battery of personality tests and counseling sessions; you can dig through piles of school catalogs and apprenticeship brochures, examining and comparing the requirements for the programs; you can search through massive databases of career information, taking pains to determine the skill requirements and the income you can expect; or you can use this book to obtain self-understanding and get concise and authoritative facts about educational/training programs that might suit you.

If the choice is not obvious already, turn to Part I and start the exercises. You'll be surprised by how quickly you'll start seeing the connections between who you are and where you want to go.

Dedication

Dedicated to Eva Shatkin, whose lifelong love of learning continues to inspire her family and everyone else who knows her.

Acknowledgments

Several thoughtful and resourceful people helped me bring this book to completion, and I thank them for their contributions:

Michael Farr set the tone for this and all the publications at JIST by showing that it is possible to balance theory and real life.

Beverly Murray Scherf helped shape the *Quick Guide to College Majors and Careers,* which served as a model for this book.

Lori Cates Hand and Stephanie Koutek kept me on schedule and provided important editorial suggestions.

Nancy Decker Shatkin, now in her fourth or fifth career, reminds me to balance career with the rest of life.

Contents

Introduction: How to Use This Book

This section shows you how to use this book for your specific needs. First, it explains who will benefit most from reading the book. Then it details the different elements of Parts I and II. Next, it describes how you can get the most out of the book depending on your needs. Sections on how to choose a training program, how various types of programs differ in their focus, and where the information in this book comes from are at the end of the Introduction.

Who Really Needs This Book?

Lots of people need to make decisions about training for careers. Read over the following list to see where you fit in:

- **Young people choosing an educational/training program or career who don't have a clear idea which program or career might be best for them.** This book can help you look at yourself and see what programs or careers might be good choices for you. For example, you may be a high school student trying to decide what to do after graduation. Your choice may depend partly on your intended career and its possible training programs. This book can help you narrow your choices by getting you interested in some specific careers and programs. It can also broaden your choices by informing you about certain programs and careers that are new to you.

- **Young people who are exploring their options:** whether to go to college, go to a trade school, sign up for an apprenticeship, or join the military. This book may get you excited about certain career paths and help make the decision easier.

- **Young people who have a program in mind but are not yet certain about it.** You can get facts that will help you make up your mind and start planning. For example, you may be interested in a certain program at your local community college but may still be unsure about the careers it might lead to. This book may suggest programs and careers that you haven't considered before or it may give you concrete facts to help you evaluate programs that you already have in mind.

- **Midlife career changers.** You can find ways to use your accumulated skills and experience in a new career. For example, perhaps you're considering taking night classes and you want to find a program that can help advance your career. This book gives you dollar figures about careers and useful information about coursework in programs.

- **People who already have a degree** and want to (or need to) change careers while still taking advantage of their educational/training credentials. You don't have to let yourself be boxed in by traditional connections between programs and careers. With the information about skills and work groups in this book, you may explore non-traditional career pathways that you have not previously considered.

- **People who are making the transition from education/training to a career.** You can see which careers might make good use of what you've learned. For example, perhaps you'll soon be leaving the Armed Forces, and you're wondering how you might use the training you've acquired. Be sure to look at the career suggestions in this book and think about using the information about skills when you start preparing your resume.

- **People who are applying for jobs.** You can get ideas for your resume, cover letter, or job interviews. For example, you can review the Career Snapshots in the book so that you can use appropriate job-related terms when you write your cover letter and resume.

- **Professionals who help people make decisions about programs and careers.** You can help them clarify their priorities, explore options, and plan their next steps. For example, maybe you're a guidance counselor, academic advisor, or librarian and you need to help other people make these decisions. You can see from the bulleted items above that this book can help a broad variety of people.

What's in This Book?

This book is set up so that you can find information quickly in a variety of ways. Look at the Table of Contents and you'll see that the book is divided into two main parts. Part I asks "What Programs and Careers Might Suit You?" Each section in it offers an exercise to help you assemble a Hot List of programs to explore in Part II. Part II offers "Facts About Training Programs and Careers," and it lists the 104 programs alphabetically.

Here are the kinds of information you'll find for each program in Part II:

- **Career Snapshot:** A one-paragraph definition of the subject and an explanation of what sorts of careers (and additional education) graduates typically go into.

- **Related Specialties and Careers:** This is a list of areas of concentration that people in this field pursue, both in college or training and later, in jobs. Depending on your interests, you could go in many different directions.

- **Related Job Titles, Educational/Training Requirements, Projected Growth, and Earnings:** Here you get very specific facts about the jobs that the program most frequently leads to. You see what kind of education or training is most commonly required; whether the job openings are growing, shrinking, or holding steady; and what the average income is. There's also a code number for each job (for an explanation of this code, see the paragraph on the next page about "Other Information Sources").

- **Typical Postsecondary Courses:** This is a list of the courses that are often required for this program. Naturally, each educational or training institution has its own set of requirements, but this is a general look at what to expect.

- **Suggested High School Courses:** If you're still in high school, this list can recommend coursework that would be good preparation. If you're beyond high school, you can see whether you have an appropriate background. If your school offers school-to-work programs based on U.S. Department of Education clusters, you'll want to see which cluster is identified here.

- **Essential Knowledge and Skills:** These are the skills that are most important for the careers related to this program. Keep in mind that while you are in a program, it requires a somewhat different set of skills for doing research, completing projects, and so on.

- **Values/Work Environment:** Here you can see some of the rewards of being in the related jobs—such as creativity, achievement, or recognition. You'll also see whether the work will have you mainly sitting, standing, working outdoors, and so on.

- **Other Information Sources:** Here each program is linked to a program in the Classification of Instructional Programs (CIP), a naming scheme used by the U.S. Department of Education. You can get additional information about any CIP program on the Web at ftp://ftp.xwalkcenter.org/download/cip2000/. For each program, you'll also see one or more GOE Work Group codes that show a related family of jobs. You can learn more about these work groups in JIST's *Guide for Occupational Exploration*, Third Edition.

  The O*NET occupation names listed under "Related Job Titles, Projected Growth, and Earnings" can lead you to resources with detailed information about each job—for example, JIST's *O*NET Dictionary of Occupational Titles,* Second Edition.

You can use the index to look up occupations and find the related programs in Part II. See JIST's Web site for crosswalks between all the programs and their CIP code numbers and between all the programs and related O*NET occupations (www.jist.com/excerpt/J9813A.pdf).

How You Can Benefit from This Book

This isn't the only book about careers or educational/training programs, but it is specially designed to knit the two tightly together so you can decide about both at the same time. You can benefit from these special features:

- Do the quick exercises in Part I to help you zero in on what is most important to you in a program and a career. Tables that accompany the exercises will help you assemble a "Hot List" of programs that may offer what you want.

- Browse the book for quick and effective information. This is easy because the description of each program begins with a "Career Snapshot" that quickly defines the program and explains its relationship to various career tracks.

- Use the Introduction for suggestions on how to follow the link from a career to a program and then to a different career.

- Also, use the Introduction to clarify your understanding of the various educational/training options—for example, what an apprenticeship is and how a trade school differs from a technical college.

- See specific and up-to-date career facts derived from the U.S. Department of Labor's databases.

- Easily compare majors and careers with the consistent naming scheme used for work-related skills, values, and environments (derived from the Department of Labor's databases).

How to Make This Book Work for You

Different people will use this book differently. The following section explains how you can use this book to serve several different functions, depending on your particular needs:

- **Use it as a complete guide.** Starting with Part I, work your way through the exercises and assemble your Hot List of programs. Then move into Part II to explore the programs and annotate your Hot List with notes about the related careers. This method is particularly useful for people who are undecided and like to do things in an orderly way. Or you can merely do one or two exercises to quickly generate programs to investigate.

- **Use it as an evaluation tool.** Go directly to Part II to review a program and its related careers. Take note of the required courses and skills, the value rewards, and the work environment. Then you may want to do some or all of the exercises in Part I to see if your choice is a good fit for your personality. Or create a Hot List for a more thorough evaluation; then compare your tentative choice to other programs on that list. This method is particularly useful to those who are decided but not 100-percent committed to a program.

- **Use it as a skill identifier.** Use the index to locate a program you have already taken or one that corresponds to your career. If it is not there, use the "Your Interests" exercise in Part I to find the appropriate work group for your career and then go to the programs listed in Part II to find the closest equivalent(s) to your experience. Jot down the skill requirements for the program(s). Then use the "Your Skills" exercise to find programs and careers that use those skills. This method is particularly useful for people who want to make a career change.

- **Use it as a program-career linker.** Jump directly to Part II and consult the "Related Job Titles" tables to see which careers are associated with specific programs.

If you really want to open up your thinking, make a note of the GOE codes (work groups) listed in the "Other Information Sources" box and then go to the "Your Interests" exercise in Part I to see what other programs are associated with that work group. Then see what careers are linked to those programs. This method is particularly useful for those who want to see what careers "use" a program that they have already completed (or will soon complete).

- **Use it as a resume stimulus.** Go to Part II and look at the program you have completed (or will soon complete) and make note of the skills listed for the related careers. If you have these skills, use those terms on your resume or in cover letters and job interviews. Also, look at the "Related Specialties and Careers" and "Typical Postsecondary Courses" sections. This method is most useful for those who are looking for a job.

How Do I Choose Where and How to Get Education/Training?

The programs that are included in this book are offered to students and/or trainees in a variety of formats (which are defined in the next section, "How Do the Various Educational/Training Formats Differ?"). For example, you may study Food Service Management in a career-oriented program at a trade school, in an associate's degree program at a community college, in a certification or diploma program at a technical college, in the Armed Forces, in an apprenticeship, or through informal on-the-job training at a work site. Which option you choose may depend on a number of factors:

- **What's available to you locally.** Not all of these options may be easily accessible to you geographically.

- **What's affordable to you.** Some of these options involve tuition costs, whereas others pay you for work you do as you learn.

- **What you qualify for.** Some of these educational/training programs— including the Armed Forces—have minimal requirements that you must meet before you are admitted.

- **Which learning style you prefer.** Some people learn better in a classroom environment, whereas others learn better in a setting where they can get their hands on the work. Keep in mind that since most of the programs in this book are very career-oriented, most of them involve a good amount of hands-on work no matter what setting they are taught in.

- **What employers prefer.** Rightly or wrongly, some employers prefer hiring people who have been educated or trained in a particular format—even at a particular institution. Understandably, this should be a major consideration when you choose how to prepare, and a little research before you choose can have a big payoff later.

- **What the occupation requires.** In some occupations, it is difficult to find work unless you are certified or licensed. A professional organization or licensing agency may set certain requirements for coursework or supervised work experience, and therefore you may need to check that any educational or training program you sign up for gives you good preparation to meet those requirements.

- **Your long-range plans.** If you plan to get an academic degree eventually but want to get some other form of education or training now, you may want to select a program that grants credit that you can transfer to an academic program later. Keep in mind that some colleges and universities grant academic credit for learning that has been acquired in non-academic settings, but not all do, and you may have to prove your knowledge by taking an exam or submitting a portfolio of your work for evaluation.

Don't be discouraged by this long list of considerations. In Part II of this book, the "Career Snapshot" for each program indicates when employers' preferences or certification/licensing are especially important.

How Do the Various Educational/Training Formats Differ?

You may be somewhat confused about exactly what an apprenticeship is or how a certification program differs from a diploma program. Here are some of the terms most commonly used for the formats of educational/training programs:

- **Apprenticeship: A structured program in which trainees learn necessary work skills from fully qualified workers** (who are called "journeyworkers" or "journeymen"—the latter term sometimes is applied to both men and women). Apprenticeships are often created by unions or large employers.

An apprenticeship that is registered with a state or federal agency is more likely to be recognized by multiple employers than one that is not. Apprentices usually must complete a certain amount of classroom learning in addition to on-the-job learning and may require three or four years of training before being recognized as journeyworkers. Apprentices earn while they learn, often being paid a certain fraction of a journeyworker's wages that increases over time. Apprentices are not just helpers or observers; they do a variety of meaningful, challenging tasks so that they will learn all aspects of the job. Admission to an apprenticeship program may be competitive and may require meeting certain age and/or physical requirements.

- **Workplace-based training: Training that is offered at a place of work.** (This is sometimes called on-the-job training.) The term covers a wide variety of formats, from formal apprenticeships to informal arrangements. Some employers offer formal courses or set aside time for workers to learn new skills, whereas others expect employees to devise their own methods of learning. Some training that is called "workplace-based" is done on company time but actually takes place away from the worksite at a community college or other training facility, perhaps even in another city. The truth is that no matter what education or training you have acquired, when you start a new job you will learn a large percentage of the skills on the job. This is partly because each workplace is unique and partly because jobs are constantly evolving, especially with new technology, so there are always new skills that must be learned.

- **Associate degree: An academic degree earned for a program that typically is the equivalent of two (sometimes three) years of full-time study.** It is most commonly earned at a community college, although some other kinds of institutions offer it. Career-oriented associate degree programs usually include supervised work experience at a real worksite. But even if a degree program is very career-oriented, it includes some "general education" requirements in subjects such as public speaking, mathematics, sciences, social/behavioral studies, or humanities. These subjects help you become a well-rounded person, and they also will be important if at a later time you decide to enter a bachelor's degree program. Keep in mind that not every institution that calls itself a "college"—or even a "university"—is officially accredited and can give you credits that will be transferable to a four-year college. If the institution grants a degree, its bulletin should indicate how the institution is accredited.

- **Diploma: Most commonly, an academic award earned for a program that is less comprehensive than an associate degree program,** although it may include some general education courses and may take as much as two years to complete. A diploma program usually has curriculum that is designed to meet entry requirements for an occupation, although it would be wise to check with local employers to confirm that they value the diploma. Some diploma programs are targeted at students who have prior postsecondary course work or even a prior degree.

- **Certification: A formal acknowledgement that someone meets the standards of knowledge and skill that are required by a specific occupation.** The standards for certification are usually set by a professional organization and may exceed the requirements for licensure (in occupations for which a license is mandated by law). A certification program is designed to match the curriculum requirements that the professional organization has set for coursework and work experience. Graduates of the program often have to pass a certification exam at the end, but they can expect to be well prepared for the exam if they have a reasonable record of achievement in the program.

- **Trade school (or career school): An institution, usually privately owned (hence sometimes called a "proprietary school"), that specializes in training students for a specific occupation or group of occupations.** Examples are schools that teach truck driving, bartending, cosmetology, court reporting, winemaking, and taxidermy. Trade schools often offer both stand-alone courses and diploma programs.

- **Community college: A public educational/training institution that serves a city or county.** Usually the highest degree it grants is an associate degree, but it also offers diploma and certification programs, as well as a variety of stand-alone courses. Its most important roles usually are to provide a trained work force for local industry and a low-cost way for local citizens to complete the first two years of college, but it may also offer enrichment courses unrelated to work or to degrees.

- **Technical college: A public educational/training institution that is similar to a community college, but it may be affiliated with state rather than with local government, and it focuses more on career-related curricula.** Its programs (diploma, certification, and associate degree) are more likely to lead directly to jobs than serve as the first half of a four-year program completed elsewhere, and it is less likely to offer enrichment courses. Nevertheless, in some states there is little or no distinction between community and technical colleges.

- **Armed Forces training: Training that is acquired while serving in the military.** People sometimes forget that the Armed Forces are one of our biggest educational institutions and teach skills that are relevant to many fields of work: technology, management, health care, and transportation, to name just a few. Armed Forces training is occasionally more narrowly focused than equivalent programs taught elsewhere, but often it is accepted as equivalent to other formats of classroom and on-the-job training.

Where Does This Information Come From?

The information in this book comes from the best and most current sources available. The U.S. Department of Labor (DOL) is the nation's number-one source of information about careers. For valuable facts about the skills, values, satisfactions, and working environments of careers, the *Quick Guide to Career Training in Two Years or Less* draws on the DOL's O*NET database. The information about whether job openings in a career are growing, shrinking, or holding steady is from the DOL's Office of Employment Projections. The information regarding the average earnings in the careers is from another office of the DOL, Occupational Employment Statistics. Finally, much of the information about career paths and opportunities is from the DOL's best-selling *Occupational Outlook Handbook,* published by JIST. Taken together, these facts will give you a good introduction to the wide range of careers linked to the programs in this book.

Some information can be acquired only from research in actual catalogs and brochures published by colleges and trade schools. This is how the information was obtained for the "Typical Postsecondary Courses" section. Several catalogs were examined and compared, and commonly required courses were identified. You may notice some variation in the number of courses listed. Some programs have fairly standard requirements that can be listed in detail; in some cases, a professional association mandates that certain courses be included. For other programs, requirements are so varied that it is difficult to list more than a handful of typical courses.

The "Suggested High School Courses" are based on a general understanding of what high school courses are considered prerequisites for the postsecondary courses required by the program. They are "suggestions" because they are often helpful but not required for entering the program.

When you read the information in this book about a program or career, keep in mind that the description covers what is average or typical. For example, one trade school may offer a program with an unusual emphasis not mentioned here. And if you start looking at "help-wanted" advertisements, you may learn about jobs that require a somewhat different mix of skills than the ones listed here. Use this book as an introduction to the programs and careers. When you've found some choices that interest you, explore them in greater detail. You may be able to find a way to carve out a niche within a program or career to suit your particular abilities and interests.

Part I

What Programs and Careers Might Suit You?

Before you can figure out where you're going, it helps to understand who you are. This section will help you do that. With the help of some quick and easy exercises, you'll take a look at yourself and what matters most to you. You'll examine your priorities from several different angles:

- Your interests
- Your skills
- Your favorite high school courses
- Your work-related values

Each time you draw conclusions about your priorities, you'll get immediate feedback in terms of educational and training programs and work groups (families of careers) that you should consider.

Then, in the section "The Hot List," you'll put together the suggestions from all four factors to create a Hot List of programs that you should explore in Part II.

As you do the exercises in the following sections, keep in mind that there are no "right" or "wrong" answers for exercises about career planning. The most important thing they require is honesty.

Your Interests

Surely you have been in a situation where someone you knew, perhaps even a close friend, was bored by something you found fascinating. Different people have different interests. Becoming aware of your interests is an important first step in career planning.

It is important not to exaggerate the importance of interests. In the past, people have attempted to base career guidance entirely on interests. Yet most of us are happy enough with jobs that fail to satisfy every one of our interests because we can compensate by pursuing those extra interests in our spare time as *hobbies*. Therefore, the *Quick Guide to Career Training in Two Years or Less* does not let interests alone determine your choices. You will have the chance to look at educational/training programs from three other perspectives: skills, high school courses, and work-related values.

We're not discussing just any kind of interests here, but work-related interests. Consider the interests described in the *Guide for Occupational Exploration*, Third Edition (JIST Works), which expands and updates the work originally done by a government task force. Under this interest classification, the world of work is divided into 14 broad areas of interest. The interest areas are further divided into a total of 83 work groups.

The following table lists and defines the 14 interest areas and the 62 work groups that are closely associated with educational/training programs found in this book. Read over the table and find the work groups that interest you the most. They may all be in the same interest area, or they may be from two or even three different interest areas. Note the programs that are related to the work groups that interest you. At the end of this section, you can list the three areas of your greatest interest.

Interest Areas with Job Descriptions and Related Programs

1 Arts, Entertainment, and Media: An interest in creatively expressing feelings or ideas, in communicating news or information, or in performing.

Work Groups (GOE)	Workers in This Field...	Programs
01.01 Managerial Work in Arts, Entertainment, and Media	Manage people who work in the field of arts, entertainment, and media.	Graphic Design, Commercial Art, and Illustration; Multimedia Design and Production
01.04 Visual Arts	Draw, paint, or sculpt works of art or design consumer goods in which visual appeal is important.	Fashion Design; Graphic Design, Commercial Art, and Illustration; Interior Design; Multimedia Design and Production
01.06 Craft Arts	Create visually appealing objects from clay, glass, fabric, and other materials.	Graphic Design, Commercial Art, and Illustration; Taxidermy
01.07 Graphic Arts	Produce printed materials, specializing in text, in pictures, or in combining both.	Graphic and Printing Equipment Operations; Graphic Design, Commercial Art, and Illustration
01.08 Media	Perform the technical tasks that create photographs, movies and videos, radio and television broadcasts, and sound recordings.	Broadcasting Technology; Photography
01.09 Modeling and Personal Appearance	Pose before a camera or a live audience or prepare makeup or costuming for models or performers.	Cosmetology /Barbering

2 Science, Math, and Engineering: An interest in discovering, collecting, and analyzing information about the natural world, in applying scientific research findings, in imagining and manipulating quantitative data, and in applying technology.		
Work Groups (GOE)	**Workers in This Field...**	**Programs**
02.05 Laboratory Technology	Use special laboratory techniques and equipment to perform tests in such fields as chemistry, biology, and physics; record information resulting from experiments and tests.	Photography
02.06 Mathematics and Computers	Use advanced math, statistics, and computer programs to solve problems and conduct research.	Accounting Technician; Computer Programming
02.08 Engineering Technology	Perform a variety of technical tasks in support of engineering.	Architectural Technology; Chemical Engineering Technology; Civil (Engineering) Technology; Computer Programming; Construction Inspection; Construction Technology; Drafting; Electrical Engineering Technology; Mechanical Engineering Technology; Network and Telecommunications Technology; Surveying Technology
3 Plants and Animals: An interest in working with plants and animals, usually outdoors.		
Work Groups (GOE)	**Workers in This Field...**	**Programs**
03.01 Managerial Work in Plants and Animals	Operate or manage farms, ranches, hatcheries, nurseries, forests, and other plant and animal businesses.	Farm and Ranch Management; Ornamental Horticulture
03.02 Animal Care and Training	Care for and train animals of many kinds.	Pet Grooming; Veterinary Technology

(continues)

(continued)

4 Law, Law Enforcement, and Public Safety: An interest in upholding people's rights or in protecting people and property by using authority, inspecting, or monitoring.

Work Groups (GOE)	Workers in This Field...	Programs
04.01 Managerial Work in Law, Law Enforcement, and Public Safety	Manage fire and police departments.	Corrections; Investigative Services
04.02 Law	Provide legal advice and representation to clients, hear and make decisions on court cases, help individuals and groups reach agreements, and conduct investigations into legal matters.	Paralegal Services
04.03 Law Enforcement	Enforce laws and regulations to protect people, animals, and property.	Corrections; Fire Science/Fire-fighting; Investigative Services; Law Enforcement
04.04 Public Safety	Protect the public by responding to emergencies and by assuring that people are not exposed to unsafe products or facilities.	Emergency Medical Services; Fire Science/Firefighting; Investigative Services

5 Mechanics, Installers, and Repairers: An interest in applying mechanical and electrical/electronic principles to practical situations by use of machines or hand tools.

Work Groups (GOE)	Workers in This Field...	Programs
05.02 Electrical and Electronic Systems	Repair and install electrical devices and systems such as motors, transformers, appliances, and power lines and electronic devices and systems such as radios, computers, and telephone networks.	Aircraft Mechanic Technology; Automotive Technology; Avionics Technology; Casino Slot Technician Training; Computer Maintenance; Electrician Training; Home Appliance Repair

Work Groups (GOE)	Workers in This Field...	Programs
05.03 Mechanical Work	Install, service, and repair various kinds of machinery.	Aircraft Mechanic Technology; Automotive Body Repair; Automotive Technology; Casino Slot Technician Training; Diesel Technology; Electrician Training; Heating, Ventilation, A/C Technology; Home Appliance Repair; Instrumentation Technology; Optical Laboratory Technology; Watchmaking and Jewelrymaking

6 Construction, Mining, and Drilling: An interest in assembling components of buildings and other structures or in using mechanical devices to drill or excavate.

Work Groups (GOE)	Workers in This Field...	Programs
06.01 Managerial Work in Construction, Mining, and Drilling	Directly supervise and coordinate activities of workers who construct buildings, roads, or other structures or who drill or dig for oil and minerals.	Business Management; Carpentry; Construction Inspection; Construction Technology; Electrician Training; Masonry; Plumbing and Pipefitting; Property Management
06.02 Construction	Construct buildings and other large structures.	Carpentry; Construction Equipment Operation; Electrician Training; Masonry; Plumbing and Pipefitting
06.03 Mining and Drilling	Operate drilling or other excavating and pumping equipment, usually in oilfields, quarries, or mines.	Construction Equipment Operation
06.04 Hands-on Work in Construction, Extraction, and Maintenance	Perform a variety of tasks requiring little skill, such as moving materials, cleaning work areas, doing routine installations, operating simple tools, and helping skilled workers.	Carpentry; Construction Equipment Operation; Masonry; Plumbing and Pipefitting

(continues)

(continued)

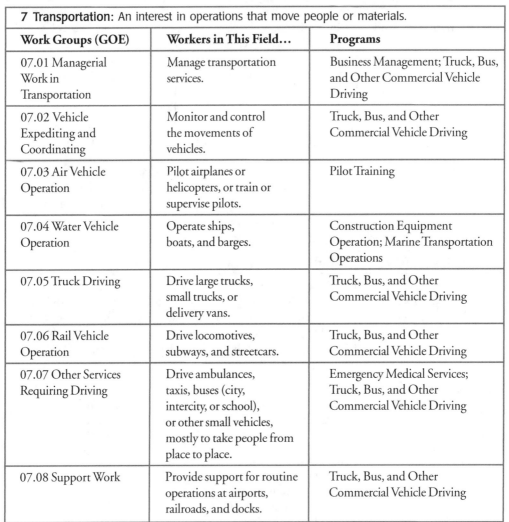

7 Transportation: An interest in operations that move people or materials.		
Work Groups (GOE)	**Workers in This Field…**	**Programs**
07.01 Managerial Work in Transportation	Manage transportation services.	Business Management; Truck, Bus, and Other Commercial Vehicle Driving
07.02 Vehicle Expediting and Coordinating	Monitor and control the movements of vehicles.	Truck, Bus, and Other Commercial Vehicle Driving
07.03 Air Vehicle Operation	Pilot airplanes or helicopters, or train or supervise pilots.	Pilot Training
07.04 Water Vehicle Operation	Operate ships, boats, and barges.	Construction Equipment Operation; Marine Transportation Operations
07.05 Truck Driving	Drive large trucks, small trucks, or delivery vans.	Truck, Bus, and Other Commercial Vehicle Driving
07.06 Rail Vehicle Operation	Drive locomotives, subways, and streetcars.	Truck, Bus, and Other Commercial Vehicle Driving
07.07 Other Services Requiring Driving	Drive ambulances, taxis, buses (city, intercity, or school), or other small vehicles, mostly to take people from place to place.	Emergency Medical Services; Truck, Bus, and Other Commercial Vehicle Driving
07.08 Support Work	Provide support for routine operations at airports, railroads, and docks.	Truck, Bus, and Other Commercial Vehicle Driving

8 Industrial Production: An interest in repetitive, concrete, organized activities most often done in a factory setting.

Work Groups (GOE)	Workers in This Field…	Programs
08.01 Managerial Work in Industrial Production	Manage industrial processing and manufacturing plants.	Business Management
08.02 Production Technology	Perform highly skilled hand and/or machine work requiring special techniques, training, and experience.	Aircraft Mechanic Technology; Avionics Technology; Cabinet making; Dental Laboratory Technology; Diesel Technology; Electromechanical Engineering Technology; Graphic and Printing Equipment Operations; Machinist Training; Optical Laboratory Technology; Watchmaking and Jewelrymaking; Welding Technology
08.03 Production Work	Use hands and hand tools with skill to make or process materials, products, and parts.	Brewing; Cabinetmaking; Graphic and Printing Equipment Operations; Graphic Design, Commercial Art, and Illustration; Machinist Training; Welding Technology; Winemaking
08.04 Metal and Plastics Machining Technology	Cut and grind metal and plastic parts to desired shapes and measurements, usually following specifications that require very precise work.	Machinist Training; Tool and Die Maker Training
08.05 Woodworking Technology	Follow specifications as they cut, shape, and finish wood products such as furniture and cabinets.	Cabinetmaking

(continues)

(continued)

Work Groups (GOE)	Workers in This Field...	Programs
08.06 Systems Operation	Operate and maintain equipment in systems that generate and distribute electricity, provide water and process wastewater, and pump oil and gas from oil fields to storage tanks.	Water/Wastewater Treatment Technology
08.07 Hands-on Work: Loading, Moving, Hoisting, and Conveying	Use hands, machinery, tools, and other equipment to package or move products or materials.	Construction Equipment Operation

9 Business Detail: An interest in organized, clearly defined activities requiring accuracy and attention to details, primarily in an office setting.

Work Groups (GOE)	Workers in This Field...	Programs
09.01 Managerial Work in Business Detail	Supervise and coordinate certain high-level business activities: contracts for buying or selling goods and services, office support services, facilities planning and maintenance, customer service, administrative support.	Business Management
09.03 Bookkeeping, Auditing, and Accounting	Collect, organize, compute, and record numerical information used in business and financial transactions.	Accounting Technician
09.05 Customer Service	Deal with people in person, often standing behind a window or in a booth.	Accounting Technician; Travel Services Marketing Operations

Work Groups (GOE)	Workers in This Field...	Programs
09.07 Records Processing	Prepare, review, file, and coordinate recorded information.	Court Reporting; Graphic and Printing Equipment Operations; Health Information Systems Technology; Medical Transcription
09.09 Clerical Machine Operation	Use business machines to record or process data.	Accounting Technician; Computer Maintenance; Graphic and Printing Equipment Operations; Graphic Design, Commercial Art, and Illustration; Office Technology

10 Sales and Marketing: An interest in bringing others to a particular point of view by personal persuasion, using sales and promotional techniques.

Work Groups (GOE)	Workers in This Field...	Programs
10.01 Managerial Work in Sales and Marketing	Direct or manage various kinds of selling and/or advertising operations—either a department within a business or a specialized business firm that contracts to provide selling and/or advertising services.	Business Management; Marketing
10.02 Sales Technology	Sell products such as industrial machinery, data processing equipment, and pharmaceuticals, plus services such as investment counseling, insurance, and advertising.	Auctioneering
10.03 General Sales	Sell, demonstrate, and solicit orders for products and services of many kinds.	Auctioneering; Fashion Merchandising; Real Estate; Travel Services Marketing Operations

(continues)

(continued)

11 Recreation, Travel, and Other Personal Services: An interest in catering to the personal wishes and needs of others so that they may enjoy cleanliness, good food and drink, comfortable lodging away from home, and enjoyable recreation.		
Work Groups (GOE)	**Workers in This Field...**	**Programs**
11.01 Managerial Work in Recreation, Travel, and Other Personal Services	Manage, through lower-level personnel, all or part of the activities in restaurants, hotels, resorts, and other places where people expect good personal service.	Food Service Management; Hotel/Motel and Restaurant Management
11.02 Recreational Services	Provide services to help people enjoy their leisure activities.	Casino Gaming Training; Personal Trainer
11.03 Transportation and Lodging Services	Help visitors, travelers, and customers get acquainted with and feel at ease in an unfamiliar setting.	Flight Attendant Training; Travel Services Marketing Operations
11.04 Barber and Beauty Services	Cut and style hair and provide a variety of other services to improve people's appearance or physical condition.	Cosmetology/Barbering
11.05 Food and Beverage Services	Prepare and serve food.	Bartending; Culinary Arts
11.08 Other Personal Services	Provide personal services to people who need a lot of attention: young children, people with chronic health problems, people in mourning, or very busy people.	Culinary Arts; Funeral Services and Mortuary Science

12 Education and Social Service: An interest in teaching people or improving their social or spiritual well-being.		
Work Groups (GOE)	**Workers in This Field…**	**Programs**
12.01 Managerial Work in Education and Social Service	Are employed at colleges, school districts, corporations, parks, and social service agencies.	Business Management; Human Services
12.03 Educational Services	Do general and specialized teaching, vocational training, and advising about education, career planning, or finances.	Business Management; Cardio-vascular Technology; Clinical Lab Technician; Computer Programming; Corrections; Dental Assisting; Dental Hygiene; Dental Laboratory Technology; Early Childhood Education; Electrocardiograph Technology; Electroencephalograph Technology; Emergency Medical Services; Farm and Ranch Management; Fashion Design; Graphic Design, Commercial Art, and Illustration; Interior Design; Law Enforcement; Library Technology; Marketing; Massage Therapy; Medical Laboratory Technology; Multimedia Design and Production; Nuclear Medicine Technology; Occupational Therapy Assisting; Ornamental Horticulture; Pharmacy Technology; Photography; Physical Therapist Assisting; Radiologic Technology; Respiratory Therapy Technology; Surgical Technology; Teacher Aide Training; Veterinary Technology

(continues)

(continued)

13 General Management and Support: An interest in making an organization run smoothly.

Work Groups (GOE)	Workers in This Field...	Programs
13.01 General Management Work and Management of Support	Are top-level and middle-level administrators who direct, through lower-level personnel, all or part of the activities in business establishments, government agencies, and labor unions.	Business Management; Farm and Ranch Management; Funeral Services and Mortuary Science; Ornamental Horticulture; Real Estate
13.02 Management Support	Plan, manage, analyze, evaluate, and make decisions about personnel, purchases, and financial transactions and records.	Business Management; Construction Technology; Fashion Merchandising; Real Estate

14 Medical and Health Services: An interest in helping people be healthy.

Work Groups (GOE)	Workers in This Field...	Programs
14.02 Medicine and Surgery	Diagnose and treat human diseases, disorders, and injuries.	Medical Assistant Training; Pharmacy Technology; Surgical Technology
14.03 Dentistry	Provide health care for patients' teeth and mouth tissues.	Dental Assisting; Dental Hygiene
14.04 Health Specialties	Are health professionals and technicians who specialize in certain parts of the human body.	Opticianry
14.05 Medical Technology	Use technology mostly to detect signs of disease.	Cardiovascular Technology; Clinical Lab Technician; Electrocardiograph Technology; Electroencephalograph Technology; Medical Assistant Training; Medical Laboratory Technology; Nuclear Medicine Technology; Radiologic Technology

Work Groups (GOE)	Workers in This Field...	Programs
14.06 Medical Therapy	Care for, treat, or train people to improve their physical and emotional well-being.	Massage Therapy; Occupational Therapy Assisting; Physical Therapist Assisting; Radiologic Technology; Respiratory Therapy Technology
14.07 Patient Care and Assistance	Are concerned with the physical needs and welfare of others.	Home Health Aide Training; Nurse Aide/Assistant Training; Practical Nursing (L.P.N. Training)
14.08 Health Protection and Promotion	Help people maintain good health and fitness.	Dietetic Technology

Write down the three work groups in which you have the greatest interest in the left column of the list that follows. In the right column, put the programs that are related to the work groups that interest you.

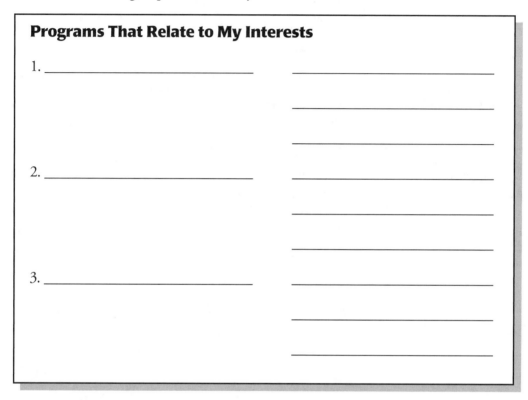

Programs That Relate to My Interests

1. _____   _____

   _____

   _____

2. _____   _____

   _____

   _____

3. _____   _____

   _____

   _____

Your Skills

Different kinds of work demand different skills. Most people want to go into a kind of work where they will be able to handle the skill requirements. Of course, you don't yet have all the skills you will need for your career—that's why you are planning to get further training. Nevertheless, based on your experiences in school and at work, you probably have a good idea of what skills you learn easily and which come harder.

The following table lists and defines 31 skills that the U.S. Department of Labor (USDOL) describes in the O*NET database. For each skill in the table, ask yourself, "What were some things I've done where I've used this skill at a high level and enjoyed using it?" If you can think of several good examples, mark the name of the skill with a plus sign or an underline; otherwise, move on to another skill.

Which Skills Are Most Important to You?

Skill	Description
Active Learning	Working with new material or information to grasp its implications
Active Listening	Listening to what other people are saying and asking questions as appropriate
Coordination	Adjusting actions in relation to others' actions
Critical Thinking	Using logic and analysis to identify the strengths and weaknesses of different approaches
Equipment Maintenance	Performing routine maintenance on equipment and determining when and what kind of maintenance is needed
Equipment Selection	Determining the kind of tools and equipment needed to do a job
Installation	Installing equipment, machines, wiring, or programs to meet specifications
Instructing	Teaching others how to do something
Judgment and Decision Making	Weighing the relative costs and benefits of a potential action
Learning Strategies	Using multiple approaches when learning or teaching new things
Management of Financial Resources	Determining how money will be spent to get the work done and accounting for these expenditures
Management of Personnel Resources	Motivating, developing, and directing people as they work, identifying the best people for the job
Mathematics	Using mathematics to solve problems
Monitoring	Assessing your performance or that of other individuals or organizations to make improvements or take corrective action
Operation and Control	Controlling operations of equipment or systems
Operation Monitoring	Watching gauges, dials, or other indicators to make sure a machine is working properly
Operations Analysis	Analyzing needs and product requirements to create a design
Persuasion	Persuading others to change their minds or behavior
Programming	Writing computer programs for various purposes

(continues)

(continued)

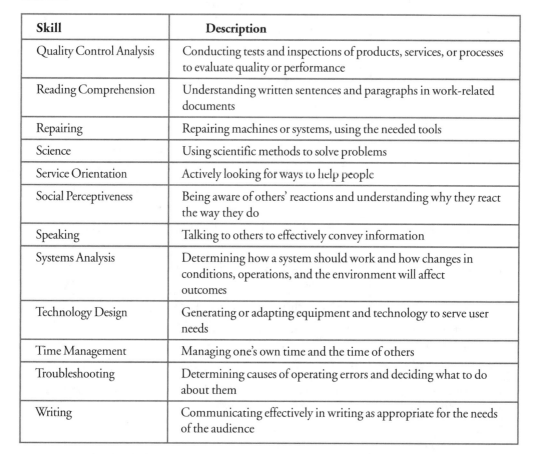

Skill	Description
Quality Control Analysis	Conducting tests and inspections of products, services, or processes to evaluate quality or performance
Reading Comprehension	Understanding written sentences and paragraphs in work-related documents
Repairing	Repairing machines or systems, using the needed tools
Science	Using scientific methods to solve problems
Service Orientation	Actively looking for ways to help people
Social Perceptiveness	Being aware of others' reactions and understanding why they react the way they do
Speaking	Talking to others to effectively convey information
Systems Analysis	Determining how a system should work and how changes in conditions, operations, and the environment will affect outcomes
Technology Design	Generating or adapting equipment and technology to serve user needs
Time Management	Managing one's own time and the time of others
Troubleshooting	Determining causes of operating errors and deciding what to do about them
Writing	Communicating effectively in writing as appropriate for the needs of the audience

Now that you've looked at all the skills, determine the three skills that you would most like to use in your career and list them below.

Most Desirable Skills for My Career

1. _____

2. _____

3. _____

The following table relates these 31 skills to educational/training programs and to the *Guide for Occupational Exploration (GOE)* work groups. Find the programs and work groups that correspond to the three skills that you listed. At the end of this section, write the programs and work groups that match your skills.

Note A skill applies to a program because it is required by the occupations to which the program is linked. You do not necessarily need this skill in the program, but it is likely that learning this skill will be part of what you do in the program.

Relationship of Skills to Programs and Work Groups

Skill	Programs	Work Groups, GOE Codes
Active Learning	Electrical Engineering Technology; Network and Telecommunications Technology	Animal Care and Training, 03.02 Customer Service, 09.05 General Sales, 10.03 Health Specialties, 14.04 Law, 04.02 Law Enforcement, 04.03 Managerial Work in Business Detail, 09.01 Sales Technology, 10.02 Social Services, 12.02 Vehicle Expediting and Coordinating, 07.02 Visual Arts, 01.04
Active Listening	Cosmetology/Barbering; Dental Assisting; Dietetic Technology; Early Childhood Education; Fashion Merchandising; Human Services; Interior Design; Law Enforcement; Multimedia Design and Production; Pet Grooming; Respiratory Therapy Technology; Teacher Aide Training	General Sales, 10.03 Law, 04.02 Law Enforcement, 04.03 Managerial Work in Business Detail, 09.01 Social Services, 12.02 Vehicle Expediting and Coordinating, 07.02

(continues)

(continued)

Skill	Programs	Work Groups, GOE Codes
Coordination	Business Management; Culinary Arts; Emergency Medical Services; Farm and Ranch Management; Fashion Design; Food Service Management; Hotel/Motel and Restaurant Management; Interior Design; Marine Transportation Operations; Marketing; Ornamental Horticulture; Personal Trainer; Property Management	Food and Beverage Services, 11.05 General Management Work and Management of Support Functions, 13.01 Managerial Work in Arts, Entertainment, and Media, 01.01 Managerial Work in Business Detail, 09.01 Managerial Work in Construction, Mining, and Drilling, 06.01 Managerial Work in Education and Social Service, 12.01 Managerial Work in Industrial Production, 08.01 Managerial Work in Law, Law Enforcement, and Public Safety, 04.01 Managerial Work in Plants and Animals, 03.01 Managerial Work in Recreation, Travel, and Other Personal Services, 11.01 Managerial Work in Sales and Marketing, 10.01 Managerial Work in Transportation, 07.01 Public Safety, 04.04 Recreational Services, 11.02 Visual Arts, 01.04 Water Vehicle Operation, 07.04
Critical Thinking	Investigative Services; Paralegal Services	[No GOE group related to the programs in this book is rated high on this skill.]

Skill	Programs	Work Groups, GOE Codes
Equipment Maintenance	Aircraft Mechanic Technology; Avionics Technology; Computer Maintenance; Diesel Technology	Electrical and Electronic Systems, 05.02 Mechanical Work, 05.03
Equipment Selection	Masonry; Optical Laboratory Technology; Photography; Tool and Die Maker Training; Watchmaking and Jewelrymaking	Graphic Arts, 01.07 Metal and Plastics Machining Technology, 08.04 Woodworking Technology, 08.05
Installation	Aircraft Mechanic Technology; Automotive Technology; Avionics Technology; Carpentry; Casino Slot Technician Training; Electrician Training; Electromechanical Engineering Technology; Heating, Ventilation, A/C Technology; Home Appliance Repair; Plumbing and Pipefitting	Construction, 06.02 Electrical and Electronic Systems, 05.02
Instructing	Broadcasting Technology; Personal Trainer; Pilot Training	Food and Beverage Services, 11.05
Judgment and Decision Making	Business Management; Marine Transportation Operations; Marketing	General Management Work and Management of Support Functions, 13.01 Law, 04.02 Management Support, 13.02 Managerial Work in Industrial Production, 08.01 Managerial Work in Law, Law Enforcement, and Public Safety, 04.01 Managerial Work in Sales and Marketing, 10.01

(continues)

(continued)

Skill	Programs	Work Groups, GOE Codes
Learning Strategies	Early Childhood Education; Personal Trainer; Physical Therapist Assisting; Teacher Aide Training	Managerial Work in Education and Social Service, 12.01 Media Technology, 01.08 Other Personal Services, 11.08
Management of Financial Resources	[No program is rated high on this skill.]	Food and Beverage Services, 11.05 General Management Work and Management of Support Functions, 13.01 Health Protection and Promotion, 14.08 Management Support, 13.02 Managerial Work in Education and Social Service, 12.01 Sales Technology, 10.02
Management of Personnel Resources	Farm and Ranch Management; Food Service Management; Hotel/Motel and Restaurant Management; Ornamental Horticulture; Property Management	Managerial Work in Construction, Mining, and Drilling, 06.01 Managerial Work in Industrial Production, 08.01 Managerial Work in Law, Law Enforcement, and Public Safety, 04.01 Water Vehicle Operation, 07.04
Mathematics	Accounting Technician; Architectural Technology; Civil (Engineering) Technology; Computer Programming; Construction Technology; Drafting; Mechanical Engineering Technology; Nuclear Medicine Technology; Surveying Technology	Educational Services, 12.03 Engineering Technology, 02.08 Mathematics and Computers, 02.06 Metal and Plastics Machining Technology, 08.04 Production Work, 08.03 Vehicle Expediting and Coordinating, 07.02
Monitoring	Casino Gaming Training; Food Service Management	[No GOE group related to the programs in this book is rated high on this skill.]

Skill	Programs	Work Groups, GOE Codes
Operation and Control	Brewing; Cabinetmaking; Construction Equipment Operation; Graphic and Printing Equipment Operations; Graphic Design, Commercial Art, and Illustration; Machinist Training; Marine Transportation Operations; Mechanical Engineering Technology; Pilot Training; Radiologic Technology; Tool and Die-Maker Training; Truck, Bus, and Other Commercial Vehicle Driving; Water/Wastewater Treatment Technology; Welding Technology; Winemaking	Air Vehicle Operation, 07.03 Construction, 06.02 Craft Arts, 01.06 Hands-on Work in Construction, Extraction, and Maintenance, 06.04 Hands-on Work: Loading, Moving, Hoisting, and Conveying, 08.07 Law Enforcement, 04.03 Mining and Drilling, 06.03 Other Services Requiring Driving, 07.07 Rail Vehicle Operation, 07.06 Support Work, 07.08 Systems Operation, 08.06 Truck Driving, 07.05 Vehicle Expediting and Coordinating, 07.02 Water Vehicle Operation, 07.04
Operation Monitoring	Construction Equipment Operation; Machinist Training; Pilot Training; Water/Wastewater Treatment Technology	Air Vehicle Operation, 07.03 Hands-on Work: Loading, Moving, Hoisting, and Conveying, 08.07 Mining and Drilling, 06.03 Production Work, 08.03 Rail Vehicle Operation, 07.06 Systems Operation, 08.06
Operations Analysis	Civil (Engineering) Technology; Construction Technology; Interior Design	[No GOE group related to the programs in this book is rated high on this skill.]
Persuasion	[No program is rated high on this skill.]	General Sales, 10.03
Programming	Computer Programming	Mathematics and Computers, 02.06

(continues)

(continued)

Skill	Programs	Work Groups, GOE Codes
Quality Control Analysis	Chemical Engineering Technology; Construction Inspection; Dental Laboratory Technology	Production Technology, 08.02
Reading Comprehension	Broadcasting Technology; Cardiovascular Technology; Dental Hygiene; Dental Laboratory Technology; Dietetic Technology; Electrocardiograph Technology; Health Information Systems Technology; Library Technology; Medical Assistant Training; Nuclear Medicine Technology; Office Technology; Opticianry; Paralegal Services; Pharmacy Technology; Physical Therapist Assisting; Radiologic Technology; Real Estate; Respiratory Therapy Technology; Surgical Technology; Veterinary Technology	Animal Care and Training, 03.02 Bookkeeping, Auditing, and Accounting, 09.03 Clerical Machine Operation, 09.09 Dentistry, 14.03 Educational Services, 12.03 Health Protection and Promotion, 14.08 Health Specialties, 14.04 Laboratory Technology, 02.05 Law, 04.02 Management Support, 13.02 Managerial Work in Arts, Entertainment, and Media, 01.01 Managerial Work in Business Detail, 09.01 Media Technology, 01.08 Medical Technology, 14.05 Medical Therapy, 14.06 Medicine and Surgery, 14.02 Modeling and Personal Appearance, 01.09 Public Safety, 04.04 Records Processing, 09.07 Visual Arts, 01.04
Repairing	Aircraft Mechanic Technology; Automotive Body Repair; Automotive Technology; Avionics Technology; Casino Slot Technician Training; Chemical Engineering Technology; Computer Maintenance; Diesel Technology; Heating,	Mechanical Work, 05.03

Skill	Programs	Work Groups, GOE Codes
	Ventilation, A/C Technology; Home Appliance Repair; Tool and Die Maker Training	
Science	Clinical Lab Technician; Dental Laboratory Technology; Medical Laboratory Technology; Nuclear Medicine Technology; Water/Wastewater Treatment Technology	Animal Care and Training, 03.02 Engineering Technology, 02.08 Laboratory Technology, 02.05 Medical Technology, 14.05
Service Orientation	Bartending; Emergency Medical Services; Fire Science/ Firefighting; Flight Attendant Training; Home Health Aide Training; Human Services; Physical Therapist Assisting; Practical Nursing (L.P.N. Training); Respiratory Therapy Technology; Travel Services Marketing Operations	Barber and Beauty Services, 11.04 Other Personal Services, 11.08 Other Services Requiring Driving, 07.07 Patient Care and Assistance, 14.07 Recreational Services, 11.02 Transportation and Lodging Services, 11.03
Social Perceptiveness	Corrections; Flight Attendant Training; Funeral Services and Mortuary Science; Human Services; Nurse Aide/ Assistant Training; Occupational Therapy Assisting	Medicine and Surgery, 14.02 Other Personal Services, 11.08 Patient Care and Assistance, 14.07 Social Services, 12.02
Speaking	Construction Inspection; Early Childhood Education; Fashion Merchandising; Marketing; Teacher Aide Training	General Sales, 10.03
Systems Analysis	[No program is rated high on this skill.]	Managerial Work in Sales and Marketing, 10.01 Sales Technology, 10.02
Technology Design	Electrical Engineering Technology; Mechanical Engineering Technology; Network and Telecommunications Technology	Metal and Plastics Machining Technology, 08.04

(continues)

(continued)

Skill	Programs	Work Groups, GOE Codes
Time Management	Property Management	Managerial Work in Construction, Mining, and Drilling, 06.01
Troubleshooting	Automotive Technology; Avionics Technology; Casino Slot Technician Training; Chemical Engineering Technology; Computer Maintenance; Diesel Technology; Heating, Ventilation, A/C Technology; Home Appliance Repair	Electrical and Electronic Systems, 05.02
Writing	Dietetic Technology; Paralegal Services	Educational Services, 12.03 Health Protection and Promotion, 14.08 Media Technology, 01.08 Medical Therapy, 14.06 Social Sciences, 02.04

Write down the programs and work groups that correspond with the three skills you listed. If there are many, try to find programs and work groups that are linked to more than one of your important skills and write down these names.

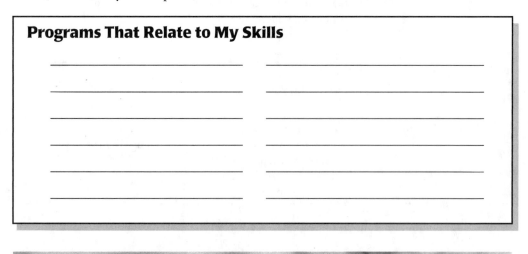

Programs That Relate to My Skills

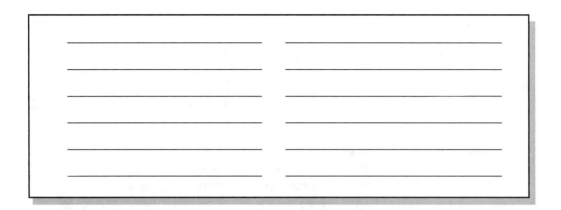

Your Favorite High School Courses

A good way to predict how well people will like postsecondary courses is to ask them how much they liked similar high school courses. Also, most people earn their highest grades in postsecondary courses that are similar to the high school courses in which they did well. Therefore, it can be useful to take note of and write down the names of three high school courses that you liked and in which you earned high grades.

My Best High School Courses

1. _____
2. _____
3. _____

Next, with those courses in mind, look over the information in the following table and find related programs and work groups (from the Work Groups, GOE Codes column). As you review this information, mark the items that most closely match your best high school courses. At the end of this section, you can make a list of the best matches.

> **Note** Many of the lower-level math courses listed in the following table are commonly required for a large number of programs. For example, if you did well in math, you should look for a high school course that represents a high level of math, such as trigonometry or pre-calculus, rather than algebra or business/applied math.

Relationship of High School Courses to Postsecondary Programs and Work Groups

High School Course	Postsecondary Programs	Work Groups, GOE Codes
Algebra	Architectural Technology; Avionics Technology; Brewing; Broadcasting Technology; Casino Slot Technician Training; Chemical Engineering Technology; Civil (Engineering) Technology; Computer Programming; Construction Inspection; Construction Technology; Dental Assisting; Dental Hygiene; Dental Laboratory Technology; Dietetic Technology; Drafting; Early Childhood Education; Electrical Engineering Technology; Electromechanical Engineering Technology; Emergency Medical Services; Farm and Ranch Management; Fashion Design; Fashion Merchandising; Funeral Services and Mortuary Science; Graphic Design, Commercial Art, and Illustration; Health Information Systems	Air Vehicle Operation, 07.03 Animal Care and Training, 03.02 Clerical Machine Operation, 09.09 Construction, 06.02 Dentistry, 14.03 Educational Services, 12.03 Electrical and Electronic Systems, 05.02 Engineering Technology, 02.08 General Management Work and Management of Support Functions, 13.01 General Sales, 10.03 Graphic Arts, 01.07 Hands-on Work in Construction, Extraction, and Maintenance, 06.04 Health Protection and Promotion, 14.08 Health Specialties, 14.04 Laboratory Technology, 02.05 Management Support, 13.02 Managerial Work in Arts, Entertainment, and Media, 01.01 Managerial Work in Construction, Mining, and Drilling, 06.01 Managerial Work in Plants and Animals, 03.01 Managerial Work in Recreation, Travel, and Other Personal Services, 11.01

High School Course	Postsecondary Programs	Work Groups, GOE Codes
	Technology; Home Appliance Repair; Hotel/Motel and Restaurant Management; Instrumentation Technology; Interior Design; Machinist Training; Marine Transportation Operations; Marketing; Mechanical Engineering Technology; Medical Assistant Training; Medical Laboratory Technology; Multimedia Design and Production; Network and Telecommunications Technology; Nuclear Medicine Technology; Nurse Aide/Assistant Training; Occupational Therapy Assisting; Optical Laboratory Technology; Opticianry; Pharmacy Technology; Photography; Physical Therapist Assisting; Pilot Training; Plumbing and Pipefitting; Practical Nursing (L.P.N. Training); Property Management; Radiologic Technology; Respiratory Therapy Technology; Surgical Technology; Surveying Technology; Teacher Aide Training; Tool and Die Maker Training; Veterinary Technology; Watchmaking and Jewelrymaking; Welding Technology; Winemaking	Managerial Work in Sales and Marketing, 10.01 Mathematics and Computers, 02.06 Mechanical Work, 05.03 Media Technology, 01.08 Medical Technology, 14.05 Medical Therapy, 14.06 Medicine and Surgery, 14.02 Metal and Plastics Machining Technology, 08.04 Other Personal Services, 11.08 Other Services Requiring Driving, 07.07 Patient Care and Assistance, 14.07 Production Technology, 08.02 Production Work, 08.03 Public Safety, 04.04 Records Processing, 09.07 Social Services, 12.02 Visual Arts, 01.04 Water Vehicle Operation, 07.04

(continues)

(continued)

High School Course	Postsecondary Programs	Work Groups, GOE Codes
Applied Communications	Accounting Technician; Architectural Technology; Automotive Body Repair; Automotive Technology; Avionics Technology; Broadcasting Technology; Business Management; Cabinetmaking; Cardiovascular Technology; Carpentry; Chemical Engineering Technology; Civil (Engineering) Technology; Clinical Lab Technician; Computer Maintenance; Computer Programming; Construction Equipment Operation; Construction Inspection; Construction Technology; Corrections; Cosmetology/Barbering; Culinary Arts; Diesel Technology; Drafting; Electrical Engineering Technology; Electrician Training; Electrocardiograph Technology; Electro-encephalograph Technology; Electromechanical Engineering Technology; Emergency Medical Services; Farm and Ranch Management; Fashion Design; Fashion Merchandising; Fire Science/Firefighting; Flight Attendant Training; Food Service Management; Funeral Services and	Barber and Beauty Services, 11.04 Bookkeeping, Auditing, and Accounting, 09.03 Clerical Machine Operation, 09.09 Construction, 06.02 Customer Service, 09.05 Educational Services, 12.03 Electrical and Electronic Systems, 05.02 Engineering Technology, 02.08 Food and Beverage Services, 11.05 General Management Work and Management of Support Functions, 13.01 General Sales, 10.03 Hands-on Work in Construction, Extraction, and Maintenance, 06.04 Hands-on Work: Loading, Moving, Hoisting, and Conveying, 08.07 Health Specialties, 14.04 Laboratory Technology, 02.05 Law Enforcement, 04.03 Management Support, 13.02 Managerial Work in Arts, Entertainment, and Media, 01.01 Managerial Work in Business Detail, 09.01 Managerial Work in Construction, Mining, and Drilling, 06.01 Managerial Work in Education and Social Service, 12.01 Managerial Work in Industrial Production, 08.01 Managerial Work in Law, Law Enforcement, and Public Safety, 04.01

High School Course	Postsecondary Programs	Work Groups, GOE Codes
	Mortuary Science; Heating, Ventilation, A/C Technology; Home Appliance Repair; Home Health Aide Training; Human Services; Instrumentation Technology; Interior Design; Investigative Services; Library Technology; Masonry; Massage Therapy; Mechanical Engineering Technology; Multimedia Design and Production; Network and Telecommunications Technology; Office Technology; Opticianry; Ornamental Horticulture; Photography; Plumbing and Pipefitting; Property Management; Real Estate; Surveying Technology; Travel Services Marketing Operations; Truck, Bus, and Other Commercial Vehicle Driving; Water/Wastewater Treatment Technology	Managerial Work in Plants and Animals, 03.01 Managerial Work in Recreation, Travel, and Other Personal Services, 11.01 Managerial Work in Sales and Marketing, 10.01 Managerial Work in Transportation, 07.01 Mathematics and Computers, 02.06 Mechanical Work, 05.03 Media Technology, 01.08 Medical Technology, 14.05 Medical Therapy, 14.06 Mining and Drilling, 06.03 Modeling and Personal Appearance, 01.09 Other Personal Services, 11.08 Other Services Requiring Driving, 07.07 Patient Care and Assistance, 14.07 Production Technology, 08.02 Production Work, 08.03 Public Safety, 04.04 Rail Vehicle Operation, 07.06 Support Work, 07.08 Systems Operation, 08.06 Transportation and Lodging Services, 11.03 Truck Driving, 07.05 Vehicle Expediting and Coordinating, 07.02 Visual Arts, 01.04 Water Vehicle Operation, 07.04 Woodworking Technology, 08.05
Art	Dental Laboratory Technology; Fashion Design; Funeral Services and Mortuary Science;	Clerical Machine Operation, 09.09 Craft Arts, 01.06 Educational Services, 12.03

(continues)

(continued)

High School Course	Postsecondary Programs	Work Groups, GOE Codes
	Graphic Design, Commercial Art, and Illustration; Interior Design; Multimedia Design and Production; Photography; Taxidermy; Watchmaking and Jewelrymaking	General Management Work and Management of Support Functions, 13.01 Graphic Arts, 01.07 Laboratory Technology, 02.05 Managerial Work in Arts, Entertainment, and Media, 01.01 Mechanical Work, 05.03 Media Technology, 01.08 Other Personal Services, 11.08 Production Technology, 08.02 Production Work, 08.03 Visual Arts, 01.04
Auto Shop	Automotive Body Repair; Automotive Technology; Construction Equipment Operation; Diesel Technology; Truck, Bus, and Other Commercial Vehicle Driving	Construction, 06.02 Electrical and Electronic Systems, 05.02 Hands-on Work in Construction, Extraction, and Maintenance, 06.04 Hands-on Work: Loading, Moving, Hoisting, and Conveying, 08.07 Managerial Work in Transportation, 07.01 Mechanical Work, 05.03 Mining and Drilling, 06.03 Other Services Requiring Driving, 07.07 Production Technology, 08.02 Rail Vehicle Operation, 07.06 Support Work, 07.08 Truck Driving, 07.05 Vehicle Expediting and Coordinating, 07.02 Water Vehicle Operation, 07.04
Biology	Brewing; Cardiovascular Technology; Clinical Lab Technician; Dental Assisting; Dental Hygiene;	Animal Care and Training, 03.02 Craft Arts, 01.06 Dentistry, 14.03 Educational Services, 12.03

High School Course	Postsecondary Programs	Work Groups, GOE Codes
	Dental Laboratory Technology; Dietetic Technology; Early Childhood Education; Electrocardiograph Technology; Electroencephalograph Technology; Emergency Medical Services; Farm and Ranch Management; Food Service Management; Funeral Services and Mortuary Science; Health Information Systems Technology; Home Health Aide Training; Massage Therapy; Medical Assistant Training; Medical Laboratory Technology; Medical Transcription; Nuclear Medicine Technology; Nurse Aide/Assistant Training; Occupational Therapy Assisting; Opticianry; Ornamental Horticulture; Personal Trainer; Pet Grooming; Pharmacy Technology; Physical Therapist Assisting; Practical Nursing (L.P.N. Training); Radiologic Technology; Respiratory Therapy Technology; Surgical Technology; Taxidermy; Veterinary Technology; Water/Wastewater Treatment Technology; Winemaking	General Management Work and Management of Support Functions, 13.01 Health Protection and Promotion, 14.08 Health Specialties, 14.04 Managerial Work in Plants and Animals, 03.01 Managerial Work in Recreation, Travel, and Other Personal Services, 11.01 Medical Technology, 14.05 Medical Therapy, 14.06 Medicine and Surgery, 14.02 Other Personal Services, 11.08 Other Services Requiring Driving, 07.07 Patient Care and Assistance, 14.07 Production Technology, 08.02 Production Work, 08.03 Public Safety, 04.04 Records Processing, 09.07 Recreational Services, 11.02 Systems Operation, 08.06

(continues)

(continued)

High School Course	Postsecondary Programs	Work Groups, GOE Codes
Business/Applied Math	Accounting Technician; Auctioneering; Automotive Body Repair; Automotive Technology; Bartending; Broadcasting Technology; Business Management; Cabinetmaking; Cardiovascular Technology; Carpentry; Casino Gaming Training; Clinical Lab Technician; Computer Maintenance; Construction Equipment Operation; Cosmetology/Barbering; Culinary Arts; Diesel Technology; Electrician Training; Electrocardiograph Technology; Electroencephalograph Technology; Fashion Design; Fashion Merchandising; Fire Science/Firefighting; Food Service Management; Graphic and Printing Equipment Operations; Heating, Ventilation, A/C Technology; Human Services; Investigative Services; Library Technology; Masonry; Massage Therapy; Medical Transcription; Office Technology; Ornamental Horticulture; Paralegal Services; Personal Trainer; Pet Grooming; Plumbing and Pipefitting;	Animal Care and Training, 03.02 Barber and Beauty Services, 11.04 Bookkeeping, Auditing, and Accounting, 09.03 Clerical Machine Operation, 09.09 Construction, 06.02 Craft Arts, 01.06 Customer Service, 09.05 Educational Services, 12.03 Electrical and Electronic Systems, 05.02 Food and Beverage Services, 11.05 General Management Work and Management of Support Functions, 13.01 General Sales, 10.03 Graphic Arts, 01.07 Hands-on Work in Construction, Extraction, and Maintenance, 06.04 Hands-on Work: Loading, Moving, Hoisting, and Conveying, 08.07 Law Enforcement, 04.03 Law, 04.02 Management Support, 13.02 Managerial Work in Business Detail, 09.01 Managerial Work in Construction, Mining, and Drilling, 06.01 Managerial Work in Education and Social Service, 12.01 Managerial Work in Industrial Production, 08.01 Managerial Work in Law, Law Enforcement, and Public Safety, 04.01 Managerial Work in Plants and Animals, 03.01

High School Course	Postsecondary Programs	Work Groups, GOE Codes
	Real Estate; Taxidermy; Travel Services Marketing Operations; Truck, Bus, and Other Commercial Vehicle Driving; Water/ Wastewater Treatment Technology	Managerial Work in Recreation, Travel, and Other Personal Services, 11.01 Managerial Work in Sales and Marketing, 10.01 Managerial Work in Transportation, 07.01 Mathematics and Computers, 02.06 Mechanical Work, 05.03 Media Technology, 01.08 Medical Technology, 14.05 Medical Therapy, 14.06 Mining and Drilling, 06.03 Modeling and Personal Appearance, 01.09 Other Personal Services, 11.08 Other Services Requiring Driving, 07.07 Production Technology, 08.02 Production Work, 08.03 Public Safety, 04.04 Rail Vehicle Operation, 07.06 Records Processing, 09.07 Recreational Services, 11.02 Sales Technology, 10.02 Support Work, 07.08 Systems Operation, 08.06 Transportation and Lodging Services, 11.03 Truck Driving, 07.05 Vehicle Expediting and Coordinating, 07.02 Visual Arts, 01.04 Water Vehicle Operation, 07.04 Woodworking Technology, 08.05
Chemistry	Brewing; Cardiovascular Technology; Chemical Engineering Technology;	Animal Care and Training, 03.02 Craft Arts, 01.06 Dentistry, 14.03

(continues)

(continued)

High School Course	Postsecondary Programs	Work Groups, GOE Codes
	Clinical Lab Technician; Dental Assisting; Dental Hygiene; Dental Laboratory Technology; Dietetic Technology; Electrocardiograph Technology; Electroencephalograph Technology; Emergency Medical Services; Farm and Ranch Management; Fire Science/Firefighting; Funeral Services and Mortuary Science; Health Information Systems Technology; Massage Therapy; Medical Assistant Training; Medical Laboratory Technology; Medical Transcription; Nuclear Medicine Technology; Nurse Aide/Assistant Training; Occupational Therapy Assisting; Ornamental Horticulture; Pharmacy Technology; Photography; Physical Therapist Assisting; Practical Nursing (L.P.N. Training); Radiologic Technology; Respiratory Therapy Technology; Surgical Technology; Taxidermy; Veterinary Technology; Water/Wastewater Treatment Technology; Winemaking	Educational Services, 12.03 Engineering Technology, 02.08 General Management Work and Management of Support Functions, 13.01 Health Protection and Promotion, 14.08 Laboratory Technology, 02.05 Law Enforcement, 04.03 Managerial Work in Plants and Animals, 03.01 Media Technology, 01.08 Medical Technology, 14.05 Medical Therapy, 14.06 Medicine and Surgery, 14.02 Other Personal Services, 11.08 Other Services Requiring Driving, 07.07 Patient Care and Assistance, 14.07 Production Technology, 08.02 Production Work, 08.03 Public Safety, 04.04 Records Processing, 09.07 Systems Operation, 08.06

High School Course	Postsecondary Programs	Work Groups, GOE Codes
Computer Science	Automotive Technology; Avionics Technology; Brewing; Broadcasting Technology; Business Management; Casino Slot Technician Training; Chemical Engineering Technology; Civil (Engineering) Technology; Clinical Lab Technician; Computer Maintenance; Computer Programming; Drafting; Electrical Engineering Technology; Electrocardiograph Technology; Electroencephalograph Technology; Electromechanical Engineering Technology; Graphic Design, Commercial Art, and Illustration; Health Information Systems Technology; Hotel/ Motel and Restaurant Management; Instrumentation Technology; Investigative Services; Library Technology; Machinist Training; Marine Transportation Operations; Marketing; Mechanical Engineering Technology; Medical Assistant Training; Multimedia Design and Production; Network and Telecommunications Technology; Photography; Surveying Technology;	Clerical Machine Operation, 09.09 Educational Services, 12.03 Electrical and Electronic Systems, 05.02 Engineering Technology, 02.08 General Management Work and Management of Support Functions, 13.01 Graphic Arts, 01.07 Laboratory Technology, 02.05 Law Enforcement, 04.03 Management Support, 13.02 Managerial Work in Arts, Entertainment, and Media, 01.01 Managerial Work in Business Detail, 09.01 Managerial Work in Construction, Mining, and Drilling, 06.01 Managerial Work in Education and Social Service, 12.01 Managerial Work in Industrial Production, 08.01 Managerial Work in Law, Law Enforcement, and Public Safety, 04.01 Managerial Work in Recreation, Travel, and Other Personal Services, 11.01 Managerial Work in Sales and Marketing, 10.01 Managerial Work in Transportation, 07.01 Mathematics and Computers, 02.06 Mechanical Work, 05.03 Media Technology, 01.08 Medical Technology, 14.05 Medicine and Surgery, 14.02 Metal and Plastics Machining Technology, 08.04

(continues)

(continued)

High School Course	Postsecondary Programs	Work Groups, GOE Codes
	Tool and Die Maker Training; Winemaking	Production Technology, 08.02 Production Work, 08.03 Public Safety, 04.04 Records Processing, 09.07 Social Services, 12.02 Visual Arts, 01.04 Water Vehicle Operation, 07.04
Distributive Education	Auctioneering; Bartending; Fashion Design; Fashion Merchandising; Food Service Management; Opticianry; Pet Grooming; Property Management; Real Estate; Taxidermy; Travel Services Marketing Operations	Animal Care and Training, 03.02 Craft Arts, 01.06 Customer Service, 09.05 Educational Services, 12.03 Food and Beverage Services, 11.05 General Management Work and Management of Support Functions, 13.01 General Sales, 10.03 Health Specialties, 14.04 Management Support, 13.02 Managerial Work in Construction, Mining, and Drilling, 06.01 Managerial Work in Recreation, Travel, and Other Personal Services, 11.01 Sales Technology, 10.02 Transportation and Lodging Services, 11.03 Visual Arts, 01.04
Drafting	Construction Inspection; Construction Technology; Electrician Training; Interior Design; Plumbing and Pipefitting; Surveying Technology; Welding Technology	Construction, 06.02 Educational Services, 12.03 Electrical and Electronic Systems, 05.02 Engineering Technology, 02.08 Hands-on Work in Construction, Extraction, and Maintenance, 06.04 Management Support, 13.02 Managerial Work in Construction, Mining, and Drilling, 06.01 Mechanical Work, 05.03

High School Course	Postsecondary Programs	Work Groups, GOE Codes
		Production Technology, 08.02 Production Work, 08.03 Visual Arts, 01.04
Driver Education	Construction Equipment Operation; Emergency Medical Services; Truck, Bus, and Other Commercial Vehicle Driving	Construction, 06.02 Educational Services, 12.03 Hands-on Work in Construction, Extraction, and Maintenance, 06.04 Hands-on Work: Loading, Moving, Hoisting, and Conveying, 08.07 Managerial Work in Transportation, 07.01 Mining and Drilling, 06.03 Other Services Requiring Driving, 07.07 Public Safety, 04.04 Rail Vehicle Operation, 07.06 Support Work, 07.08 Truck Driving, 07.05 Vehicle Expediting and Coordinating, 07.02 Water Vehicle Operation, 07.04
Electronics Shop	Automotive Technology; Avionics Technology; Broadcasting Technology; Cardiovascular Technology; Casino Slot Technician Training; Chemical Engineering Technology; Computer Maintenance; Diesel Technology; Electrical Engineering Technology; Electrocardiograph Technology; Electroencephalograph Technology; Electromechanical Engineering Technology; Heating, Ventilation, A/C Technology; Home Appliance	Clerical Machine Operation, 09.09 Educational Services, 12.03 Electrical and Electronic Systems, 05.02 Engineering Technology, 02.08 Mechanical Work, 05.03 Media Technology, 01.08 Medical Technology, 14.05 Production Technology, 08.02

(continues)

(continued)

High School Course	Postsecondary Programs	Work Groups, GOE Codes
	Repair; Instrumentation Technology; Network and Telecommunications Technology	
English	Court Reporting; Dental Hygiene; Dietetic Technology; Early Childhood Education; Graphic and Printing Equipment Operations; Graphic Design, Commercial Art, and Illustration; Health Information Systems Technology; Hotel/Motel and Restaurant Management; Interior Design; Law Enforcement; Marine Transportation Operations; Marketing; Medical Assistant Training; Medical Laboratory Technology; Medical Transcription; Nuclear Medicine Technology; Nurse Aide/Assistant Training; Occupational Therapy Assisting; Paralegal Services; Physical Therapist Assisting; Practical Nursing (L.P.N. Training); Radiologic Technology; Respiratory Therapy Technology; Surgical Technology; Teacher Aide Training; Veterinary Technology	Animal Care and Training, 03.02 Clerical Machine Operation, 09.09 Dentistry, 14.03 Educational Services, 12.03 Graphic Arts, 01.07 Health Protection and Promotion, 14.08 Law Enforcement, 04.03 Law, 04.02 Managerial Work in Arts, Entertainment, and Media, 01.01 Managerial Work in Recreation, Travel, and Other Personal Services, 11.01 Managerial Work in Sales and Marketing, 10.01 Medical Technology, 14.05 Medical Therapy, 14.06 Medicine and Surgery, 14.02 Patient Care and Assistance, 14.07 Production Technology, 08.02 Production Work, 08.03 Records Processing, 09.07 Social Services, 12.02 Visual Arts, 01.04 Water Vehicle Operation, 07.04
Foreign Language	Culinary Arts; Flight Attendant Training; Hotel/Motel and Restaurant Management; Human Services; Library Technology; Marketing; Travel Services	Customer Service, 09.05 Educational Services, 12.03 Food and Beverage Services, 11.05 General Sales, 10.03 Managerial Work in Education and Social Service, 12.01

High School Course	Postsecondary Programs	Work Groups, GOE Codes
	Marketing Operations	Managerial Work in Recreation, Travel, and Other Personal Services, 11.01 Managerial Work in Sales and Marketing, 10.01 Other Personal Services, 11.08 Social Services, 12.02 Transportation and Lodging Services, 11.03
French	Winemaking	Educational Services, 12.03 Production Work, 08.03 Public Safety, 04.04
Geography	Marine Transportation Operations; Travel Services Marketing Operations; Winemaking	Customer Service, 09.05 Educational Services, 12.03 General Sales, 10.03 Production Work, 08.03 Public Safety, 04.04 Transportation and Lodging Services, 11.03 Water Vehicle Operation, 07.04
Geometry	Aircraft Mechanic Technology; Architectural Technology; Brewing; Casino Slot Technician Training; Chemical Engineering Technology; Civil (Engineering) Technology; Construction Inspection; Construction Technology; Drafting; Electrical Engineering Technology; Electromechanical Engineering Technology; Graphic Design, Commercial Art, and Illustration; Hotel/Motel and Restaurant Management; Instrumentation Technology;	Air Vehicle Operation, 07.03 Animal Care and Training, 03.02 Clerical Machine Operation, 09.09 Educational Services, 12.03 Electrical and Electronic Systems, 05.02 Engineering Technology, 02.08 Graphic Arts, 01.07 Health Specialties, 14.04 Laboratory Technology, 02.05 Management Support, 13.02 Managerial Work in Arts, Entertainment, and Media, 01.01 Managerial Work in Construction, Mining, and Drilling, 06.01 Managerial Work in Recreation, Travel, and Other Personal Services, 11.01

(continues)

(continued)

High School Course	Postsecondary Programs	Work Groups, GOE Codes
	Interior Design; Machinist Training; Marine Transportation Operations; Marketing; Mechanical Engineering Technology; Network and Telecommunications Technology; Optical Laboratory Technology; Opticianry; Photography; Pilot Training; Surveying Technology; Tool and Die Maker Training; Veterinary Technology; Welding Technology; Winemaking	Managerial Work in Sales and Marketing, 10.01 Mechanical Work, 05.03 Media Technology, 01.08 Metal and Plastics Machining Technology, 08.04 Production Technology, 08.02 Production Work, 08.03 Public Safety, 04.04 Social Services, 12.02 Visual Arts, 01.04 Water Vehicle Operation, 07.04
History	Teacher Aide Training	Educational Services, 12.03
Home Economics	Culinary Arts; Dietetic Technology; Fashion Design; Fashion Merchandising; Food Service Management; Interior Design	Educational Services, 12.03 Food and Beverage Services, 11.05 General Sales, 10.03 Health Protection and Promotion, 14.08 Management Support, 13.02 Managerial Work in Recreation, Travel, and Other Personal Services, 11.01 Other Personal Services, 11.08 Visual Arts, 01.04
Industrial Arts	Aircraft Mechanic Technology; Cabinetmaking; Carpentry; Carpentry; Casino Slot Technician Training; Diesel Technology; Electrician Training; Graphic and Printing Equipment Operations; Home Appliance Repair; Machinist Training; Masonry; Plumbing and Pipefitting; Tool and Die Maker Training;	Clerical Machine Operation, 09.09 Construction, 06.02 Electrical and Electronic Systems, 05.02 Graphic Arts, 01.07 Hands-on Work in Construction, Extraction, and Maintenance, 06.04 Managerial Work in Construction, Mining, and Drilling, 06.01 Mechanical Work, 05.03 Metal and Plastics

High School Course	Postsecondary Programs	Work Groups, GOE Codes
	Watchmaking and Jewelry-making; Welding Technology	Machining Technology, 08.04 Production Technology, 08.02 Production Work, 08.03 Records Processing, 09.07 Woodworking Technology, 08.05
Keyboarding	Accounting Technician; Business Management; Computer Maintenance; Computer Programming; Court Reporting; Emergency Medical Services; Health Information Systems Technology; Library Technology; Medical Assistant Training; Medical Transcription; Office Technology; Paralegal Services; Travel Services Marketing Operations	Bookkeeping, Auditing, and Accounting, 09.03 Clerical Machine Operation, 09.09 Customer Service, 09.05 Educational Services, 12.03 Electrical and Electronic Systems, 05.02 Engineering Technology, 02.08 General Management Work and Management of Support Functions, 13.01 General Sales, 10.03 Law, 04.02 Management Support, 13.02 Managerial Work in Business Detail, 09.01 Managerial Work in Construction, Mining, and Drilling, 06.01 Managerial Work in Education and Social Service, 12.01 Managerial Work in Industrial Production, 08.01 Managerial Work in Sales and Marketing, 10.01 Managerial Work in Transportation, 07.01 Mathematics and Computers, 02.06 Medical Technology, 14.05 Medicine and Surgery, 14.02 Other Services Requiring Driving, 07.07 Public Safety, 04.04 Records Processing, 09.07 Transportation and Lodging Services, 11.03

(continues)

(continued)

High School Course	Postsecondary Programs	Work Groups, GOE Codes
Mechanical Drawing	Architectural Technology; Automotive Body Repair; Cabinetmaking; Carpentry; Drafting; Graphic Design, Commercial Art, and Illustration; Heating, Ventilation, A/C Technology; Machinist Training; Masonry; Mechanical Engineering Technology; Tool and Die Maker Training; Welding Technology	Clerical Machine Operation, 09.09 Construction, 06.02 Educational Services, 12.03 Engineering Technology, 02.08 Graphic Arts, 01.07 Hands-on Work in Construction, Extraction, and Maintenance, 06.04 Managerial Work in Arts, Entertainment, and Media, 01.01 Managerial Work in Construction, Mining, and Drilling, 06.01 Mechanical Work, 05.03 Metal and Plastics Machining Technology, 08.04 Production Technology, 08.02 Production Work, 08.03 Visual Arts, 01.04 Woodworking Technology, 08.05
Metal Shop	Aircraft Mechanic Technology; Automotive Body Repair; Diesel Technology; Heating, Ventilation, A/C Technology; Machinist Training; Plumbing and Pipefitting; Tool and Die Maker Training; Watchmaking and Jewelrymaking; Welding Technology	Construction, 06.02 Electrical and Electronic Systems, 05.02 Hands-on Work in Construction, Extraction, and Maintenance, 06.04 Managerial Work in Construction, Mining, and Drilling, 06.01 Mechanical Work, 05.03 Metal and Plastics Machining Technology, 08.04 Production Technology, 08.02 Production Work, 08.03
Office Computer Applications	Accounting Technician; Auctioneering; Bartending; Business Management; Computer Programming; Court Reporting; Dental Assisting; Farm and Ranch	Air Vehicle Operation, 07.03 Animal Care and Training, 03.02 Bookkeeping, Auditing, and Accounting, 09.03 Clerical Machine Operation, 09.09 Customer Service, 09.05

High School Course	Postsecondary Programs	Work Groups, GOE Codes
	Management; Fashion Design; Fashion Merchandising; Funeral Services and Mortuary Science; Graphic and Printing Equipment Operations; Home Appliance Repair; Human Services; Interior Design; Library Technology; Medical Assistant Training; Medical Transcription; Office Technology; Optical Laboratory Technology; Opticianry; Ornamental Horticulture; Paralegal Services; Pet Grooming; Pharmacy Technology; Photography; Pilot Training; Property Management; Real Estate; Surveying Technology; Travel Services Marketing Operations; Veterinary Technology	Dentistry, 14.03 Educational Services, 12.03 Electrical and Electronic Systems, 05.02 Engineering Technology, 02.08 Food and Beverage Services, 11.05 General Management Work and Management of Support Functions, 13.01 General Sales, 10.03 Graphic Arts, 01.07 Health Specialties, 14.04 Laboratory Technology, 02.05 Law, 04.02 Management Support, 13.02 Managerial Work in Business Detail, 09.01 Managerial Work in Construction, Mining, and Drilling, 06.01 Managerial Work in Education and Social Service, 12.01 Managerial Work in Industrial Production, 08.01 Managerial Work in Plants and Animals, 03.01 Managerial Work in Sales and Marketing, 10.01 Managerial Work in Transportation, 07.01 Mathematics and Computers, 02.06 Mechanical Work, 05.03 Media Technology, 01.08 Medical Technology, 14.05 Medicine and Surgery, 14.02 Other Personal Services, 11.08 Production Technology, 08.02 Production Work, 08.03 Records Processing, 09.07 Sales Technology, 10.02

(continues)

(continued)

High School Course	Postsecondary Programs	Work Groups, GOE Codes
		Transportation and Lodging Services, 11.03 Visual Arts, 01.04
Photography	Broadcasting Technology; Graphic and Printing Equipment Operations; Graphic Design, Commercial Art, and Illustration; Investigative Services; Multimedia Design and Production; Optical Laboratory Technology; Photography	Clerical Machine Operation, 09.09 Educational Services, 12.03 Graphic Arts, 01.07 Laboratory Technology, 02.05 Law Enforcement, 04.03 Managerial Work in Arts, Entertainment, and Media, 01.01 Managerial Work in Law, Law Enforcement, and Public Safety, 04.01 Mechanical Work, 05.03 Media Technology, 01.08 Production Technology, 08.02 Production Work, 08.03 Records Processing, 09.07 Visual Arts, 01.04
Physics/Principles of Technology	Marine Transportation Operations; Aircraft Mechanic Technology; Architectural Technology; Avionics Technology; Broadcasting Technology; Cabinetmaking; Cardiovascular Technology; Carpentry; Casino Slot Technician Training; Chemical Engineering Technology; Civil (Engineering) Technology; Clinical Lab Technician; Computer Maintenance; Construction Equipment Operation; Construction Inspection; Construction Technology; Diesel Technology; Drafting; Electrical Engineering Technology; Electrician	Air Vehicle Operation, 07.03 Clerical Machine Operation, 09.09 Construction, 06.02 Educational Services, 12.03 Electrical and Electronic Systems, 05.02 Engineering Technology, 02.08 General Management Work and Management of Support Functions, 13.01 Graphic Arts, 01.07 Hands-on Work in Construction, Extraction, and Maintenance, 06.04 Hands-on Work: Loading, Moving, Hoisting, and Conveying, 08.07 Health Specialties, 14.04 Laboratory Technology, 02.05 Law Enforcement, 04.03 Management Support, 13.02

High School Course	Postsecondary Programs	Work Groups, GOE Codes
	Training; Electrocardiograph Technology; Electro-encephalograph Technology; Electromechanical Engineering Technology; Emergency Medical Services; Fire Science/Firefighting; Graphic and Printing Equipment Operations; Heating, Ventilation, A/C Technology; Home Appliance Repair; Instrumentation Technology; Machinist Training; Masonry; Massage Therapy; Mechanical Engineering Technology; Medical Laboratory Technology; Network and Telecommunications Technology; Nuclear Medicine Technology; Optical Laboratory Technology; Opticianry; Ornamental Horticulture; Personal Trainer; Pharmacy Technology; Photography; Physical Therapist Assisting; Pilot Training; Plumbing and Pipefitting; Radiologic Technology; Respiratory Therapy Technology; Surgical Technology; Surveying Technology; Tool and Die Maker Training; Watchmaking and Jewelrymaking; Welding Technology	Managerial Work in Construction, Mining, and Drilling, 06.01 Managerial Work in Plants and Animals, 03.01 Mechanical Work, 05.03 Media Technology, 01.08 Medical Technology, 14.05 Medical Therapy, 14.06 Medicine and Surgery, 14.02 Metal and Plastics Machining Technology, 08.04 Mining and Drilling, 06.03 Other Services Requiring Driving, 07.07 Production Technology, 08.02 Production Work, 08.03 Public Safety, 04.04 Records Processing, 09.07 Recreational Services, 11.02 Water Vehicle Operation, 07.04 Woodworking Technology, 08.05
Pre-Calculus	Brewing; Graphic Design, Commercial Art, and Illustration; Instrumentation Technology; Surveying Technology	Clerical Machine Operation, 09.09 Educational Services, 12.03 Engineering Technology, 02.08 Graphic Arts, 01.07 Managerial Work

(continues)

(continued)

High School Course	Postsecondary Programs	Work Groups, GOE Codes
		in Arts, Entertainment, and Media, 01.01 Mechanical Work, 05.03 Production Work, 08.03 Public Safety, 04.04 Visual Arts, 01.04
Public Speaking	Auctioneering; Bartending; Broadcasting Technology; Business Management; Cardiovascular Technology; Casino Gaming Training; Corrections; Dental Assisting; Dental Hygiene; Early Childhood Education; Flight Attendant Training; Funeral Services and Mortuary Science; Graphic Design, Commercial Art, and Illustration; Health Information Systems Technology; Hotel/Motel and Restaurant Management; Interior Design; Investigative Services; Law Enforcement; Library Technology; Massage Therapy; Medical Assistant Training; Multimedia Design and Production; Occupational Therapy Assisting; Opticianry; Paralegal Services; Personal Trainer; Physical Therapist Assisting; Practical Nursing (L.P.N. Training); Property Management; Radiologic Technology; Real Estate; Respiratory Therapy Technology; Teacher Aide Training; Travel Services Marketing Operations; Veterinary Technology	Animal Care and Training, 03.02 Clerical Machine Operation, 09.09 Customer Service, 09.05 Dentistry, 14.03 Educational Services, 12.03 Food and Beverage Services, 11.05 General Management Work and Management of Support Functions, 13.01 General Sales, 10.03 Graphic Arts, 01.07 Health Specialties, 14.04 Law, 04.02 Law Enforcement, 04.03 Management Support, 13.02 Managerial Work in Arts, Entertainment, and Media, 01.01 Managerial Work in Business Detail, 09.01 Managerial Work in Construction, Mining, and Drilling, 06.01 Managerial Work in Education and Social Service, 12.01 Managerial Work in Industrial Production, 08.01 Managerial Work in Law, Law Enforcement, and Public Safety, 04.01 Managerial Work in Recreation, Travel, and Other Personal Services, 11.01 Managerial Work in Sales and Marketing, 10.01

High School Course	Postsecondary Programs	Work Groups, GOE Codes
		Managerial Work in Transportation, 07.01 Media Technology, 01.08 Medical Technology, 14.05 Medical Therapy, 14.06 Medicine and Surgery, 14.02 Other Personal Services, 11.08 Patient Care and Assistance, 14.07 Production Work, 08.03 Records Processing, 09.07 Recreational Services, 11.02 Sales Technology, 10.02 Social Services, 12.02 Transportation and Lodging Services, 11.03 Visual Arts, 01.04
Science	Hotel/Motel and Restaurant Management; Marketing; Teacher Aide Training	Educational Services, 12.03 Managerial Work in Recreation, Travel, and Other Personal Services, 11.01 Managerial Work in Sales and Marketing, 10.01 Social Services, 12.02
Social Science	Early Childhood Education; Emergency Medical Services; Fashion Design; Fashion Merchandising; Flight Attendant Training; Funeral Services and Mortuary Science; Home Health Aide Training; Human Services; Interior Design; Investigative Services; Law Enforcement; Occupational Therapy Assisting; Paralegal Services; Physical Therapist Assisting; Property Management; Real Estate; Teacher Aide Training; Travel Services Marketing Operations	Customer Service, 09.05 Educational Services, 12.03 General Management Work and Management of Support Functions, 13.01 General Sales, 10.03 Law Enforcement, 04.03 Law, 04.02 Management Support, 13.02 Managerial Work in Construction, Mining, and Drilling, 06.01 Managerial Work in Education and Social Service, 12.01 Managerial Work in Law, Law Enforcement, and Public Safety, 04.01 Medical Therapy, 14.06

(continues)

(continued)

High School Course	Postsecondary Programs	Work Groups, GOE Codes
		Other Personal Services, 11.08 Other Services Requiring Driving, 07.07 Patient Care and Assistance, 14.07 Public Safety, 04.04 Transportation and Lodging Services, 11.03 Visual Arts, 01.04
Spanish	Farm and Ranch Management	Educational Services, 12.03 General Management Work and Management of Support Functions, 13.01 Managerial Work in Plants and Animals, 03.01
Trigonometry	Avionics Technology; Brewing; Casino Slot Technician Training; Chemical Engineering Technology; Civil (Engineering) Technology; Construction Technology; Drafting; Electrical Engineering Technology; Electromechanical Engineering Technology; Graphic Design, Commercial Art, and Illustration; Hotel/Motel and Restaurant Management; Instrumentation Technology; Machinist Training; Marine Transportation Operations; Marketing; Mechanical Engineering Technology; Network and Telecommunications Technology; Optical Laboratory Technology; Opticianry; Photography; Surveying Technology; Tool and Die	Clerical Machine Operation, 09.09 Educational Services, 12.03 Electrical and Electronic Systems, 05.02 Engineering Technology, 02.08 Graphic Arts, 01.07 Health Specialties, 14.04 Laboratory Technology, 02.05 Management Support, 13.02 Managerial Work in Arts, Entertainment, and Media, 01.01 Managerial Work in Construction, Mining, and Drilling, 06.01 Managerial Work in Recreation, Travel, and Other Personal Services, 11.01 Managerial Work in Sales and Marketing, 10.01 Mechanical Work, 05.03 Media Technology, 01.08 Metal and Plastics Machining Technology, 08.04 Production Technology, 08.02 Production Work, 08.03 Public Safety, 04.04

High School Course	Postsecondary Programs	Work Groups, GOE Codes
	Maker Training; Winemaking	Social Services, 12.02 Visual Arts, 01.04 Water Vehicle Operation, 07.04

Look over the items that you marked in the table. Determine the programs and work groups that best fit with the high school courses you listed at the beginning of this section and enter them below. If there are many, try to find programs and work groups that are linked to *more than one* of your best high school courses and enter these names.

Similar Programs and Work Groups

_____

_____

_____

_____

_____

_____

Your Work-Related Values

People rarely talk about values, except occasionally when politicians boast about their "family values." Yet values affect every decision we make. A *value* is something that we consider desirable to gain or keep. When we choose between two things that we have the chance to gain or keep, we base our preference on our values. Sometimes it is obvious that one choice is better aligned with our values than another one. But a lot of the time we have to make trade-offs, accepting less of one thing that we value to get something else that we value more.

For example, when choosing what to have for lunch, we make trade-offs between several values: good taste, good nutrition, reasonable price, convenient location, something different from what we had yesterday, and perhaps trying to impress our lunch date. It may be impossible to find one meal that will fit *all* of these values perfectly, but we usually can find a compromise choice that will satisfy our most important values. Note that our lunch-related values may change over time, as we might become more nutrition-conscious or short on lunch money. Most important of all, consider that there is no one right set of lunch-related values for all people. Some people enjoy having the same lunch every day, and others don't care what their lunch date thinks of their choice. Lunch-related values are a matter of personal preference.

The same applies to work-related values. People have their own unique preferences, they often need to make trade-offs, and they may find that their values change over time. But in fact most people don't consciously know what their work-related values are. If you ask them what makes one job better than another, they can usually name only one or two things—such as the salary or the working conditions.

This is where this section can help you: by making you more aware of your work-related values. In the following chart, look over the names and definitions of 19 work-related values that the U.S. Department of Labor (USDOL) uses to describe jobs in its O*NET database. (The work-related values in this book are particular to the listed educational/training programs. The USDOL uses additional values that are unrelated.) When you compare the importance of two values, ask yourself, "Would I quit a job that had a lot of Value X if I could get a job with a lot of Value Y?"

Work-Related Values	
Value	**Description**
Ability Utilization	Making use of your individual abilities
Achievement	Getting a feeling of accomplishment
Activity	Being busy all the time
Authority	Giving directions and instructions to others
Autonomy	Planning your work with little supervision
Company Policies and Practices	Being treated fairly by the company
Compensation	Being paid well in comparison with other workers
Coworkers	Having coworkers who are easy to get along with
Creativity	Getting chances to try out your own ideas
Good Working Conditions	Having good working conditions
Independence	Doing your work alone
Moral Values	Never being pressured to do things that go against your sense of right and wrong
Recognition	Receiving recognition for the work you do
Responsibility	Making decisions on your own
Security	Having steady employment
Social Service	Having work where you do things to improve other people's lives
Social Status	Being looked up to by others in your company and your community
Supervision, Human Relations	Having supervisors who back you up with management
Supervision, Technical	Having supervisors who train you well

When you've decided which three of these are most important for you to get from your work, list them here:

Work Values for My Career

1. _____

2. _____

3. _____

In the following table, start by drawing a large box around each row containing the work-related values that you listed above as your most important. Now look in the second and third columns of these rows and circle any programs and work groups that appear in two or more of your selected rows. At the end of this section, you can list the names of those programs and work groups, because they correspond well to your three most important work-related values. If *none* of them appears more than once in the selected rows, list some of the programs and work groups that correspond to your number-one value.

Note The work-related values are related to programs insofar as they characterize the occupations to which the programs are linked. They do not necessarily reflect the experience of being in the program.

Work-Related Values and Their Relationship to Postsecondary Programs and Work Groups		
Work-Related Values	Programs	Work Groups, GOE Codes
Ability Utilization— Making use of your individual abilities	Broadcasting Technology; Fashion Design; Interior Design; Medical Laboratory Technology; Multimedia Design and Production; Nuclear Medicine Technology; Photography; Pilot Training	Air Vehicle Operation, 07.03 Dentistry, 14.03 Managerial Work in Education and Social Service, 12.01 Mathematics and Computers, 02.06 Media Technology, 01.08 Medicine and Surgery, 14.02 Visual Arts, 01.04

Work-Related Values	Programs	Work Groups, GOE Codes
Achievement—Getting a feeling of accomplishment	Emergency Medical Services; Fashion Design; Fire Science/Firefighting; Interior Design; Opticianry; Photography; Practical Nursing (L.P.N. Training); Respiratory Therapy Technology	Air Vehicle Operation, 07.03 Dentistry, 14.03 Educational Services, 12.03 Health Specialties, 14.04 Managerial Work in Arts, Entertainment, and Media, 01.01 Managerial Work in Education and Social Service 12.01 Managerial Work in Law, Law Enforcement, and Public Safety, 04.01 Medical Therapy, 14.06 Medicine and Surgery, 14.02 Social Services, 12.02 Visual Arts, 01.04
Activity—Being busy all the time	Construction Technology	Managerial Work in Education and Social Service, 12.01
Authority—Giving directions and instructions to others	Business Management; Corrections; Farm and Ranch Management; Food Service Management; Hotel/Motel and Restaurant Management; Marine Transportation Operations; Ornamental Horticulture; Personal Trainer; Property Management	Educational Services, 12.03 General Management Work and Management of Support Functions, 13.01 Managerial Work in Business Detail, 09.01 Managerial Work in Construction, Mining, and Drilling, 06.01 Managerial Work in Industrial Production, 08.01 Managerial Work in Law, Law Enforcement, and Public Safety, 04.01 Managerial Work in Plants and Animals, 03.01 Managerial Work in Recreation, Travel, and Other Personal Services, 11.01 Managerial Work in Sales and Marketing, 10.01 Managerial Work in Transportation, 07.01

(continues)

(continued)

Work-Related Values	Programs	Work Groups, GOE Codes
Autonomy—Planning your work with little supervision	Business Management; Farm and Ranch Management; Fashion Merchandising; Food Service Management; Hotel/Motel and Restaurant Management; Marine Transportation Operations; Multimedia Design and Production; Ornamental Horticulture; Property Management	General Management Work and Management of Support Functions, 13.01 Law, 04.02 Managerial Work in Arts, Entertainment, and Media, 01.01 Managerial Work in Business Detail, 09.01 Managerial Work in Construction, Mining, and Drilling, 06.01 Managerial Work in Industrial Production, 08.01 Managerial Work in Plants and Animals, 03.01 Managerial Work in Sales and Marketing, 10.01 Managerial Work in Transportation, 07.01 Mathematics and Computers, 02.06 Sales Technology, 10.02 Social Services, 12.02
Company Policies and Practices—Being treated fairly by the company	Paralegal Services; Pilot Training	Managerial Work in Transportation, 07.01
Compensation—Being paid well in comparison with other workers	Computer Programming; Marketing; Pilot Training	Truck Driving, 07.05
Coworkers—Having coworkers who are easy to get along with	Corrections; Dietetic Technology; Flight Attendant Training; Pharmacy Technology; Practical Nursing (L.P.N. Training); Respiratory Therapy Technology; Teacher Aide Training	Medical Therapy, 14.06

Work-Related Values	Programs	Work Groups, GOE Codes
Creativity—Getting chances to try out your own ideas	Fashion Design; Interior Design; Marketing; Multimedia Design and Production; Personal Trainer; Photography	Visual Arts, 01.04
Good Working Conditions—Having good working conditions	Accounting Technician; Architectural Technology; Business Management; Casino Gaming Training; Drafting; Library Technology; Marketing; Pharmacy Technology; Travel Services Marketing Operations	Bookkeeping, Auditing, and Accounting, 09.03 Customer Service, 09.05 Educational Services, 12.03 General Management Work and Management of Support Functions, 13.01 General Sales, 10.03 Management Support, 13.02 Managerial Work in Business Detail, 09.01 Managerial Work in Sales and Marketing, 10.01 Mathematics and Computers, 02.06 Records Processing, 09.07
Independence—Doing your work alone	Cabinetmaking; Chemical Engineering Technology; Computer Programming; Dental Laboratory Technology; Electromechanical Engineering Technology; Graphic and Printing Equipment Operations; Graphic Design, Commercial Art, and Illustration; Office Technology; Optical Laboratory Technology; Watchmaking and Jewelrymaking	Clerical Machine Operation, 09.09 Craft Arts, 01.06 Graphic Arts, 01.07 Truck Driving, 07.05
Moral Values—Never being pressured to do things that go against your sense of right and wrong	Aircraft Mechanic Technology; Architectural Technology; Automotive Body Repair; Automotive Technology; Avionics Technology;	Animal Care and Training, 03.02 Clerical Machine Operation, 09.09 Construction, 06.02 Craft Arts, 01.06 Electrical and Electronic

(continues)

(continued)

Work-Related Values	Programs	Work Groups, GOE Codes
	Bartending; Brewing; Cabinetmaking; Carpentry; Casino Slot Technician Training; Chemical Engineering Technology; Civil (Engineering) Technology; Clinical Lab Technician; Computer Maintenance; Computer Programming; Construction Equipment Operation; Culinary Arts; Dental Laboratory Technology; Diesel Technology; Drafting; Electrical Engineering Technology; Electrician Training; Electromechanical Engineering Technology; Graphic and Printing Equipment Operations; Graphic Design, Commercial Art, and Illustration; Health Information Systems Technology; Heating, Ventilation, A/C Technology; Home Appliance Repair; Investigative Services; Library Technology; Machinist Training; Masonry; Mechanical Engineering Technology; Medical Assistant Training; Network and Telecommunications Technology; Office Technology; Optical Laboratory Technology; Pet Grooming; Plumbing and Pipefitting; Radiologic Technology; Surgical Technology; Surveying Technology; Tool	Systems, 05.02 Engineering Technology, 02.08 Food and Beverage Services, 11.05 Graphic Arts, 01.07 Hands-on Work in Construction, Extraction, and Maintenance, 06.04 Hands-on Work: Loading, Moving, Hoisting, and Conveying, 08.07 Laboratory Technology, 02.05 Mechanical Work, 05.03 Medical Technology, 14.05 Metal and Plastics Machining Technology, 08.04 Mining and Drilling, 06.03 Modeling and Personal Appearance, 01.09 Other Personal Services, 11.08 Other Services Requiring Driving, 07.07 Production Technology, 08.02 Production Work, 08.03 Records Processing, 09.07 Recreational Services, 11.02 Support Work, 07.08 Systems Operation, 08.06 Vehicle Expediting and Coordinating, 07.02 Water Vehicle Operation, 07.04 Woodworking Technology, 08.05

Work-Related Values	Programs	Work Groups, GOE Codes
	and Die Maker Training; Veterinary Technology; Water/Wastewater Treatment Technology; Welding Technology; Winemaking	
Recognition— Receiving recognition for the work you do	[No program is rated high on this value.]	Air Vehicle Operation, 07.03
Responsibility— Making decisions on your own	Construction Inspection; Farm and Ranch Management; Marine Transportation Operations; Ornamental Horticulture; Personal Trainer; Property Management; Real Estate	Health Specialties, 14.04 Managerial Work in Arts, Entertainment, and Media, 01.01 Managerial Work in Construction, Mining, and Drilling, 06.01 Managerial Work in Industrial Production, 08.01 Managerial Work in Law, Law Enforcement, and Public Safety, 04.01 Managerial Work in Plants and Animals, 03.01
Security—Having steady employment	Corrections; Fire Science/Firefighting; Food Service Management; Funeral Services and Mortuary Science; Law Enforcement; Occupational Therapy Assisting; Physical Therapist Assisting; Surgical Technology	Law, 04.02 Law Enforcement, 04.03 Public Safety, 04.04
Social Service— Having work where you do things to improve other people's lives	Bartending; Cardiovascular Technology; Cosmetology/ Barbering; Dental Assisting; Dental Hygiene; Dietetic Technology; Early Childhood Education; Electrocardiograph Technology; Emergency Medical Services; Flight Attendant Training; Home	Barber and Beauty Services, 11.04 Dentistry, 14.03 Health Protection and Promotion, 14.08 Health Specialties, 14.04 Medical Therapy, 14.06 Medicine and Surgery, 14.02 Patient Care and Assistance, 14.07 Social Services, 12.02

(continues)

(continued)

Work-Related Values	Programs	Work Groups, GOE Codes
	Health Aide Training; Human Services; Nurse Aide/Assistant Training; Occupational Therapy Assisting; Opticianry; Physical Therapist Assisting; Practical Nursing (L.P.N. Training); Respiratory Therapy Technology; Occupational Therapy Assisting; Surgical Technology; Teacher Aide Training	Transportation and Lodging Services, 11.03
Social Status—Being looked up to by others in your company and your community	Fire Science/Firefighting; Opticianry	[No GOE group is rated high on this value.]
Supervision, Human Relations—Having supervisors who back you up with management	Law Enforcement; Truck, Bus, and Other Commercial Vehicle Driving	Rail Vehicle Operation, 07.06
Supervision, Technical—Having supervisors who train you well	Flight Attendant Training	[No GOE group is rated high on this value.]

Write down the names of the programs and work groups that most closely correspond to the three values you listed at the beginning of this section.

Programs That Relate to My Values

_____

_____

_____

_____

_____

_____

_____

_____

_____

_____

The Hot List

Now that you've done the four exercises in this part of the book, it's time for you
to assemble a Hot List of programs and careers that deserve active consideration in
Part II.

At the end of each of the four exercises—interests, skills, high school courses, and
work-related values—you made a list of the programs and work groups that were
most strongly suggested by each exercise. Look these over now and decide which of
the following statements best characterizes what you see:

- **Certain programs and work groups appear in all four, or three of the four, outputs of the exercises.** If this is what you find, congratulations! These programs obviously correspond well to your personality, and you should write them on your Hot List at the end of this section.

- **Certain programs and work groups appear in two outputs of the exercises, but none appear in three or four.** This is still a meaningful finding; these programs probably belong on your Hot List below. If a large number of programs fit this description, you might ask yourself whether you feel more confident about one kind of exercise than another. For example, do you feel you have a clearer notion of your interests and high school courses than of your skills and values? In that case, you might want to give greater weight to the programs that are shared by the outputs of the exercises relating to interests and high school courses.

- **There's no pattern at all—no programs or work groups appear in more than one output of the exercises.** In this case, you need to decide which exercise you trust the most. Different people have different styles of thinking about themselves, and some have a much keener awareness of (for example) their interests than their values. Or perhaps the terms used in one exercise seem easier to understand than the terms in the others. Go with the results of the exercise that you feel most confident about and write those programs on your Hot List.

- **One of the preceding three statements applies to me, but the problem is that I get a very large number of programs for my Hot List.** Here's where the work groups can help you. Find the work group that appears most often in the results of the exercises for skills, high school courses, and values. Then go back to the interest exercise and see which programs are linked to that work group. These are strong candidates for your Hot List.

Note No skills or values data is available for the following programs:

- Auctioneering
- Chemical Engineering Technology
- Court Reporting
- Electroencephalograph Technology

- Instrumentation Technology

- Massage Therapy

- Medical Transcription

- Taxidermy

- Veterinary Technology

That means that if any of these was suggested by the exercises for Interests and high school courses (especially if it was suggested by both), it is also a candidate for your Hot List.

After you have filled in your Hot List below and you start investigating these programs in Part II, you can also use the Hot List as an informal way of recording your impressions:

- If a program appeals to you when you read about it, put a star next to the name on the Hot List. The stars can serve to remind you which programs are the hottest of the hot!

- One of the important facts you'll read about the program is what jobs it is linked to. When you see a job that looks interesting to you, write its name next to the name of the program on the Hot List. Later, you can use other resources to investigate these jobs in greater detail.

My Hot List

_____

_____

_____

_____

_____

_____

_____

_____

Facts About Training Programs and Careers

In this section, you can get the facts about 104 postsecondary training programs and the careers related to them. You may learn new things about training that you thought you were knowledgeable about. You may also encounter programs that you have never heard of before or that you don't know much about.

The Hot List you created in Part I can help you choose programs to explore here. But even if you just browse at random, the facts are organized in a way that makes it easy for you to get an understanding of the program and related careers.

Here are the kinds of information you'll find for each training program:

- **Program/Training Duration** and **Location:** How long this training takes and the type of place where you might get the training

- **Career Snapshot:** What the training program is and what careers are related to it

- **Related Specialties and Careers:** Common areas of concentration

- **Related Job Titles, Educational Requirements, Projected Growth, and Earnings:** Specific facts about the jobs from the U.S. Department of Labor

- **Typical Postsecondary Courses:** Courses often required for this program (varies by institution)

- **Some Suggested High School Courses:** High school coursework that is considered good preparation

- **Essential Knowledge and Skills:** Skills that are most important for the careers related to this training program

- **Values/Work Environment:** The rewards of being in the related jobs; also, the typical work setting and physical demands

- **Other Information Sources:** Where to look in other reference materials for additional facts

Accounting Technician

Program/Training Duration: One month to a year

Location: Workplace

Career Snapshot

Accounting technicians and bookkeepers record the transactions of an organization and maintain its financial records. Under the supervision of accountants, they provide information about the fiscal condition and trends of the organization and figures for tax forms and financial reports. They advise senior accountants and management, and therefore, they need good communications skills. The job outlook is considered generally good for those who can work with computers rather than do only routine tasks.

Related Specialties and Careers

Accounts payable/receivable, auditing, banking, bookkeeping, computerized accounting systems, payroll.

Related Job Titles, Educational Requirements, Projected Growth, and Earnings			
Job Title	Educational Requirements	Projected Growth	Average Earnings
Billing and Posting Clerks and Machine Operators (O*NET code 43-3021.00)	Moderate-term on-the-job training	Little or none	$25,350
Billing, Cost, and Rate Clerks (O*NET code 43-3021.02)	Short-term on-the-job training	Little or none	$25,350
Billing, Posting, and Calculating Machine Operators (O*NET code 43-3021.03)	Short-term on-the-job training	Little or none	$25,350
Bookkeeping, Accounting, and Auditing Clerks (O*NET code 43-3031.00)	Moderate-term on-the-job training	Little or none	$26,540
Brokerage Clerks (O*NET code 43-4011.00)	Moderate-term on-the-job training	Declining	$32,470

(continues)

(continued)

Related Job Titles, Educational Requirements, Projected Growth, and Earnings			
Job Title	**Educational Requirements**	**Projected Growth**	**Average Earnings**
Gaming Cage Workers (O*NET code 43-3041.00)	Moderate-term on-the-job training	Faster than average	$21,540
Payroll and Timekeeping Clerks (O*NET code 43-3051.00)	Short-term on-the-job training	Little or none	$28,250
Statement Clerks (O*NET code 43-3021.01)	Short-term on-the-job training	Little or none	$25,350
Statistical Assistants (O*NET code 43-9111.00)	Moderate-term on-the-job training	Little or none	$28,990
Tax Preparers (O*NET code 13-2082.00)	Moderate-term on-the-job training	Average	$27,680

Typical Postsecondary Courses

Business finance; business information processing; business reports and communi-cation; college algebra; computer spreadsheet; co-op work experience; English composition; financial accounting; introduction to accounting; introduction to business; introduction to economics; legal environment of business; managerial accounting; oral communication; taxation of corporations, partnerships, and estates; taxation of individuals.

Suggested High School Courses

Applied communications; bookkeeping; business/applied math; keyboarding; office computer applications. **Dept. of Education School-to-Work Cluster:** Business and Administration; Finance and Insurance.

Essential Knowledge and Skills

Clerical; economics and accounting; mathematics. **Values/Work Environment:** Indoors, environmentally controlled; spend time sitting; good working conditions.

Other Information Sources

Many career and education information sources use the standard cross-referencing systems noted below. You can use the codes to obtain substantial additional information on the program (via CIP code) and related occupations (via GOE code). The O*NET codes on the opposite page refer to another major career information system. See the Introduction for details on obtaining additional information.

Classification of Instructional Programs (CIP) code(s): 520302 Accounting Technology/Technician and Bookkeeping

Guide for Occupational Exploration (GOE) code(s): 02.06 Mathematics and Computers; 09.03 Bookkeeping, Auditing, and Accounting; 09.05 Customer Service; 09.09 Clerical Machine Operation

 **Aircraft Mechanic Technology**

Program/Training Duration: A year or more

Location: Vocational classroom and workplace

Career Snapshot

The nation's fleet of airplanes depends on aircraft mechanics to perform scheduled maintenance, conduct regular safety inspections, and make repairs as needed. These mechanics are trained at trade schools approved by the Federal Aviation Administration (FAA) and are certified by passing an FAA exam. Some begin their training in the military, but the work there tends to be too specialized to teach all the necessary skills. Aircraft mechanics often need to take classes throughout their careers to keep abreast of changing technologies. Airlines generally prefer mechanics who are certified for both airframe and powerplant work (A&P), although some mechanics specialize in one or the other. The job outlook looks good, although competition will be keen for the best-paying jobs with large airlines.

Related Specialties and Careers

Airframe, powerplant.

Related Job Titles, Educational Requirements, Projected Growth, and Earnings			
Job Title	**Educational Requirements**	**Projected Growth**	**Average Earnings**
Aircraft Body and Bonded Structure Repairers (O*NET code 49-3011.03)	Postsecondary vocational training	Average	$41,990
Aircraft Engine Specialists (O*NET code 49-3011.02)	Postsecondary vocational training	Average	$41,990
Aircraft Mechanics and Service Technicians (O*NET code 49-3011.00)	Postsecondary vocational training	Average	$41,990
Aircraft Rigging Assemblers (O*NET code 51-2011.03)	Long-term on-the-job training	Average	$37,190
Aircraft Structure Assemblers, Precision (O*NET code 51-2011.01)	Long-term on-the-job training	Average	$37,190

Job Title	Educational Requirements	Projected Growth	Average Earnings
Aircraft Structure, Surfaces, Rigging, and Systems Assemblers (O*NET code 51-2011.00)	Long-term on-the-job training	Average	$37,190
Aircraft Systems Assemblers, Precision (O*NET code 51-2011.02)	Long-term on-the-job training	Average	$37,190
Airframe-and-Power-Plant Mechanics (O*NET code 49-3011.01)	Postsecondary vocational training	Average	$41,990
Avionics Technicians (O*NET code 49-2091.00)	Postsecondary vocational training	Average	$41,450

Typical Postsecondary Courses

Aircraft basic science; aircraft hydraulic, pneumatic, and fuel systems; aircraft materials and processes; aircraft powerplant inspection; aircraft powerplant maintenance; aircraft powerplant theory; aircraft structural materials; airframe electrical systems; airframe inspection; airframe maintenance; blueprint reading; propellers; technical writing.

Suggested High School Courses

Geometry; industrial arts; metal shop; physics/principles of technology. **Dept. of Education School-to-Work Cluster:** Transportation, Distribution, and Logistics.

Essential Knowledge and Skills

Design; engineering and technology; equipment maintenance; installation; mechanical devices; repairing. **Values/Work Environment:** Exposed to hazardous equipment; moral values; spend time standing.

Other Information Sources

Many career and education information sources use the standard cross-referencing systems noted below. You can use the codes to obtain substantial additional information on the program (via CIP code) and related occupations (via GOE code). The O*NET codes on the opposite page refer to another major career information system. See the Introduction for details on obtaining additional information.

Classification of Instructional Programs (CIP) code(s): 470608 Aircraft Powerplant Technology/Technician; 470607 Airframe Mechanics and Aircraft Maintenance Technology/Technician

Guide for Occupational Exploration (GOE) code(s): 05.02 Electrical and Electronic Systems; 05.03 Mechanical Work; 08.02 Production Technology

Architectural Technology

Program/Training Duration: One to two years

Location: Vocational classroom

Career Snapshot

Architectural drafters prepare technical drawings and plans that architects use to present their designs to clients and government agencies and that builders follow during construction. Employment opportunities are best for those who have been trained at a community college or vocational school. Some schools offer much better preparation than others, so you should be careful when you select where to study. Skill with computer-aided drafting (CAD) has become essential.

Related Specialties and Careers

Commercial buildings, computer-aided drafting (CAD), residential buildings.

Related Job Titles, Educational Requirements, Projected Growth, and Earnings			
Job Title	Educational Requirements	Projected Growth	Average Earnings
Architectural and Civil Drafters (O*NET code 17-3011.00)	Postsecondary vocational training	Faster than average	$37,010
Architectural Drafters (O*NET code 17-3011.01)	Associate degree	Faster than average	$37,010
Civil Drafters (O*NET code 17-3011.02)	Postsecondary vocational training	Faster than average	$37,010

Typical Postsecondary Courses

Architectural computer graphics; architectural construction documents; architectural design; architectural drafting; architectural graphics; building materials and systems; building structural analysis; codes, permits, and government regulations; geometry and trigonometry; history of architecture; introduction to architecture.

Suggested High School Courses

Algebra; applied communications; geometry; mechanical drawing; physics/ principles of technology. **Dept. of Education School-to-Work Cluster:** Architecture and Construction.

Essential Knowledge and Skills

Design; engineering and technology; mathematics. **Values/Work Environment:** Indoors, environmentally controlled; moral values; spend time sitting; good working conditions.

Other Information Sources

Many career and education information sources use the standard cross-referencing systems noted below. You can use the codes to obtain substantial additional information on the program (via CIP code) and related occupations (via GOE code). The O*NET codes on the opposite page refer to another major career information system. See the Introduction for details on obtaining additional information.

Classification of Instructional Programs (CIP) code(s): 040901 Architectural Technology/Technician

Guide for Occupational Exploration (GOE) code(s): 02.08 Engineering Technology

---

 Auctioneering

Program/Training Duration: A few weeks to a year or more

Location: Vocational classroom or workplace

Career Snapshot

Many different kinds of goods, from artwork to automobiles, are sold at auctions. Auctioneers generate interest in the merchandise, partly by describing the item and partly by using a singsong patter as they take bids. Often they need to appraise the value of an item before bidding begins. This means that they have to be knowledgeable about the kind of merchandise and have to develop an effective calling style. Some of them learn on the job by working for an auction firm, but many complete a course at a specialized auctioneering school. Licensure is required in many states. Auctioneering offers opportunities for self-employment. Travel is often required, and physical stamina may be needed for the work.

Related Specialties and Careers

Antiques and furniture, appraising, auction management, automobiles, estates and bankruptcies, farm equipment and livestock, real estate.

Related Job Titles, Educational Requirements, Projected Growth, and Earnings			
Job Title	Educational Requirements	Projected Growth	Average Earnings
Sales and Related Workers, All Other (O*NET code 41-9099.99)	No data available	Faster than average	No salary data available

Typical Postsecondary Courses

Advertising and managing auctions; auction industry legalities; auctions of antiques and furniture; auto auctions; bid calling and voice control; business liquidations; clerking and cashiering; estate and bankruptcy auctions; farm equipment and livestock auctions; getting started in auctioneering; real estate auctions.

Suggested High School Courses

Business/applied math; distributive education; office computer applications; public speaking. **Dept. of Education School-to-Work Cluster:** Retail and Wholesale Sales and Service.

Essential Knowledge and Skills

No data available. **Values/Work Environment:** No data available.

Other Information Sources

Many career and education information sources use the standard cross-referencing systems noted below. You can use the codes to obtain substantial additional information on the program (via CIP code) and related occupations (via GOE code). The O*NET codes on the opposite page refer to another major career information system. See the Introduction for details on obtaining additional information.

Classification of Instructional Programs (CIP) code(s): 521901 Auctioneering

Guide for Occupational Exploration (GOE) code(s): 10.02 Sales Technology

---

Automotive Body Repair

Program/Training Duration: A year or more

Location: Workplace

Career Snapshot

Although cars don't rust as easily as they once did, they continue to get into accidents and need to have their bodies repaired. Automotive body repairers straighten bent frames and fenders, smooth out dents, replace glass and parts that are damaged beyond repair, and repaint and refinish the exterior. They also need to make careful examinations and measurements of damaged vehicles to plan the method of repair and estimate the costs. In large shops, they may specialize in one aspect of the business, such as estimating, painting, or realigning unibody structures. As more sophisticated body materials come on the market, the best job prospects will be for those with formal training.

Related Specialties and Careers

Estimating, frame realignment, glass, painting, welding.

Related Job Titles, Educational Requirements, Projected Growth, and Earnings			
Job Title	Educational Requirements	Projected Growth	Average Earnings
Automotive Body and Related Repairers (O*NET code 49-3021.00)	Long-term on-the-job training	Average	$32,490
Automotive Glass Installers and Repairers (O*NET code 49-3022.00)	Long-term on-the-job training	Average	$27,160
Painters, Transportation Equipment (O*NET code 51-9122.00)	Moderate-term on-the-job training	Average	$32,330

Typical Postsecondary Courses

Auto body repair estimating; auto body repair materials; basic welding; body shop operations; glass and trim repair; painting and refinishing; structural damage and repair; workplace communications; workplace math.

Suggested High School Courses

Applied communications; auto shop; business/applied math; mechanical drawing; metal shop. **Dept. of Education School-to-Work Cluster:** Manufacturing.

Essential Knowledge and Skills

Mechanical devices; repairing. **Values/Work Environment:** Moral values; spend time standing.

Other Information Sources

Many career and education information sources use the standard cross-referencing systems noted below. You can use the codes to obtain substantial additional information on the program (via CIP code) and related occupations (via GOE code). The O*NET codes on the opposite page refer to another major career information system. See the Introduction for details on obtaining additional information.

Classification of Instructional Programs (CIP) code(s): 470603 Autobody/Collision and Repair Technology/ Technician

Guide for Occupational Exploration (GOE) code(s): 05.03 Mechanical Work

---

Automotive Technology

Program/Training Duration: A few weeks to more than a year

Location: Workplace

Career Snapshot

Cars are staying on the road longer and therefore need more service. They are also getting more technologically sophisticated each year, with complex computerized controls and anti-pollution systems. Weekend driveway tinkerers are increasingly handing over service jobs to trained professionals. For all these reasons, the job outlook for automotive mechanics and service technicians appears very good, provided they are willing to get the formal training required to learn and keep up with the latest technologies.

Related Specialties and Careers

Brakes, engine systems, exhaust systems, front end, transmissions.

Related Job Titles, Educational Requirements, Projected Growth, and Earnings			
Job Title	**Educational Requirements**	**Projected Growth**	**Average Earnings**
Automotive Master Mechanics (O*NET code 49-3023.01)	Postsecondary vocational training	Average	$29,510
Automotive Service Technicians and Mechanics (O*NET code 49-3023.00)	Postsecondary vocational training	Average	$29,510
Automotive Specialty Technicians (O*NET code 49-3023.02)	Postsecondary vocational training	Average	$29,510
Electrical and Electronics Installers and Repairers, Transportation Equipment (O*NET code 49-2093.00)	Postsecondary vocational training	Average	$37,910
Electronic Equipment Installers and Repairers, Motor Vehicles (O*NET code 49-2096.00)	Postsecondary vocational training	Average	$25,250

Typical Postsecondary Courses

Advanced engine performance; automotive electrical systems; automotive electronics; automotive heating and air conditioning systems; basic engine diagnosis and tune-up; brake systems; electronic tune-up and emissions control; fundamentals of automotive service; physical principles of heating and refrigeration; power train overhaul and rebuilding; suspension, steering, and alignment; transaxles and drive systems; workplace communications; workplace math.

Suggested High School Courses

Applied communications; auto shop; business/applied math; computer science; electronics shop. **Dept. of Education School-to-Work Cluster:** Transportation, Distribution, and Logistics.

Essential Knowledge and Skills

Computers and electronics; engineering and technology; installation; mechanical devices; repairing; troubleshooting. **Values/Work Environment:** Indoors, environmentally controlled; moral values.

Other Information Sources

Many career and education information sources use the standard cross-referencing systems noted below. You can use the codes to obtain substantial additional information on the program (via CIP code) and related occupations (via GOE code). The O*NET codes on the opposite page refer to another major career information system. See the Introduction for details on obtaining additional information.

Classification of Instructional Programs (CIP) code(s): 470604 Automobile/Automotive Mechanics Technology/Technician

Guide for Occupational Exploration (GOE) code(s): 05.02 Electrical and Electronic Systems; 05.03 Mechanical Work

---

 **Avionics Technology**

Program/Training Duration: A few weeks to more than a year

Location: Vocational classroom

Career Snapshot

Each new generation of airplanes contains more electronic equipment than ever before for communications, flight control, control of internal systems, measurement of weather conditions, and navigation. The Federal Aviation Administration (FAA) requires periodic checkups of this equipment, and avionics technicians do the job, working mostly at airports near large cities. Some work at aircraft assembly plants. Although it is possible to acquire job skills and qualify for the FAA certifying exam through work experience, most avionics technicians complete a course at an FAA-certified trade school and then take the certifying exam. Training in the Armed Forces is usually too specialized to provide all the knowledge and skills required for the exam. FAA certification standards require technicians to take courses throughout their careers so their skills remain current.

Related Specialties and Careers

Communications systems, instrumentation systems, microprocessors, navigation systems, radar systems.

Related Job Titles, Educational Requirements, Projected Growth, and Earnings			
Job Title	Educational Requirements	Projected Growth	Average Earnings
Aircraft Rigging Assemblers (O*NET code 51-2011.03)	Long-term on-the-job training	Average	$37,190
Aircraft Structure Assemblers, Precision (O*NET code 51-2011.01)	Long-term on-the-job training	Average	$37,190
Aircraft Structure, Surfaces, Rigging, and Systems Assemblers (O*NET code 51-2011.00)	Long-term on-the-job training	Average	$37,190

Job Title	Educational Requirements	Projected Growth	Average Earnings
Aircraft Systems Assemblers, Precision (O*NET code 51-2011.02)	Long-term on-the-job training	Average	$37,190
Avionics Technicians (O*NET code 49-2091.00)	Postsecondary vocational training	Average	$41,450

Typical Postsecondary Courses

Aircraft instrumentation; college algebra; digital systems; direct and alternating current; introduction to communications systems; introduction to electronics; introduction to physics; linear circuit analysis; pulse components and circuit applications; radio-frequency communication.

Suggested High School Courses

Algebra; applied communications; computer science; electronics shop; physics/ principles of technology; trigonometry. **Dept. of Education School-to-Work Cluster:** Scientific Research/Engineering; Transportation, Distribution, and Logistics.

Essential Knowledge and Skills

Computers and electronics; engineering and technology; equipment maintenance; repairing; troubleshooting. **Values/Work Environment:** Exposed to hazardous conditions; moral values; spend time standing.

Other Information Sources

Many career and education information sources use the standard cross-referencing systems noted below. You can use the codes to obtain substantial additional information on the program (via CIP code) and related occupations (via GOE code). The O*NET codes on the opposite page refer to another major career information system. See the Introduction for details on obtaining additional information.

Classification of Instructional Programs (CIP) code(s): 470609 Avionics Maintenance Technology/Technician

Guide for Occupational Exploration (GOE) code(s): 05.02 Electrical and Electronic Systems; 08.02 Production Technology

---

 **Bartending**

Program/Training Duration: One month or less

Location: Workplace or vocational classroom

Career Snapshot

Bartenders prepare mostly standard mixed drinks, and they must know a wide variety of recipes and be able to prepare drinks quickly, accurately, and neatly. Since customers come to bars largely for the friendly atmosphere, bartenders also need good social skills. They usually need to set up and clean up the glasses and equipment used in the bar. They take payments and use the cash register. Sometimes they also serve food. They may learn their skills by working as a bartender's helper or by attending a vocational or specialized bartender's school. There is frequent turnover in this occupation, so there are usually many job opportunities, although competition may be keen for jobs where tips are greatest. About half of bartenders work full time. Working conditions vary and may include loud music or cigarette smoke.

Related Specialties and Careers

Bar management, mixology.

Related Job Titles, Educational Requirements, Projected Growth, and Earnings			
Job Title	Educational Requirements	Projected Growth	Average Earnings
Bartenders (O*NET code 35-3011.00)	Short-term on-the-job training	Average	$14,610

Typical Postsecondary Courses

Bar cleaning and sanitation; bar equipment and setup; bar industry legalities; bar restocking and maintenance; handling money; interviewing techniques; personal presentation and etiquette; preparation of mixed drinks.

Suggested High School Courses

Business/applied math; distributive education; office computer applications; public speaking. **Dept. of Education School-to-Work Cluster:** Hospitality and Tourism.

Essential Knowledge and Skills

Customer and personal service; law and government; sales and marketing; service orientation. **Values/Work Environment:** Moral values; social service; spend time standing.

Other Information Sources

Many career and education information sources use the standard cross-referencing systems noted below. You can use the codes to obtain substantial additional information on the program (via CIP code) and related occupations (via GOE code). The O*NET codes on the opposite page refer to another major career information system. See the Introduction for details on obtaining additional information.

Classification of Instructional Programs (CIP) code(s): 120502 Bartending/Bartender

Guide for Occupational Exploration (GOE) code(s): 11.05 Food and Beverage Services

---

 # Brewing

Program/Training Duration: At least one year

Location: College/vocational classroom and workplace

Career Snapshot

The boom in microbreweries has created many job openings in brewing, although it is still a small industry compared to bread baking or soft drink production. Training courses are available at a few specialized technical schools. Prior coursework in math, biology, and chemistry is useful, and work experience in a brewery is an important part of the learning process.

Related Specialties and Careers

Bottling and packaging, distribution, fermentation, malting, quality control, sales.

Related Job Titles, Educational Requirements, Projected Growth, and Earnings			
Job Title	Educational Requirements	Projected Growth	Average Earnings
Food and Tobacco Roasting, Baking, and Drying Machine Operators and Tenders (O*NET code 51-3091.00)	Short-term on-the-job training	Declining	$23,210
Food Batchmakers (O*NET code 51-3092.00)	Short-term on-the-job training	Little or none	$21,690
Food Cooking Machine Operators and Tenders (O*NET code 51-3093.00)	Short-term on-the-job training	Little or none	$21,420
Mixing and Blending Machine Setters, Operators, and Tenders (O*NET code 51-9023.00)	Moderate-term on-the-job training	Little or none	$26,860

Typical Postsecondary Courses

Brewery product packaging; brewery sanitation and cleaning; brewhouse processes; college algebra; conditioning and filtration; general biology; microbiology; quality control; raw materials for brewing; yeast management.

Suggested High School Courses

Algebra; biology; chemistry; computer science; geometry; pre-calculus; trigonometry. **Dept. of Education School-to-Work Cluster:** Agriculture/Natural Resources; Manufacturing.

Essential Knowledge and Skills

Operation and control; production and processing. **Values/Work Environment:** Indoors, environmentally controlled; moral values; spend time making repetitive motions; spend time standing.

Other Information Sources

Many career and education information sources use the standard cross-referencing systems noted below. You can use the codes to obtain substantial additional information on the program (via CIP code) and related occupations (via GOE code). The O*NET codes on the opposite page refer to another major career information system. See the Introduction for details on obtaining additional information.

Classification of Instructional Programs (CIP) code(s): 010401 Agricultural and Food Products Processing

Guide for Occupational Exploration (GOE) code(s): 08.03 Production Work; 12.03 Educational Services

Broadcasting Technology

Program/Training Duration: One month to more than a year

Location: Workplace or vocational classroom

Career Snapshot

The broadcast media surround us throughout the day, and a wide range of technicians and specialists are required to make the sights and sounds appealing. Some of them specialize more in the technical aspects of recording and transmitting sound and video. Others focus more on the artistic aspects of production, although they also need to understand the technical factors that contribute to the quality of the output. Job openings are expected to be highest in small towns and in the cable industry.

Related Specialties and Careers

Radio operation, radio production, recording engineering, sound mixing, TV and video production, video operation.

Related Job Titles, Educational Requirements, Projected Growth, and Earnings			
Job Title	Educational Requirements	Projected Growth	Average Earnings
Broadcast Technicians (O*NET code 27-4012.00)	Postsecondary vocational training	Average	$27,750
Camera Operators, Television, Video, and Motion Picture (O*NET code 27-4031.00)	Moderate-term on-the-job training	Faster than average	$28,980

Typical Postsecondary Courses

Broadcast journalism; broadcast law and ethics; broadcast writing; introduction to broadcasting; introduction to electronics; radio production; television production.

Suggested High School Courses

Algebra; applied communications; business/applied math; computer science; electronics shop; photography; physics/principles of technology; public speaking.

Dept. of Education School-to-Work Cluster: Arts, A/V Technology, and Communication.

Essential Knowledge and Skills

Communications and media; instructing; physics; reading comprehension; telecommunications. **Values/Work Environment:** Ability utilization; indoors, environmentally controlled.

Other Information Sources

Many career and education information sources use the standard cross-referencing systems noted below. You can use the codes to obtain substantial additional information on the program (via CIP code) and related occupations (via GOE code). The O*NET codes on the opposite page refer to another major career information system. See the Introduction for details on obtaining additional information.

Classification of Instructional Programs (CIP) code(s): 100202 Radio and Television Broadcasting Technology/Technician

Guide for Occupational Exploration (GOE) code(s): 01.08 Media Technology

---

Business Management

Program/Training Duration: At least two years
Location: College classroom

Career Snapshot

Students of business management learn about the basic principles of economics, the legal and social environment in which business operates, and quantitative methods for measuring and projecting business activity. The major covers a number of specialized business functions, including accounting, marketing, human resources, operations, and finance. Later, you may want to complete a bachelor's program (and even a master's) in one of these specializations. Job opportunities vary, depending on specialization, and employment is often sensitive to economic ups and downs.

Related Specialties and Careers

International business, management, marketing, operations.

Related Job Titles, Educational Requirements, Projected Growth, and Earnings			
Job Title	**Educational Requirements**	**Projected Growth**	**Average Earnings**
Administrative Services Managers (O*NET code 11-3011.00)	Work experience plus degree	Average	$49,810
Chief Executives (O*NET code 11-1011.00)	Work experience plus degree	Average	$120,450
General and Operations Managers (O*NET code 11-1021.00)	Work experience plus degree	Average	$65,010
Government Service Executives (O*NET code 11-1011.01)	Work experience plus degree	Average	$120,450
Management Analysts (O*NET code 13-1111.00)	Work experience plus degree	Faster than average	$57,970
Managers, All Other (O*NET code 11-9199.99)	No data available	Little or none	No salary data available
Private Sector Executives (O*NET code 11-1011.02)	Work experience plus degree	Average	$120,450
Sales Managers (O*NET code 11-2022.00)	Work experience plus degree	Faster than average	$71,620

Job Title	Educational Requirements	Projected Growth	Average Earnings
Storage and Distribution Managers (O*NET code 11-3071.02)	Work experience in a related occupation	Average	$57,240
Transportation Managers (O*NET code 11-3071.01)	Work experience in a related occupation	Average	$57,240
Transportation, Storage, and Distribution Managers (O*NET code 11-3071.00)	Work experience in a related occupation	Average	$57,240

Typical Postsecondary Courses

Business finance; business information processing; business math; business reports and communication; college algebra; computer spreadsheet; co-op work experience; financial accounting; human resource management; introduction to accounting; introduction to business management; introduction to economics; introduction to marketing; introduction to psychology; legal environment of business; managerial accounting; operations management; oral communication; organizational behavior; principles of management and organization; statistics for business and social sciences; strategic management.

Suggested High School Courses

Applied communications; bookkeeping; business/applied math; computer science; keyboarding; office computer applications; public speaking. **Dept. of Education School-to-Work Cluster:** Business and Administration; Government and Public Administration.

Essential Knowledge and Skills

Administration and management; coordination; judgment and decision making; mathematics; personnel and human resources. **Values/Work Environment:** Authority; autonomy; indoors, environmentally controlled; good working conditions.

Other Information Sources

Many career and education information sources use the standard cross-referencing systems noted below. You can use the codes to obtain substantial additional information on the program (via CIP code) and related occupations (via GOE code). The O*NET codes on the opposite page refer to another major career information system. See the Introduction for details on obtaining additional information.

Classification of Instructional Programs (CIP) code(s): 520201 Business Administration and Management, General

Guide for Occupational Exploration (GOE) code(s): 06.01 Managerial Work in Construction, Mining, and Drilling; 07.01 Managerial Work in Transportation; 08.01 Managerial Work in Industrial Production; 09.01 Managerial Work in Business Detail; 10.01 Managerial Work in Sales and Marketing; 12.01 Managerial Work in Education and Social Service; 12.03 Educational Services; 13.01 General Management Work and Management of Support Functions; 13.02 Management Support

Cabinetmaking

Program/Training Duration: One month to more than a year

Location: Workplace, perhaps vocational classroom

Career Snapshot

Woodworkers are employed by manufacturers of cabinets and furniture and by companies that install and repair cabinets and other wooden components and trim in residences and businesses. Some are self-employed. They work not only with wood, but also with finishes, laminates, and various materials used for countertops. Most learn on the job, which may take two years or more. Some certification programs are available at community colleges and trade schools. In production, job opportunities will be best for those who are trained in computer-assisted design and manufacture (CAD/CAM); in installation, for those who specialize in moldings, cabinets, stairs, and windows. Jobs in this field are sensitive to the ups and downs of the economy.

Related Specialties and Careers

Cabinets, detailing, furniture, installation, millwork, shaper operation, windows.

Related Job Titles, Educational Requirements, Projected Growth, and Earnings			
Job Title	**Educational Requirements**	**Projected Growth**	**Average Earnings**
Cabinetmakers and Bench Carpenters (O*NET code 51-7011.00)	Long-term on-the-job training	Average	$23,500
Model Makers, Wood (O*NET code 51-7031.00)	Long-term on-the-job training	Average	$24,990
Patternmakers, Wood (O*NET code 51-7032.00)	Long-term on-the-job training	Average	$28,690
Sawing Machine Operators and Tenders (O*NET code 51-7041.02)	Moderate-term on-the-job training	Average	$21,740
Sawing Machine Setters and Set-Up Operators (O*NET code 51-7041.01)	Moderate-term on-the-job training	Average	$21,740
Sawing Machine Setters, Operators, and Tenders, Wood (O*NET code 51-7041.00)	Moderate-term on-the-job training	Average	$21,740

Job Title	Educational Requirements	Projected Growth	Average Earnings
Woodworking Machine Operators and Tenders, Except Sawing (O*NET code 51-7042.02)	Moderate-term on-the-job training	Little or none	$21,600
Woodworking Machine Setters and Set-Up Operators, Except Sawing (O*NET code 51-7042.01)	Moderate-term on-the-job training	Little or none	$21,600
Woodworking Machine Setters, Operators, and Tenders, Except Sawing (O*NET code 51-7042.00)	Moderate-term on-the-job training	Little or none	$21,600

Typical Postsecondary Courses

Blueprint reading; cabinet and furniture construction; cabinet design and layout; cabinet finishing and installation; computer-aided design/manufacturing (CAD/CAM); computers for the vocational trades; door, drawer, and hardware installation; machining and milling wood; plastic laminates and wood veneers; power equipment; shop safety; wood joints; wood materials; workplace communications; workplace math.

Suggested High School Courses

Applied communications; business/applied math; industrial arts; mechanical drawing; physics/principles of technology. **Dept. of Education School-to-Work Cluster:** Architecture and Construction; Manufacturing.

Essential Knowledge and Skills

Building and construction; operation and control. **Values/Work Environment:** Exposed to hazardous equipment; independence; indoors, environmentally controlled; moral values.

Other Information Sources

Many career and education information sources use the standard cross-referencing systems noted below. You can use the codes to obtain substantial additional information on the program (via CIP code) and related occupations (via GOE code). The O*NET codes on the opposite page refer to another major career information system. See the Introduction for details on obtaining additional information.

Classification of Instructional Programs (CIP) code(s): 480703 Cabinetmaking and Millwork/Millwright

Guide for Occupational Exploration (GOE) code(s): 08.02 Production Technology; 08.03 Production Work; 08.05 Woodworking Technology

---

Cardiovascular Technology

Program/Training Duration: Two years

Location: College/vocational classroom

Career Snapshot

Cardiovascular technologists help physicians in the diagnosis and treatment of patients with disease of the heart or blood vessels. They work in catheterization labs and in cardiovascular diagnostic labs. Their tests may be invasive (using cardiac catheterization) or noninvasive (using ultrasound, exercise, and electrocardiographic testing). Some specialists also help physicians with repair procedures such as coronary angioplasty, stent implantation, and pacemaker insertion. They also provide extensive personal care to patients before, during, and after a cardiovascular procedure. The educational program takes two years, although people with experience in related allied health care may need only one year. Demand for new workers is expected to increase as the population ages.

Related Specialties and Careers

Cardiac catheterization lab support, cardiovascular invasive specialist, monitor (telemetry) technician, pacemaker technician.

Related Job Titles, Educational Requirements, Projected Growth, and Earnings			
Job Title	Educational Requirements	Projected Growth	Average Earnings
Cardiovascular Technologists and Technicians (O*NET code 29-2031.00)	Associate degree	Faster than average	$35,010

Typical Postsecondary Courses

Cardiovascular anatomy and physiology; cardiovascular clinical practicum; cardiovascular pharmacology; computer applications in health care; critical care applications; echocardiography; English composition; human anatomy and physiology; introduction to cardiovascular technology; introduction to electrocardiography; introduction to psychology; invasive cardiology; noninvasive cardiology; performing electrocardiography; technical mathematics.

Suggested High School Courses

Applied communications; biology; business/applied math; chemistry; electronics shop; physics/principles of technology; public speaking. **Dept. of Education School-to-Work Cluster:** Health Science.

Essential Knowledge and Skills

Biology; computers and electronics; medicine and dentistry; reading comprehension. **Values/Work Environment:** Indoors, environmentally controlled; social service.

Other Information Sources

Many career and education information sources use the standard cross-referencing systems noted below. You can use the codes to obtain substantial additional information on the program (via CIP code) and related occupations (via GOE code). The O*NET codes on the opposite page refer to another major career information system. See the Introduction for details on obtaining additional information.

Classification of Instructional Programs (CIP) code(s): 510901 Cardiovascular Technology/Technologist

Guide for Occupational Exploration (GOE) code(s): 12.03 Educational Services; 14.05 Medical Technology

---

 **Carpentry**

Program/Training Duration: One month to a year or more

Location: Workplace

Career Snapshot

Carpenters work not only at building sites, but also to make wooden frames in various manufacturing and mining sites. More than one-fourth of them are self-employed. Most learn informally on the job, but apprenticeships and vocational training programs are also available. The job outlook is expected to be excellent, especially for those who are not overly specialized and can do a variety of tasks for a subcontractor. Job openings in this field tend to be sensitive to economic ups and downs.

Related Specialties and Careers

Brattice building, commercial construction, construction estimating, finish work, residential construction, rough work.

Related Job Titles, Educational Requirements, Projected Growth, and Earnings			
Job Title	**Educational Requirements**	**Projected Growth**	**Average Earnings**
Boat Builders and Shipwrights (O*NET code 47-2031.05)	Long-term on-the-job training	Little or none	$33,470
Brattice Builders (O*NET code 47-2031.06)	Moderate-term on-the-job training	Little or none	$33,470
Carpenter Assemblers and Repairers (O*NET code 47-2031.03)	Moderate-term on-the-job training	Little or none	$33,470
Carpenters (O*NET code 47-2031.00)	Long-term on-the-job training	Little or none	$33,470
Construction Carpenters (O*NET code 47-2031.01)	Long-term on-the-job training	Little or none	$33,470
First-Line Supervisors and Manager/Supervisors— Construction Trades Workers (O*NET code 47-1011.01)	Work experience in a related occupation	Average	$46,570

Job Title	Educational Requirements	Projected Growth	Average Earnings
First-Line Supervisors/Managers of Construction Trades and Extraction Workers (O*NET code 47-1011.00)	Work experience in a related occupation	Average	$46,570
Helpers—Carpenters (O*NET code 47-3012.00)	Short-term on-the-job training	Little or none	$21,200
Rough Carpenters (O*NET code 47-2031.02)	Moderate-term on-the-job training	Little or none	$33,470
Ship Carpenters and Joiners (O*NET code 47-2031.04)	Moderate-term on-the-job training	Little or none	$33,470

Typical Postsecondary Courses

Basic welding; blueprint reading; carpentry procedures; exterior finish; hand tools; interior finish; introduction to carpentry; power tools; workplace communications; workplace math.

Suggested High School Courses

Applied communications; business/applied math; industrial arts; mechanical drawing; physics/principles of technology. **Dept. of Education School-to-Work Cluster:** Architecture and Construction.

Essential Knowledge and Skills

Building and construction; installation. **Values/Work Environment: Exposed** to hazardous equipment; moral values; outdoors, exposed to weather; spend time standing.

Other Information Sources

Many career and education information sources use the standard cross-referencing systems noted below. You can use the codes to obtain substantial additional information on the program (via CIP code) and related occupations (via GOE code). The O*NET codes on the opposite page refer to another major career information system. See the Introduction for details on obtaining additional information.

Classification of Instructional Programs (CIP) code(s): 460201 Carpentry/Carpenter

Guide for Occupational Exploration (GOE) code(s): 06.01 Managerial Work in Construction, Mining, and Drilling; 06.02 Construction; 06.04 Hands-on Work in Construction, Extraction, and Maintenance

 Casino Gaming Training

Program/Training Duration: A few weeks to more than a year

Location: Vocational classroom

Career Snapshot

The gaming industry continues to boom and create jobs for people who deal cards, run roulette wheels, and run other kinds of casino games. The job often involves evening and weekend work, and it requires integrity with money and a friendly personality. Competition for jobs often is intense. Large casinos and specialized casino trade schools offer training programs that consist mostly of simulations of actual casino games and settings.

Related Specialties and Careers

Card games, craps, keno, roulette.

Related Job Titles, Educational Requirements, Projected Growth, and Earnings			
Job Title	Educational Requirements	Projected Growth	Average Earnings
Gaming and Sports Book Writers and Runners (O*NET code 39-3012.00)	Postsecondary vocational training	Faster than average	$18,240
Gaming Dealers (O*NET code 39-3011.00)	Postsecondary vocational training	Faster than average	$13,680
Gaming Supervisors (O*NET code 39-1011.00)	Postsecondary vocational training	Average	$39,240
Slot Key Persons (O*NET code 39-1012.00)	Short-term on-the-job training	Faster than average	$22,510

Typical Postsecondary Courses

Baccarat; blackjack; introduction to casino games; legal environment of casino operations; poker; roulette.

Suggested High School Courses

Business/applied math; public speaking. **Dept. of Education School-to-Work Cluster:** Hospitality and Tourism.

Essential Knowledge and Skills

Customer and personal service; mathematics; monitoring. **Values/Work Environment:** Indoors, environmentally controlled; good working conditions.

Other Information Sources

Many career and education information sources use the standard cross-referencing systems noted below. You can use the codes to obtain substantial additional information on the program (via CIP code) and related occupations (via GOE code). The O*NET codes on the opposite page refer to another major career information system. See the Introduction for details on obtaining additional information.

Classification of Instructional Programs (CIP) code(s): 319999 Parks, Recreation, Leisure, and Fitness Studies, Other

Guide for Occupational Exploration (GOE) code(s): 11.02 Recreational Services

---

Casino Slot Technician Training

Program/Training Duration: At least one year

Location: Workplace, perhaps following vocational classroom

Career Snapshot

The rapid growth of the casino industry has created a growing demand for slot technicians to maintain and repair the ever-popular "one-armed bandits." Most of the skills acquired in this job can also be applied to a job repairing coin-operated vending machines. A good route to preparation is to get general training in electronics at a technical college or trade school, followed by on-the-job training at a large casino or slot machine sales and service company.

Related Specialties and Careers

Bench repair, on-site service.

Related Job Titles, Educational Requirements, Projected Growth, and Earnings			
Job Title	**Educational Requirements**	**Projected Growth**	**Average Earnings**
Battery Repairers (O*NET code 49-2092.03)	Moderate-term on-the-job training	Little or none	$31,010
Electric Home Appliance and Power Tool Repairers (O*NET code 49-2092.01)	Long-term on-the-job training	Little or none	$31,010
Electric Motor and Switch Assemblers and Repairers (O*NET code 49-2092.02)	Long-term on-the-job training	Little or none	$31,010
Electric Motor, Power Tool, and Related Repairers (O*NET code 49-2092.00)	Long-term on-the-job training	Little or none	$31,010
Electrical Parts Reconditioners (O*NET code 49-2092.05)	Moderate-term on-the-job training	Little or none	$31,010
Hand and Portable Power Tool Repairers (O*NET code 49-2092.06)	Moderate-term on-the-job training	Little or none	$31,010
Transformer Repairers (O*NET code 49-2092.04)	Long-term on-the-job training	Little or none	$31,010

Typical Postsecondary Courses

Introduction to slots; legal environment of casino operations; money validation; slot machine electronics; slot machine microprocessor operations; slot machine operation and troubleshooting; slot mechanical operations.

Suggested High School Courses

Algebra; computer science; electronics shop; geometry; industrial arts; physics/principles of technology; trigonometry. **Dept. of Education School-to-Work Cluster:** Manufacturing.

Essential Knowledge and Skills

Computers and electronics; installation; mechanical devices. **Values/Work Environment:** Indoors, environmentally controlled; moral values.

Other Information Sources

Many career and education information sources use the standard cross-referencing systems noted below. You can use the codes to obtain substantial additional information on the program (via CIP code) and related occupations (via GOE code). The O*NET codes on the opposite page refer to another major career information system. See the Introduction for details on obtaining additional information.

Classification of Instructional Programs (CIP) code(s): 470101 Electrical/Electronics Equipment Installation and Repair, General

Guide for Occupational Exploration (GOE) code(s): 05.02 Electrical and Electronic Systems; 05.03 Mechanical Work

---

Chemical Engineering Technology

Program/Training Duration: Two years

Location: College/vocational classroom

Career Snapshot

Many of the products we use every day are created from processed chemicals. Chemical engineering technicians work in the chemical, pharmaceutical, and petroleum industries, helping engineers solve problems in research and industrial processing. A good preparation route is two or three years at a community college or technical school in a program approved by the Technology Accreditation Commission of the Accreditation Board for Engineering and Technology (TAC/ABET).

Related Specialties and Careers

Process controls, processes, quality control, research, sales.

Related Job Titles, Educational Requirements, Projected Growth, and Earnings			
Job Title	Educational Requirements	Projected Growth	Average Earnings
Electro-Mechanical Technicians (O*NET code 17-3024.00)	Associate degree	Average	$38,150
Engineering Technicians, Except Drafters, All Other (O*NET code 17-3029.99)	Associate degree	Faster than average	No salary data available

Typical Postsecondary Courses

Chemical separation processes; general chemistry; general physics; industrial chemical processes; instrumentation and process control; introduction to chemical engineering technology; process safety, quality, environmental issues; statistics in process technology; technical mathematics; technical writing; undergraduate research project.

Suggested High School Courses

Algebra; applied communications; chemistry; computer science; electronics shop; geometry; physics/principles of technology; trigonometry. **Dept. of Education School-to-Work Cluster:** Manufacturing.

Essential Knowledge and Skills

Engineering and technology; mechanical devices; production and processing; quality control analysis; repairing; troubleshooting. **Values/Work Environment:** Exposed to hazardous equipment; independence; indoors, environmentally controlled; moral values.

Other Information Sources

Many career and education information sources use the standard cross-referencing systems noted below. You can use the codes to obtain substantial additional information on the program (via CIP code) and related occupations (via GOE code). The O*NET codes on the opposite page refer to another major career information system. See the Introduction for details on obtaining additional information.

Classification of Instructional Programs (CIP) code(s): 159999 Engineering Technologies/Technicians, Other

Guide for Occupational Exploration (GOE) code(s): 02.08 Engineering Technology

---

Civil (Engineering) Technology

Program/Training Duration: Two years

Location: College/vocational classroom

Career Snapshot

Civil engineering technicians help engineers plan and construct highways, bridges, buildings, earthworks, and other structures. They often specialize in one aspect of the process, such as surveying, drafting plans, or estimating costs. Formal education, especially in the latest computer-based technology, is probably the best preparation route, and it typically takes two years. Because programs can vary in quality, it is advisable to look for one approved by the Technology Accreditation Commission of the Accreditation Board for Engineering and Technology (TAC/ABET).

Related Specialties and Careers

Computer-aided drafting and design (CADD), construction, estimating, photogrammetry, research, surveying and mapping, transportation.

Related Job Titles, Educational Requirements, Projected Growth, and Earnings			
Job Title	Educational Requirements	Projected Growth	Average Earnings
Civil Engineering Technicians (O*NET code 17-3022.00)	Associate degree	Average	$37,410

Typical Postsecondary Courses

Advanced surveying; architectural drafting; computer-aided drafting and design (CADD); construction math and estimating; descriptive geometry; drainage design; elementary surveying; engineering graphics; highway and transportation engineering; soil mechanics; strength of materials; technical mathematics; technical writing.

Suggested High School Courses

Algebra; applied communications; computer science; geometry; physics/ principles of technology; trigonometry. **Dept. of Education School-to-Work Cluster:** Manufacturing.

Essential Knowledge and Skills

Building and construction; design; engineering and technology; mathematics; operations analysis. **Values/Work Environment:** Indoors, environmentally controlled; moral values.

Other Information Sources

Many career and education information sources use the standard cross-referencing systems noted below. You can use the codes to obtain substantial additional information on the program (via CIP code) and related occupations (via GOE code). The O*NET codes on the opposite page refer to another major career information system. See the Introduction for details on obtaining additional information.

Classification of Instructional Programs (CIP) code(s): 150201 Civil Engineering Technology/Technician

Guide for Occupational Exploration (GOE) code(s): 02.08 Engineering Technology

---

Clinical Lab Technician

Program/Training Duration: Two years

Location: College/vocational classroom

Career Snapshot

Medical and clinical laboratory technicians perform laboratory tests on body fluids and tissue samples, often using automated equipment. They usually have either an associate degree from a two-year college or a certificate from a hospital or vocational/technical school. Some get training in the Armed Forces. (A medical laboratory technologist has a bachelor's degree.) They may specialize in one procedure or perform several.

Related Specialties and Careers

Blood banking, histology, phlebotomy.

Related Job Titles, Educational Requirements, Projected Growth, and Earnings			
Job Title	**Educational Requirements**	**Projected Growth**	**Average Earnings**
Medical and Clinical Laboratory Technicians (O*NET code 29-2012.00)	Associate degree	Average	$28,810

Typical Postsecondary Courses

Clinical experience as laboratory technician; clinical immunology and serology; English composition; general chemistry; hematology and coagulation; human anatomy and physiology; immunohematology; introduction to clinical laboratory technician; introduction to psychology; introduction to speech communication; microbiology; parasitology; urinalysis.

Suggested High School Courses

Applied communications; biology; business/applied math; chemistry; computer science; physics/principles of technology. **Dept. of Education School-to-Work Cluster:** Health Science.

Essential Knowledge and Skills

Biology; chemistry; medicine and dentistry; science. **Values/Work Environment:**
Exposed to disease or infections; indoors, environmentally controlled; moral values.

Other Information Sources

Many career and education information sources use the standard cross-referencing systems noted below. You can use the codes to obtain substantial additional information on the program (via CIP code) and related occupations (via GOE code). The O*NET codes on the opposite page refer to another major career information system. See the Introduction for details on obtaining additional information.

Classification of Instructional Programs (CIP) code(s): 511001 Blood Bank Technology Specialist; 511004 Clinical/Medical Laboratory Technician

Guide for Occupational Exploration (GOE) code(s): 12.03 Educational Services; 14.05 Medical Technology

---

Computer Maintenance

Program/Training Duration: A few weeks to more than one year

Location: Workplace or vocational classroom

Career Snapshot

Computer technicians set up, maintain, upgrade, and repair computers, networks, and peripheral equipment. Nowadays they are vital to keeping offices and industries in operation and working productively. Although they usually must understand both hardware and software, hardware tends to be more reliable and predictable; they are needed more for software tasks such as managing a network and configuring workstations. Employment opportunities will be very good for those skilled with the latest technology.

Related Specialties and Careers

Hardware maintenance, network systems, telecommunications.

Related Job Titles, Educational Requirements, Projected Growth, and Earnings			
Job Title	Educational Requirements	Projected Growth	Average Earnings
Automatic Teller Machine Servicers (O*NET code 49-2011.01)	Long-term on-the-job training	Average	$32,890
Computer, Automated Teller, and Office Machine Repairers (O*NET code 49-2011.00)	Postsecondary vocational training	Average	$32,890
Data Processing Equipment Repairers (O*NET code 49-2011.02)	Postsecondary vocational training	Average	$32,890
Electrical and Electronics Repairers, Commercial and Industrial Equipment (O*NET code 49-2094.00)	Postsecondary vocational training	Little or none	$38,800
Office Machine and Cash Register Servicers (O*NET code 49-2011.03)	Long-term on-the-job training	Average	$32,890

Typical Postsecondary Courses

Business reports and communication; college algebra; computer upgrade and repair fundamentals; data communications and networking; digital systems; electronic devices and circuits; English composition; introduction to electric circuits; introduction to microprocessors; manufacturer-specific network administration; operating systems; programming in a language (e.g., C, PASCAL, COBOL).

Suggested High School Courses

Applied communications; business/applied math; computer science; electronics shop; keyboarding, physics/principles of technology. **Dept. of Education School-to-Work Cluster:** Information Technology.

Essential Knowledge and Skills

Computers and electronics; equipment maintenance; repairing; troubleshooting. **Values/Work Environment:** Indoors, environmentally controlled; moral values.

Other Information Sources

Many career and education information sources use the standard cross-referencing systems noted below. You can use the codes to obtain substantial additional information on the program (via CIP code) and related occupations (via GOE code). The O*NET codes on the opposite page refer to another major career information system. See the Introduction for details on obtaining additional information.

Classification of Instructional Programs (CIP) code(s): 470104 Computer Installation and Repair Technology/Technician

Guide for Occupational Exploration (GOE) code(s): 05.02 Electrical and Electronic Systems; 09.09 Clerical Machine Operation

---

 **Computer Programming**

Program/Training Duration: More than one year

Location: Workplace or college/vocational classroom

Career Snapshot

Computer programmers write, test, and maintain the complex instructions called programs that computers use to perform useful functions. Programmers analyze a data-related problem to devise a logical set of procedures for solving it and then write code (computer language) to execute that set of procedures. They also write notes or descriptions of how their programs work, called documentation, so other programmers can make sense of the code. The job outlook for programmers is very good, with best opportunities for college graduates with up-to-date skills.

Related Specialties and Careers

Business programming, database programming, programming for the Internet, scientific programming, security and disaster recovery, systems programming.

Related Job Titles, Educational Requirements, Projected Growth, and Earnings			
Job Title	Educational Requirements	Projected Growth	Average Earnings
Numerical Tool and Process Control Programmers (O*NET code 51-4012.00)	Long-term on-the-job training	Average	$37,290

Typical Postsecondary Courses

Algorithms and data structures; college algebra; data communications and networking; English composition; introduction to computer science; operating systems; operating systems; oral communication; systems analysis and design.

Suggested High School Courses

Algebra; applied communications; computer science; keyboarding; office computer applications. **Dept. of Education School-to-Work Cluster:** Manufacturing.

Essential Knowledge and Skills

Computers and electronics; design; mathematics; programming. **Values/Work Environment:** Compensation; independence; indoors, environmentally controlled; moral values; spend time sitting.

Other Information Sources

Many career and education information sources use the standard cross-referencing systems noted below. You can use the codes to obtain substantial additional information on the program (via CIP code) and related occupations (via GOE code). The O*NET codes on the opposite page refer to another major career information system. See the Introduction for details on obtaining additional information.

Classification of Instructional Programs (CIP) code(s): 110201 Computer Programming/Programmer, General

Guide for Occupational Exploration (GOE) code(s): 02.06 Mathematics and Computers; 02.08 Engineering Technology; 12.03 Educational Services

Construction Equipment Operation

Program/Training Duration: One month to a year

Location: Workplace, perhaps vocational classroom

Career Snapshot

Construction (or heavy) equipment operators generally get their training, which takes a few weeks, after they are hired. The employer either trains them on the job or sends them to a specialized school where they learn how to operate the equipment efficiently and safely. Some job-seekers prepare ahead by attending a trade school, but before you sign up for one, be sure the school has a good reputation in your area. The work is noisy and sometimes strenuous, and it is done in all kinds of weather, but the employment outlook is expected to be good.

Related Specialties and Careers

Backhoes, bulldozers, compactors, excavators, loaders, motor graders, scrapers.

Related Job Titles, Educational Requirements, Projected Growth, and Earnings			
Job Title	**Educational Requirements**	**Projected Growth**	**Average Earnings**
Construction and Related Workers, All Other (O*NET code 47-4099.99)	Moderate-term on-the-job training	Faster than average	No salary data available
Construction Drillers (O*NET code 47-5021.01)	Moderate-term on-the-job training	Average	$32,000
Continuous Mining Machine Operators (O*NET code 47-5041.00)	Moderate-term on-the-job training	Declining	$33,640
Crane and Tower Operators (O*NET code 53-7021.00)	Moderate-term on-the-job training	Little or none	$34,610
Dragline Operators (O*NET code 53-7032.02)	Moderate-term on-the-job training	Average	$32,000
Dredge Operators (O*NET code 53-7031.00)	Moderate-term on-the-job training	Declining	$27,590
Earth Drillers, Except Oil and Gas (O*NET code 47-5021.00)	Moderate-term on-the-job training	Average	$32,000

Job Title	Educational Requirements	Projected Growth	Average Earnings
Excavating and Loading Machine and Dragline Operators (O*NET code 53-7032.00)	Moderate-term on-the-job training	Average	$32,000
Excavating and Loading Machine Operators (O*NET code 53-7032.01)	Moderate-term on-the-job training	Average	$32,000
Extraction Workers, All Other (O*NET code 47-5099.99)	No data available	Declining	No salary data available
Grader, Bulldozer, and Scraper Operators (O*NET code 47-2073.01)	Moderate-term on-the-job training	Little or none	$34,160
Highway Maintenance Workers (O*NET code 47-4051.00)	Moderate-term on-the-job training	Little or none	$27,510

Typical Postsecondary Courses

Backhoes; bulldozers; calculating yardage; construction equipment preventative maintenance; construction safety; earth moving; excavators; finishing and grading; fundamentals of construction equipment operation; grade reading; soil analysis.

Suggested High School Courses

Applied communications; auto shop; business/applied math; driver education; physics/principles of technology. **Dept. of Education School-to-Work Cluster:** Architecture and Construction.

Essential Knowledge and Skills

Mechanical devices; operation and control; operation monitoring. **Values/Work Environment:** Exposed to hazardous equipment; moral values; outdoors, exposed to weather.

Other Information Sources

Many career and education information sources use the standard cross-referencing systems noted below. You can use the codes to obtain substantial additional information on the program (via CIP code) and related occupations (via GOE code). The O*NET codes on the opposite page refer to another major career information system. See the Introduction for details on obtaining additional information.

Classification of Instructional Programs (CIP) code(s): 490202 Construction/Heavy Equipment/Earthmoving Equipment Operation

Guide for Occupational Exploration (GOE) code(s): 06.02 Construction; 06.03 Mining and Drilling; 06.03 Mining and Drilling; 06.04 Hands-on Work in Construction, Extraction, and Maintenance; 07.04 Water Vehicle Operation; 08.07 Hands-on Work: Loading, Moving, Hoisting, and Conveying

 Construction Inspection

Program/Training Duration: Several years

Location: Workplace, perhaps college classroom

Career Snapshot

Construction inspectors ensure that buildings and public works are built according to specifications, meet the relevant codes for safety, and are maintained in accordance with codes. About half work for local governments. Some new hires come out of a background in a construction trade or supervising construction. Others prepare by completing coursework or a certification or associate degree program at a technical or community college. Certification by a professional organization is helpful and may be required in some locales. On-the-job training is also necessary, and inspectors need to take classes periodically to keep abreast of changing technology and codes. Job opportunities will be best for those with a mix of formal training and construction-related experience.

Related Specialties and Careers

Building inspection, electrical, elevator, mechanical, plan examination, public works, residential.

Related Job Titles, Educational Requirements, Projected Growth, and Earnings			
Job Title	Educational Requirements	Projected Growth	Average Earnings
Construction and Building Inspectors (O*NET code 47-4011.00)	Work experience in a related occupation	Average	$40,190
First-Line Supervisors and Manager/Supervisors— Construction Trades Workers (O*NET code 47-1011.01)	Work experience in a related occupation	Average	$46,570
First-Line Supervisors/ Managers of Construction Trades and Extraction Workers (O*NET code 47-1011.00)	Work experience in a related occupation	Average	$46,570

Typical Postsecondary Courses

Bridge structures inspection; construction inspection documentation; drainage inspection; electrical inspection; evaluating construction materials; excavation and embankment inspection; legal responsibilities and agencies; sampling and testing; structural plan reading.

Suggested High School Courses

Algebra; applied communications; drafting; geometry; physics/principles of technology. **Dept. of Education School-to-Work Cluster:** Architecture and Construction.

Essential Knowledge and Skills

Administration and management; building and construction; design; quality control analysis; speaking. **Values/Work Environment:** Outdoors, exposed to weather; responsibility; spend time standing; spend time walking and running.

Other Information Sources

Many career and education information sources use the standard cross-referencing systems noted below. You can use the codes to obtain substantial additional information on the program (via CIP code) and related occupations (via GOE code). The O*NET codes on the opposite page refer to another major career information system. See the Introduction for details on obtaining additional information.

Classification of Instructional Programs (CIP) code(s): 460403 Building/Home/Construction Inspection/Inspector

Guide for Occupational Exploration (GOE) code(s): 02.08 Engineering Technology; 06.01 Managerial Work in Construction, Mining, and Drilling

---

 **Construction Technology**

Program/Training Duration: Two years or more

Location: College/vocational classroom or workplace

Career Snapshot

Construction is a very large industry, and job opportunities are expected to be excellent, with ups and downs depending on the state of the economy. Many enter this field by getting training on the job or through an apprenticeship with the goal of mastering a skilled trade such as carpentry or plumbing. For those who intend to go into management, a certificate or associate degree in construction technology is often a more direct route. A graduate or certificate holder may enter as a field engineer, estimator, or scheduler and advance to assistant manager.

Related Specialties and Careers

Commercial construction, contract administration, estimating, public works construction, residential construction, scheduling.

Related Job Titles, Educational Requirements, Projected Growth, and Earnings			
Job Title	Educational Requirements	Projected Growth	Average Earnings
Civil Engineering Technicians (O*NET code 17-3022.00)	Associate degree	Average	$37,410

Typical Postsecondary Courses

Blueprint reading; computer fundamentals; computer-aided drafting (CAD); concrete pouring and finishing; construction contracts and related law; construction cost control; construction materials and methods; construction math and estimating; construction planning and scheduling; construction safety; English composition; interior finishing; layout and framing; surveying.

Suggested High School Courses

Algebra; applied communications; drafting; geometry; physics/principles of technology; trigonometry. **Dept. of Education School-to-Work Cluster:** Manufacturing.

Essential Knowledge and Skills

Design; engineering and technology; mathematics; operations analysis. **Values/Work Environment:** Activity; indoors, environmentally controlled.

Other Information Sources

Many career and education information sources use the standard cross-referencing systems noted below. You can use the codes to obtain substantial additional information on the program (via CIP code) and related occupations (via GOE code). The O*NET codes on the opposite page refer to another major career information system. See the Introduction for details on obtaining additional information.

Classification of Instructional Programs (CIP) code(s): 151001 Construction Engineering Technology/Technician

Guide for Occupational Exploration (GOE) code(s): 02.08 Engineering Technology; 06.01 Managerial Work in Construction, Mining, and Drilling; 13.02 Management Support

---

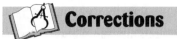

Corrections

Program/Training Duration: One month to a year

Location: Vocational classroom

Career Snapshot

America's jail and prison populations continue to grow, and this creates demand for officers who oversee the prisoners, maintaining security and order. The employment outlook is expected to be excellent. However, the job can involve night and weekend work, unpleasant people, and dangerous situations. Some community colleges offer training in corrections, but most correctional officers receive training at a correctional facility, sometimes after formal instruction at a regional academy. A written exam is often required.

Related Specialties and Careers

Detention, tactical response.

Related Job Titles, Educational Requirements, Projected Growth, and Earnings			
Job Title	Educational Requirements	Projected Growth	Average Earnings
Correctional Officers and Jailers (O*NET code 33-3012.00)	Moderate-term on-the-job training	Faster than average	$32,010
First-Line Supervisors/ Managers of Correctional Officers (O*NET code 33-1011.00)	Work experience in a related occupation	Faster than average	$44,640
First-Line Supervisors/ Managers of Police and Detectives (O*NET code 33-1012.00)	Work experience in a related occupation	Average	$59,300

Typical Postsecondary Courses

Conflict and crisis management; correction officer safety and weapons training; criminal law; emergency care; inmate security procedures; introduction to inmate management; prisoner transportation.

Suggested High School Courses

Applied communications; public speaking. **Dept. of Education School-to-Work Cluster:** Law and Public Safety.

Essential Knowledge and Skills

Law and government; public safety and security; social perceptiveness. **Values/Work Environment:** Authority; co-workers; indoors, environmentally controlled; security.

Other Information Sources

Many career and education information sources use the standard cross-referencing systems noted below. You can use the codes to obtain substantial additional information on the program (via CIP code) and related occupations (via GOE code). The O*NET codes on the opposite page refer to another major career information system. See the Introduction for details on obtaining additional information.

Classification of Instructional Programs (CIP) code(s): 430102 Corrections

Guide for Occupational Exploration (GOE) code(s): 04.01 Managerial Work in Law, Law Enforcement, and Public Safety; 04.03 Law Enforcement; 12.03 Educational Services

---

Cosmetology/Barbering

Program/Training Duration: One month to a year or more

Location: Workplace or vocational classroom

Career Snapshot

Cosmetologists mainly shampoo, cut, and style hair, but they also give manicures, pedicures, and scalp and facial treatments, and they sometimes clean and style wigs. Barbers do all of these tasks except treat skin and nails; they also shave men. These occupations offer many opportunities for part-time or flexible work, as well as for self-employment. The prospects for jobs look very good. These workers are licensed, so most of them are graduates of state-approved programs at a trade or vocational school.

Related Specialties and Careers

Barbering, facial treatments, hairstyling, makeup, manicure/pedicure.

Related Job Titles, Educational Requirements, Projected Growth, and Earnings			
Job Title	**Educational Requirements**	**Projected Growth**	**Average Earnings**
Barbers (O*NET code 39-5011.00)	Postsecondary vocational training	Declining	$18,500
Hairdressers, Hairstylists, and Cosmetologists (O*NET code 39-5012.00)	Postsecondary vocational training	Average	$18,260
Makeup Artists, Theatrical and Performance (O*NET code 39-5091.00)	Postsecondary vocational training	Average	$30,240
Manicurists and Pedicurists (O*NET code 39-5092.00)	Postsecondary vocational training	Faster than average	$16,700
Shampooers (O*NET code 39-5093.00)	Short-term on-the-job training	Average	$13,730
Skin Care Specialists (O*NET code 39-5094.00)	Short-term on-the-job training	Average	$22,060

Typical Postsecondary Courses

Cosmetology chemistry and safety; cosmetology sanitation and bacteriology; hair coloring; haircutting and design; nail care; scalp treatments and shampooing; skin care.

Suggested High School Courses

Applied communications; business/applied math. **Dept. of Education School-to-Work Cluster:** Retail and Wholesale Sales and Service.

Essential Knowledge and Skills

Active listening; customer and personal service. **Values/Work Environment:** Indoors, environmentally controlled; social service.

Other Information Sources

Many career and education information sources use the standard cross-referencing systems noted below. You can use the codes to obtain substantial additional information on the program (via CIP code) and related occupations (via GOE code). The O*NET codes on the opposite page refer to another major career information system. See the Introduction for details on obtaining additional information.

Classification of Instructional Programs (CIP) code(s): 120409 Aesthetician/Esthetician and Skin Care Specialist; 120402 Barbering/Barber; 120401 Cosmetology/Cosmetologist, General; 120408 Facial Treatment Specialist/Facialist; 120407 Hair Styling/Stylist and Hair Design; 120406 Make-Up Artist/Specialist

Guide for Occupational Exploration (GOE) code(s): 01.09 Modeling and Personal Appearance; 11.04 Barber and Beauty Services

---

Court Reporting

Program/Training Duration: Two years

Location: Vocational classroom

Career Snapshot

Court reporters transcribe the spoken word in settings such as courtrooms where an accurate written record must be kept. They use specialized machines to key in a shorthand representation of what is being spoken, and this record is translated by computer into spelled-out text (which usually needs some corrections). Training in these skills requires at least two years, and it is important to study at a school—a community or technical college, a business institute, or a court reporting school—that is approved by a reputable accrediting agency. Employment opportunities in courts may not grow as fast as the number of legal proceedings because of budget constraints. On the other hand, many jobs are expected to open outside of courtrooms: Television broadcasters need to create closed captioning, and colleges need to provide services so hearing-impaired students can follow lectures.

Related Specialties and Careers

Closed captioning, courtroom transcription, medical transcription.

Related Job Titles, Educational Requirements, Projected Growth, and Earnings			
Job Title	Educational Requirements	Projected Growth	Average Earnings
Court Reporters (O*NET code 23-2091.00)	Postsecondary vocational training	Average	$40,410

Typical Postsecondary Courses

Court reporting procedures; court reporting technology; current events; English composition; field experience/internship; introduction to medical terminology; keyboarding; legal procedures; legal terminology; machine shorthand.

Suggested High School Courses

English; keyboarding; office computer applications. **Dept. of Education School-to-Work Cluster:** Law and Public Safety.

Essential Knowledge and Skills

No data available. **Values/Work Environment:** No data available.

Other Information Sources

Many career and education information sources use the standard cross-referencing systems noted below. You can use the codes to obtain substantial additional information on the program (via CIP code) and related occupations (via GOE code). The O*NET codes on the opposite page refer to another major career information system. See the Introduction for details on obtaining additional information.

Classification of Instructional Programs (CIP) code(s): 220303 Court Reporting/Court Reporter

Guide for Occupational Exploration (GOE) code(s): 09.07 Records Processing

Culinary Arts

Program/Training Duration: One month to a year or more

Location: Workplace or vocational classroom

Career Snapshot

Chefs and cooks use a variety of tools, ingredients, and techniques to create wholesome, appealing foods according to recipes. Some specialize in a particular type of cuisine, such as French or Japanese; some specialize in a particular variety of food, such as pastries or sushi; many are generalists who can prepare many kinds of meals. The work can be hot, can be pressured, and (outside of institutional settings) is often scheduled at times when other people are relaxing. Job opportunities are expected to be very good.

Related Specialties and Careers

Asian cuisine, breads, Continental cuisine, pastries, regional American cuisine.

Related Job Titles, Educational Requirements, Projected Growth, and Earnings			
Job Title	Educational Requirements	Projected Growth	Average Earnings
Chefs and Head Cooks (O*NET code 35-1011.00)	Postsecondary vocational training	Little or none	$26,800
Cooks, All Other (O*NET code 35-2019.99)	No data available	Average	No salary data available
Cooks, Private Household (O*NET code 35-2013.00)	Short-term on-the-job training	Declining	No salary data available
Cooks, Restaurant (O*NET code 35-2014.00)	Long-term on-the-job training	Faster than average	$18,480

Typical Postsecondary Courses

Baking; contemporary American cuisine; co-op work experience; food and beverage cost control; food service sanitation and safety; garde manger; international cuisine; introduction to nutrition; introduction to the hospitality industry; stewarding/inventory management; workplace communications; workplace math.

Suggested High School Courses

Applied communications; business/applied math; foreign language; home economics. **Dept. of Education School-to-Work Cluster:** Hospitality and Tourism.

Essential Knowledge and Skills

Administration and management; coordination; customer and personal service.
Values/Work Environment: Indoors, environmentally controlled; moral values; spend time making repetitive motions; spend time standing.

Other Information Sources

Many career and education information sources use the standard cross-referencing systems noted below. You can use the codes to obtain substantial additional information on the program (via CIP code) and related occupations (via GOE code). The O*NET codes on the opposite page refer to another major career information system. See the Introduction for details on obtaining additional information.

Classification of Instructional Programs (CIP) code(s): 120503 Culinary Arts/Chef Training

Guide for Occupational Exploration (GOE) code(s): 11.05 Food and Beverage Services; 11.08 Other Personal Services

---

Dental Assisting

Program/Training Duration: One month to a year

Location: Workplace

Career Snapshot

Dental assistants perform a number of tasks to help dentists. They do not clean teeth (which is what dental hygienists do), but they may do any or all of the following: Prepare the patient and the dentist's tools and equipment, sterilize instruments and hand them to the dentist, instruct the patient on post-operative care and general oral hygiene, develop film from dental X rays, make casts of the teeth and mouth from impressions made by the dentist, bill patients, schedule appointments, or order dental supplies. The job outlook is expected to be good, as older Americans are keeping their teeth better than previous generations did, and more dentists are handing off routine tasks to assistants.

Related Specialties and Careers

Chairside assisting, dental laboratory assistant, dental office assistant.

Related Job Titles, Educational Requirements, Projected Growth, and Earnings			
Job Title	Educational Requirements	Projected Growth	Average Earnings
Dental Assistants (O*NET code 31-9091.00)	Moderate-term on-the-job training	Much faster than average	$26,720

Typical Postsecondary Courses

Chairside assisting; dental anatomy and physiology; dental materials; dental office management; oral radiology; preventive dentistry.

Suggested High School Courses

Algebra; biology; bookkeeping; chemistry; office computer applications; public speaking. **Dept. of Education School-to-Work Cluster:** Health Science.

Essential Knowledge and Skills

Active listening; clerical; medicine and dentistry. **Values/Work Environment:** Indoors, environmentally controlled; social service.

Other Information Sources

Many career and education information sources use the standard cross-referencing systems noted below. You can use the codes to obtain substantial additional information on the program (via CIP code) and related occupations (via GOE code). The O*NET codes on the opposite page refer to another major career information system. See the Introduction for details on obtaining additional information.

Classification of Instructional Programs (CIP) code(s): 510601 Dental Assisting/Assistant

Guide for Occupational Exploration (GOE) code(s): 12.03 Educational Services; 14.03 Dentistry

Dental Hygiene

Program/Training Duration: Two years

Location: College/vocational classroom

Career Snapshot

Dental hygienists clean teeth and provide other preventive dental care, as well as teaching patients how to maintain dental health. They use a variety of instruments to clean teeth and make X rays. This field offers many opportunities for part-time or flexible work schedules, and it promises to be one of the fastest-growing occupations. Dentists are tending to hand over more of their cleaning work to hygienists. The older population also increasingly tends to have retained their teeth, thus enlarging the pool of patients.

Related Specialties and Careers

Chairside assisting, dental health educator.

Related Job Titles, Educational Requirements, Projected Growth, and Earnings			
Job Title	Educational Requirements	Projected Growth	Average Earnings
Dental Hygienists (O*NET code 29-2021.00)	Associate degree	Much faster than average	$54,700

Typical Postsecondary Courses

Clinical dental hygiene; community dental health; dental hygiene theory; dental pharmacology and anesthesiology; English composition; general and oral pathology; general chemistry; head and neck anatomy; human anatomy and physiology; introduction to organic chemistry and biochemistry; introduction to psychology; introduction to sociology; microbiology; nutrition; oral communication; oral embryology and histology; oral radiology.

Suggested High School Courses

Algebra; biology; chemistry; English; public speaking. **Dept. of Education School-to-Work Cluster:** Health Science.

Essential Knowledge and Skills

Biology; education and training; medicine and dentistry; reading comprehension. **Values/Work Environment:** Indoors, environmentally controlled; social service.

Other Information Sources

Many career and education information sources use the standard cross-referencing systems noted below. You can use the codes to obtain substantial additional information on the program (via CIP code) and related occupations (via GOE code). The O*NET codes on the opposite page refer to another major career information system. See the Introduction for details on obtaining additional information.

Classification of Instructional Programs (CIP) code(s): 510602 Dental Hygiene/Hygienist

Guide for Occupational Exploration (GOE) code(s): 12.03 Educational Services; 14.03 Dentistry

Dental Laboratory Technology

Program/Training Duration: More than one year

Location: Workplace

Career Snapshot

Dental laboratory technicians create crowns, bridges, dentures, and other dental prosthetics, working from prescriptions and molds sent to them by dentists. They fashion wax models to get the right size and shape and then fabricate the actual crown using a metal core and a ceramic coating. They need very good color sense to match the patient's natural teeth. Some specialize in parts of the process or types of dental prosthetics, while others are generalists. Although job growth is expected to be modest, the occupation is not well known, so there will be many opportunities for those who wish to enter this field.

Related Specialties and Careers

Bridges, crowns, finishing, molding.

Related Job Titles, Educational Requirements, Projected Growth, and Earnings			
Job Title	Educational Requirements	Projected Growth	Average Earnings
Dental Laboratory Technicians (O*NET code 51-9081.00)	Long-term on-the-job training	Little or none	$27,970

Typical Postsecondary Courses

Complete dentures; dental ceramics; dental laboratory internship; dental laboratory management; dental morphology; dental occlusion; fixed prosthodontics; introduction to dental prosthodontics; partial denture prosthodontics.

Suggested High School Courses

Algebra; art; biology; chemistry. **Dept. of Education School-to-Work Cluster:** Manufacturing.

Essential Knowledge and Skills

Medicine and dentistry; quality control analysis; reading comprehension; science.
Values/Work Environment: Independence; indoors, environmentally controlled; moral values; spend time sitting.

Other Information Sources

Many career and education information sources use the standard cross-referencing systems noted below. You can use the codes to obtain substantial additional information on the program (via CIP code) and related occupations (via GOE code). The O*NET codes on the opposite page refer to another major career information system. See the Introduction for details on obtaining additional information.

Classification of Instructional Programs (CIP) code(s): 510603 Dental Laboratory Technology/Technician

Guide for Occupational Exploration (GOE) code(s): 08.02 Production Technology; 12.03 Educational Services

Diesel Technology

Program/Training Duration: A few weeks to a year or more

Location: College/vocational classroom or workplace

Career Snapshot

Diesel engines power the nation's trucks and buses, as well as heavy vehicles such as bulldozers and farm tractors. Technicians who service these engines work for equipment dealers, trucking companies, and bus fleets. As the technology of diesels is becoming more complex, with computerized controls and other electronic components, employers are increasingly looking for technicians who are graduates of formal training programs offered by community colleges or by trade and vocational schools. Some technicians still learn on the job, perhaps after experience with automobile engines. The standard of achievement is certification by the National Institute for Automotive Service Excellence (ASE).

Related Specialties and Careers

Bus and truck service, diesel automobile service, diesel boat service, heavy equipment service.

Related Job Titles, Educational Requirements, Projected Growth, and Earnings			
Job Title	Educational Requirements	Projected Growth	Average Earnings
Bus and Truck Mechanics and Diesel Engine Specialists (O*NET code 49-3031.00)	Postsecondary vocational training	Average	$33,570
Engine and Other Machine Assemblers (O*NET code 51-2031.00)	Short-term on-the-job training	Little or none	$28,100
Mobile Heavy Equipment Mechanics, Except Engines (O*NET code 49-3042.00)	Postsecondary vocational training	Average	$35,190
Rail Car Repairers (O*NET code 49-3043.00)	Long-term on-the-job training	Declining	$38,390

Typical Postsecondary Courses

Basic diesel engines; basic welding; computers for the vocational trades; diesel electronic controls; English composition; fuel systems; heavy-duty electrical systems; heavy-duty powertrains; hydraulics; technical mathematics.

Suggested High School Courses

Applied communications; auto shop; business/applied math; electronics shop; industrial arts; metal shop; physics/principles of technology. **Dept. of Education School-to-Work Cluster:** Manufacturing; Transportation, Distribution, and Logistics.

Essential Knowledge and Skills

Equipment maintenance; mechanical devices; repairing; troubleshooting. **Values/ Work Environment:** Exposed to hazardous equipment; moral values.

Other Information Sources

Many career and education information sources use the standard cross-referencing systems noted below. You can use the codes to obtain substantial additional information on the program (via CIP code) and related occupations (via GOE code). The O*NET codes on the opposite page refer to another major career information system. See the Introduction for details on obtaining additional information.

Classification of Instructional Programs (CIP) code(s): 470605 Diesel Mechanics Technology/Technician; 470302 Heavy Equipment Maintenance Technology/Technician

Guide for Occupational Exploration (GOE) code(s): 05.03 Mechanical Work; 08.02 Production Technology

---

 Dietetic Technology

Program/Training Duration: One month to a year or more

Location: Workplace or college/vocational classroom

Career Snapshot

Dietetic technicians work under the direction of registered dietitians in hospitals, nursing homes, institutional food services, school nutrition programs, fitness and wellness organizations, and food products manufacturers. Graduates of approved two-year programs may take an exam to become registered and thus improve their job prospects. The outlook for jobs in this field is expected to be about the same as for dietitians and nutritionists—about average, and best in settings other than hospitals.

Related Specialties and Careers

Education, health care, research, sales.

Related Job Titles, Educational Requirements, Projected Growth, and Earnings			
Job Title	Educational Requirements	Projected Growth	Average Earnings
Dietetic Technicians (O*NET code 29-2051.00)	Moderate-term on-the-job training	Faster than average	$21,790

Typical Postsecondary Courses

Clinical experience in dietetic technology; college algebra; community nutrition; diet therapy; dietetic orientation and terminology; English composition; food service operational management; food service purchasing; food service sanitation and safety; general biology; introduction to computer applications; introduction to food science and technology; introduction to nutrition; volume food preparation and service.

Suggested High School Courses

Algebra; biology; chemistry; English; home economics. **Dept. of Education School-to-Work Cluster:** Health Science.

Essential Knowledge and Skills

Active listening; biology; customer and personal service; education and training; reading comprehension; writing. **Values/Work Environment:** Co-workers; indoors, environmentally controlled; social service.

Other Information Sources

Many career and education information sources use the standard cross-referencing systems noted below. You can use the codes to obtain substantial additional information on the program (via CIP code) and related occupations (via GOE code). The O*NET codes on the opposite page refer to another major career information system. See the Introduction for details on obtaining additional information.

Classification of Instructional Programs (CIP) code(s): 513103 Dietetic Technician (DTR)

Guide for Occupational Exploration (GOE) code(s): 14.08 Health Protection and Promotion

---

 **Drafting**

Program/Training Duration: A few weeks to two years

Location: Workplace or college/vocational classroom

Career Snapshot

Drafters prepare technical drawings and plans that are followed by manufacturers and builders as they create all kinds of products and structures. They specify the dimensions and materials of the object to be produced and what processes will be used to create it. The pencils and drawing boards of yesteryear are now largely replaced by computer-aided drafting (CAD) systems, but drafters still need the ability to visualize objects, plus knowledge of materials and processes that will be used for these objects. Best job opportunities will be for those who have at least two years of formal training and a lot of experience with CAD.

Related Specialties and Careers

Aeronautical drafting, civil drafting, computer-aided drafting (CAD), electrical drafting, electronic drafting, mechanical drafting, process drafting.

Related Job Titles, Educational Requirements, Projected Growth, and Earnings			
Job Title	**Educational Requirements**	**Projected Growth**	**Average Earnings**
Architectural and Civil Drafters (O*NET code 17-3011.00)	Postsecondary vocational training	Faster than average	$37,010
Architectural Drafters (O*NET code 17-3011.01)	Associate degree	Faster than average	$37,010
Civil Drafters (O*NET code 17-3011.02)	Postsecondary vocational training	Faster than average	$37,010
Drafters, All Other (O*NET code 17-3019.99)	No data available	Faster than average	No salary data available
Electrical and Electronics Drafters (O*NET code 17-3012.00)	Associate degree	Faster than average	$40,070
Electrical Drafters (O*NET code 17-3012.02)	Associate degree	Faster than average	$40,070

Job Title	Educational Requirements	Projected Growth	Average Earnings
Electronic Drafters (O*NET code 17-3012.01)	Postsecondary vocational training	Faster than average	$40,070
Mechanical Drafters (O*NET code 17-3013.00)	Postsecondary vocational training	Average	$39,620

Typical Postsecondary Courses

Computer aided drafting (CAD); co-op work experience; descriptive geometry; engineering drawing; English composition; general physics; geometric tolerancing; introduction to computer numerical control; introduction to computer science; mechanical design; statics and strengths of materials; technical mathematics.

Suggested High School Courses

Algebra; applied communications; computer science; geometry; mechanical drawing; physics/principles of technology; trigonometry. **Dept. of Education School-to-Work Cluster:** Architecture and Construction.

Essential Knowledge and Skills

Design; engineering and technology; mathematics. **Values/Work Environment:** Indoors, environmentally controlled; moral values; spend time sitting; good working conditions.

Other Information Sources

Many career and education information sources use the standard cross-referencing systems noted below. You can use the codes to obtain substantial additional information on the program (via CIP code) and related occupations (via GOE code). The O*NET codes on the opposite page refer to another major career information system. See the Introduction for details on obtaining additional information.

Classification of Instructional Programs (CIP) code(s): 151303 Architectural Drafting and Architectural CAD/CADD; 151302 CAD/CADD Drafting and/or Design Technology/Technician; 151304 Civil Drafting and Civil Engineering CAD/CADD; 151301 Drafting and Design Technology/Technician, General; 151399 Drafting/Design Engineering Technologies/Technicians, Other; 151305 Electrical/Electronics Drafting and Electrical/Electronics CAD/CADD; 151306 Mechanical Drafting and Mechanical Drafting CAD/CADD

Guide for Occupational Exploration (GOE) code(s): 02.08 Engineering Technology

Early Childhood Education

Program/Training Duration: One month to a year or more

Location: Workplace or college/vocational classroom

Career Snapshot

Public school teachers must have a bachelor's degree, but graduates of associate degree programs in early childhood education can find work in preschools and child care centers as teachers and teacher assistants. Some work in Head Start, recreational, and social service programs. Working in education requires the ability to deal with students with a range of backgrounds and abilities. The legislative trend is toward licensing as a requirement, even for teacher aides, although states vary on specific requirements and private schools may be more flexible. The outlook for jobs is very good.

Related Specialties and Careers

Day care, early childhood teaching, Head Start teaching, kindergarten teaching, recreation assisting, teacher assisting.

Related Job Titles, Educational Requirements, Projected Growth, and Earnings			
Job Title	Educational Requirements	Projected Growth	Average Earnings
Teacher Assistants (O*NET code 25-9041.00)	Short-term on-the-job training	Faster than average	$18,070

Typical Postsecondary Courses

Child development; child health and nutrition; children with exceptional needs; classroom organization and management; educational observation, planning, assessment; English composition; expressive arts; infant and toddler programs; introduction to computer applications; introduction to early childhood education; introduction to psychology; language arts for children; math and science in early childhood education; sociology of the family; student teaching; the integrated curriculum.

Suggested High School Courses

Algebra; biology; English; public speaking; social science. **Dept. of Education School-to-Work Cluster:** Education and Training.

Essential Knowledge and Skills

Active listening; education and training; English language; learning strategies; speaking. **Values/Work Environment:** Indoors, environmentally controlled; social service.

Other Information Sources

Many career and education information sources use the standard cross-referencing systems noted below. You can use the codes to obtain substantial additional information on the program (via CIP code) and related occupations (via GOE code). The O*NET codes on the opposite page refer to another major career information system. See the Introduction for details on obtaining additional information.

Classification of Instructional Programs (CIP) code(s): 131210 Early Childhood Education and Teaching; 131501 Teacher Assistant/Aide

Guide for Occupational Exploration (GOE) code(s): 12.03 Educational Services

---

 Electrical Engineering Technology

Program/Training Duration: Two years

Location: College/vocational classroom

Career Snapshot

About half of all engineering technicians work with electric and electronic circuits, and the greatest job growth will probably be in this specialization. EE technicians work in research, manufacturing, sales, and maintenance (but not primarily repair—a different occupation). The better jobs are open to graduates of programs approved by the Technology Accreditation Commission of the Accreditation Board for Engineering and Technology (TAC/ABET), which usually require two years of study.

Related Specialties and Careers

Communications, instrumentation, manufacturing, microprocessors.

Related Job Titles, Educational Requirements, Projected Growth, and Earnings			
Job Title	Educational Requirements	Projected Growth	Average Earnings
Calibration and Instrumentation Technicians (O*NET code 17-3023.02)	Associate degree	Average	$42,130
Electrical and Electronic Engineering Technicians (O*NET code 17-3023.00)	Associate degree	Average	$42,130
Electrical Engineering Technicians (O*NET code 17-3023.03)	Associate degree	Average	$42,130
Electronics Engineering Technicians (O*NET code 17-3023.01)	Associate degree	Average	$42,130

Typical Postsecondary Courses

Communication systems; DC/AC theory; digital electronics; electronics; engineering circuit analysis; English composition; general physics; microcomputer electronics; pre-calculus; solid state circuitry.

Suggested High School Courses

Algebra; applied communications; computer science; electronics shop; geometry; physics/principles of technology; trigonometry. **Dept. of Education School-to-Work Cluster:** Manufacturing.

Essential Knowledge and Skills

Active learning; computers and electronics; design; engineering and technology; technology design. **Values/Work Environment:** Indoors, environmentally controlled; moral values.

Other Information Sources

Many career and education information sources use the standard cross-referencing systems noted below. You can use the codes to obtain substantial additional information on the program (via CIP code) and related occupations (via GOE code). The O*NET codes on the opposite page refer to another major career information system. See the Introduction for details on obtaining additional information.

Classification of Instructional Programs (CIP) code(s): 150399 Electrical and Electronic Engineering Technologies/ Technicians, Other

Guide for Occupational Exploration (GOE) code(s): 02.08 Engineering Technology

---

 **Electrician Training**

Program/Training Duration: One month to more than a year

Location: Workplace

Career Snapshot

Electricians install and maintain electrical systems for power, lighting, transportation, manufacturing, and many other applications. About two-thirds work in construction. Most train in a structured apprenticeship program, though a few learn informally by working as an electrician's helper. Licensure is required in most localities. The job outlook is expected to be excellent, although (especially in construction) it is sensitive to economic downturns.

Related Specialties and Careers

Construction, estimating, maintenance.

Related Job Titles, Educational Requirements, Projected Growth, and Earnings			
Job Title	**Educational Requirements**	**Projected Growth**	**Average Earnings**
Electricians (O*NET code 47-2111.00)	Long-term on-the-job training	Average	$40,770
First-Line Supervisors and Manager/Supervisors—Construction Trades Workers (O*NET code 47-1011.01)	Work experience in a related occupation	Average	$46,570
First-Line Supervisors/Managers of Construction Trades and Extraction Workers (O*NET code 47-1011.00)	Work experience in a related occupation	Average	$46,570
Helpers—Electricians (O*NET code 47-3013.00)	Short-term on-the-job training	Average	$22,160
Security and Fire Alarm Systems Installers (O*NET code 49-2098.00)	Postsecondary vocational training	Faster than average	$30,490
Signal and Track Switch Repairers (O*NET code 49-9097.00)	Postsecondary vocational training	Average	$42,390

Typical Postsecondary Courses

Blueprint reading; construction math and estimating; construction safety; electrical circuits; electrical theory; electrical wiring; introduction to computer applications; motors and controls; National Electrical Code.

Suggested High School Courses

Applied communications; business/applied math; drafting; industrial arts; physics/principles of technology. **Dept. of Education School-to-Work Cluster:** Architecture and Construction.

Essential Knowledge and Skills

Engineering and technology; installation. **Values/Work Environment:** Exposed to hazardous equipment; moral values; outdoors, exposed to weather; spend time standing.

Other Information Sources

Many career and education information sources use the standard cross-referencing systems noted below. You can use the codes to obtain substantial additional information on the program (via CIP code) and related occupations (via GOE code). The O*NET codes on the opposite page refer to another major career information system. See the Introduction for details on obtaining additional information.

Classification of Instructional Programs (CIP) code(s): 460302 Electrician

Guide for Occupational Exploration (GOE) code(s): 05.02 Electrical and Electronic Systems; 05.03 Mechanical Work; 06.01 Managerial Work in Construction, Mining, and Drilling; 06.02 Construction

---

Electrocardiograph Technology

Program/Training Duration: Several months to one year, often following work experience

Location: Workplace or vocational classroom

Career Snapshot

Electrocardiograph (or EKG) technicians trace electrical impulses transmitted through the heart. They attach electrodes to various parts of the patient's body and obtain a printout to be interpreted by a physician. They learn their skills either in a one-year certification program or through on-the-job training that may take from 8 to 16 weeks. Often employers prefer to train those who have previous health care educational and/or experience. Job opportunities are expected to be good as the population ages. Specialized technicians with advanced training may perform tests in which the patient wears a Holter monitor (a portable unit that measures for 24 hours) or works out on a treadmill (stress testing). These technicians have a better job outlook than those with only the basic EKG skills.

Related Specialties and Careers

Cardiac stress testing, Holter monitoring.

Related Job Titles, Educational Requirements, Projected Growth, and Earnings			
Job Title	Educational Requirements	Projected Growth	Average Earnings
Cardiovascular Technologists and Technicians (O*NET code 29-2031.00)	Associate degree	Faster than average	$35,010

Typical Postsecondary Courses

Basic electroneurodiagnostic skills; biomedical electronics; human anatomy and physiology; introduction to electrocardiography; patient preparation; performing electrocardiography; pharmacology and electrocardiography.

Suggested High School Courses

Applied communications; biology; business/applied math; chemistry; computer science; electronics shop; physics/principles of technology. **Dept. of Education School-to-Work Cluster:** Health Science.

Essential Knowledge and Skills

Biology; computers and electronics; medicine and dentistry; reading comprehension. **Values/Work Environment:** Indoors, environmentally controlled; social service.

Other Information Sources

Many career and education information sources use the standard cross-referencing systems noted below. You can use the codes to obtain substantial additional information on the program (via CIP code) and related occupations (via GOE code). The O*NET codes on the opposite page refer to another major career information system. See the Introduction for details on obtaining additional information.

Classification of Instructional Programs (CIP) code(s): 510902 Electrocardiograph Technology/Technician

Guide for Occupational Exploration (GOE) code(s): 12.03 Educational Services; 14.05 Medical Technology

---

Electroencephalograph Technology

Program/Training Duration: One to two years

Location: Workplace or college/vocational classroom

Career Snapshot

Physicians are able to assess the condition of the brain and nervous system with the help of the electroencephalograph (EEG) machine, which is operated by an electroneurodiagnostic technologist. Most work in the neurology labs of hospitals, but some work in offices of neurologists or in a center specializing in sleep disorders. On-the-job training has been the most common entry route in the past, but employers are increasingly favoring those who have received formal training (one or two years) in a hospital or community college. Job growth is expected to be slow, partly because more sophisticated equipment is improving workers' productivity.

Related Specialties and Careers

Evoked potential testing, polysomnographic testing, resting EEGs.

Related Job Titles, Educational Requirements, Projected Growth, and Earnings			
Job Title	Educational Requirements	Projected Growth	Average Earnings
Health Technologists and Technicians, All Other (O*NET code 29-2099.99)	No data available	Faster than average	No salary data available

Typical Postsecondary Courses

Basic electroneurodiagnostic skills; computer applications in health care; electroneurodiagnostic clinical education; English composition; general biology; human anatomy and physiology; introduction to psychology; introduction to speech communication; neuroanatomy and neurophysiology; neurological disorders and neuropathology; normal adult EEG and normal variants; normal neonatal and pediatric EEG; pharmacology.

Suggested High School Courses

Applied communications; biology; business/applied math; chemistry; computer science; electronics shop; physics/principles of technology. **Dept. of Education School-to-Work Cluster:** Health Science.

Essential Knowledge and Skills

No data available. **Values/Work Environment:** No data available.

Other Information Sources

Many career and education information sources use the standard cross-referencing systems noted below. You can use the codes to obtain substantial additional information on the program (via CIP code) and related occupations (via GOE code). The O*NET codes on the opposite page refer to another major career information system. See the Introduction for details on obtaining additional information.

Classification of Instructional Programs (CIP) code(s): 510903 Electroneurodiagnostic/Electroencephalographic Technology/Technologist

Guide for Occupational Exploration (GOE) code(s): 12.03 Educational Services; 14.05 Medical Technology

---

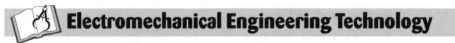

Electromechanical Engineering Technology

Program/Training Duration: Two years

Location: College/vocational classroom

Career Snapshot

Electronic and mechanical devices are combined in many automated manufacturing processes, research instruments, vehicles, and consumer goods, and increasingly they are controlled by tiny computers. Electromechanical engineering technologists are needed to help solve problems in the design and manufacture of these devices. Employers prefer graduates of programs approved by the Technology Accreditation Commission of the Accreditation Board for Engineering and Technology (TAC/ABET), which typically take two or three years.

Related Specialties and Careers

Digital controls, electronics, fluid power, instrumentation, motors, robotics.

Related Job Titles, Educational Requirements, Projected Growth, and Earnings			
Job Title	Educational Requirements	Projected Growth	Average Earnings
Electromechanical Equipment Assemblers (O*NET code 51-2023.00)	Short-term on-the-job training	Little or none	$24,690

Typical Postsecondary Courses

Analog devices and circuits; computer applications in manufacturing; computer-automated manufacturing; computer-aided drafting (CAD); DC/AC theory; digital electronics; general physics; hydraulics; motors and controls; robotics; technical mathematics; technical writing.

Suggested High School Courses

Algebra; applied communications; computer science; electronics shop; geometry; physics/principles of technology; trigonometry. **Dept. of Education School-to-Work Cluster:** Manufacturing.

Essential Knowledge and Skills

Computers and electronics; installation; mechanical devices; production and processing. **Values/Work Environment:** Exposed to hazardous equipment; independence; indoors, environmentally controlled; moral values.

Other Information Sources

Many career and education information sources use the standard cross-referencing systems noted below. You can use the codes to obtain substantial additional information on the program (via CIP code) and related occupations (via GOE code). The O*NET codes on the opposite page refer to another major career information system. See the Introduction for details on obtaining additional information.

Classification of Instructional Programs (CIP) code(s): 150403 Electromechanical Technology/Electromechanical Engineering Technology

Guide for Occupational Exploration (GOE) code(s): 08.02 Production Technology

---

 Emergency Medical Services

Program/Training Duration: A few weeks to two years

Location: Vocational classroom and workplace

Career Snapshot

Emergency medical technicians (EMTs) rush to the scene of an accident or sudden illness, make a quick diagnosis of the patient's problem, perform first aid, bring the patient aboard an ambulance (perhaps on a stretcher or gurney), and do what can be done to stabilize the patient's condition en route to the hospital. (Often the person at the wheel of the ambulance is also an EMT. Some EMTs work from helicopters.) At the hospital, EMTs transport the patient to the emergency room and give important information to the ER staff. States require EMTs to be certified, which means completing a combination of classes and work experience appropriate for the level of certification. EMT-Paramedics need two years of schooling and experience, and all EMTs must continue to take courses to remain certified. Job outlook is expected to be good, especially for those certified at the higher levels.

Related Specialties and Careers

Ambulance aide, first responder, paramedic.

Related Job Titles, Educational Requirements, Projected Growth, and Earnings			
Job Title	Educational Requirements	Projected Growth	Average Earnings
Ambulance Drivers and Attendants, Except Emergency Medical Technicians (O*NET code 53-3011.00)	Moderate-term on-the-job training	Faster than average	$18,890
Emergency Medical Technicians and Paramedics (O*NET code 29-2041.00)	Postsecondary vocational training	Faster than average	$23,170

Typical Postsecondary Courses

College algebra; emergency life support procedures; EMT pharmacology; EMT procedures for hazardous materials; English composition; human anatomy and physiology; internship in emergency medical services; introduction to medical terminology; introduction to psychology; management of emergency medical services.

Suggested High School Courses

Algebra; applied communications; biology; chemistry; driver education; keyboarding; physics/principles of technology; social science. **Dept. of Education School-to-Work Cluster:** Health Science.

Essential Knowledge and Skills

Coordination; medicine and dentistry; service orientation; therapy and counseling; transportation. **Values/Work Environment:** Achievement; exposed to disease or infections; outdoors, exposed to weather; social service.

Other Information Sources

Many career and education information sources use the standard cross-referencing systems noted below. You can use the codes to obtain substantial additional information on the program (via CIP code) and related occupations (via GOE code). The O*NET codes on the opposite page refer to another major career information system. See the Introduction for details on obtaining additional information.

Classification of Instructional Programs (CIP) code(s): 510904 Emergency Medical Technology/Technician (EMT Paramedic)

Guide for Occupational Exploration (GOE) code(s): 04.04 Public Safety; 07.07 Other Services Requiring Driving; 12.03 Educational Services

---

Farm and Ranch Management

Program/Training Duration: At least one year, perhaps several
Location: Workplace or college classroom

Career Snapshot

Farm and ranch managers oversee day-to-day agricultural activities to maximize productivity. At a large farm or ranch, they may have a very specific assignment, such as managing livestock breeding, whereas they may be in charge of most aspects of the business at a small operation. The hours are long during planting and harvesting seasons, and those who supervise several farms may divide their time between the farms, a central office, and traveling among these locations. Formal education, combined with experience, is increasingly important. Consolidation of family farms and increased efficiency of farming methods are expected to reduce the number of self-employed farmers but increase the need for farm and ranch managers.

Related Specialties and Careers

Animal breeding, aquaculture, crop production, farm labor management, fiber production, livestock production, organic farming.

Related Job Titles, Educational Requirements, Projected Growth, and Earnings			
Job Title	**Educational Requirements**	**Projected Growth**	**Average Earnings**
Agricultural Crop Farm Managers (O*NET code 11-9011.02)	Work experience in a related occupation	Little or none	$42,170
Farm, Ranch, and Other Agricultural Managers (O*NET code 11-9011.00)	Work experience in a related occupation	Little or none	$42,170
Farmers and Ranchers (O*NET code 11-9012.00)	Long-term on-the-job training	Declining	$42,170
First-Line Supervisors and Manager/Supervisors— Agricultural Crop Workers (O*NET code 45-1011.01)	Associate degree	Average	$33,330
First-Line Supervisors and Manager/Supervisors—Animal Care Workers, Except Livestock (O*NET code 45-1011.03)	Associate degree	Average	$33,330
First-Line Supervisors and Manager/Supervisors—Animal Husbandry Workers (O*NET code 45-1011.02)	Associate degree	Average	$33,330

Job Title	Educational Requirements	Projected Growth	Average Earnings
First-Line Supervisors and Manager/Supervisors—Fishery Workers (O*NET code 45-1011.06)	Associate degree	Average	$33,330
First-Line Supervisors and Manager/Supervisors—Horticultural Workers (O*NET code 45-1011.04)	Associate degree	Average	$33,330
First-Line Supervisors/Managers of Farming, Fishing, and Forestry Workers (O*NET code 45-1011.00)	Work experience in a related occupation	Average	$33,330
Fish Hatchery Managers (O*NET code 11-9011.03)	Work experience in a related occupation	Little or none	$42,170
Nursery and Greenhouse Managers (O*NET code 11-9011.01)	Work experience in a related occupation	Little or none	$42,170

Typical Postsecondary Courses

Agricultural marketing; American government; animal breeding; animal science; college algebra; computers in agriculture; English composition; feeds and feeding; general biology; introduction to accounting; introduction to agriculture industry; introduction to economics; introduction to plant science.

Suggested High School Courses

Algebra; applied communications; biology; bookkeeping; chemistry; office computer applications; Spanish. **Dept. of Education School-to-Work Cluster:** Agriculture/Natural Resources.

Essential Knowledge and Skills

Administration and management; biology; coordination; food production; management of personnel resources. **Values/Work Environment:** Authority; autonomy; outdoors, exposed to weather; responsibility; spend time standing.

Other Information Sources

Many career and education information sources use the standard cross-referencing systems noted below. You can use the codes to obtain substantial additional information on the program (via CIP code) and related occupations (via GOE code). The O*NET codes on the opposite page refer to another major career information system. See the Introduction for details on obtaining additional information.

Classification of Instructional Programs (CIP) code(s): 010104 Farm/Farm and Ranch Management

Guide for Occupational Exploration (GOE) code(s): 03.01 Managerial Work in Plants and Animals; 12.03 Educational Services; 13.01 General Management Work and Management of Support Functions

---

Fashion Design

Program/Training Duration: At least two years, usually four

Location: College classroom

Career Snapshot

A program in fashion design may lead to a career as a clothing designer, pattern maker, sample maker, alterations specialist, or theatrical costumer. Additional coursework in business can be helpful for advancement in the fashion industry, and employers actually prefer a bachelor's degree. Clothing may be manufactured mostly offshore, but fashion design continues to offer opportunities here in the U.S. Demand for fashion designers is expected to be good, although the field is very competitive and somewhat sensitive to economic ups and downs.

Related Specialties and Careers

Design, illustration, patternmaking.

Related Job Titles, Educational Requirements, Projected Growth, and Earnings			
Job Title	Educational Requirements	Projected Growth	Average Earnings
Fashion Designers (O*NET code 27-1022.00)	Bachelor's degree	Average	$49,530

Typical Postsecondary Courses

Clothing construction; color and design; creative apparel design; fashion illustration; fashion marketing and merchandising; field experience/internship; flat pattern design; history of fashion; introduction to marketing; textiles.

Suggested High School Courses

Algebra; applied communications; art; business/applied math; distributive education; home economics; office computer applications; social science. **Dept. of Education School-to-Work Cluster:** Retail and Wholesale Sales and Service.

Essential Knowledge and Skills

Coordination; design; fine arts; sales and marketing. **Values/Work Environment:** Ability utilization; achievement; creativity; indoors, environmentally controlled.

Other Information Sources

Many career and education information sources use the standard cross-referencing systems noted below. You can use the codes to obtain substantial additional information on the program (via CIP code) and related occupations (via GOE code). The O*NET codes on the opposite page refer to another major career information system. See the Introduction for details on obtaining additional information.

Classification of Instructional Programs (CIP) code(s): 500407 Fashion/Apparel Design

Guide for Occupational Exploration (GOE) code(s): 01.04 Visual Arts; 12.03 Educational Services

 **Fashion Merchandising**

Program/Training Duration: One month to a year

Location: Workplace or vocational classroom

Career Snapshot

Graduates of fashion merchandising programs often work as sales representatives or management trainees; with experience and perhaps additional education, they may become retail buyers, sales managers, store managers, market researchers, or advertising copywriters. Although the fashion industry is expected to be strong, competition for jobs may be keen. Good communication and analytical skills will be helpful for getting ahead.

Related Specialties and Careers

Market research, promotion, retail buying, sales.

Related Job Titles, Educational Requirements, Projected Growth, and Earnings			
Job Title	**Educational Requirements**	**Projected Growth**	**Average Earnings**
Sales Representatives, Wholesale and Manufacturing, Except Technical and Scientific (O*NET code 41-4012.00)	Moderate-term on-the-job training	Little or none	$41,520

Typical Postsecondary Courses

Business math; fashion marketing and merchandising; fashion promotion; financial accounting; introduction to advertising; introduction to business; introduction to business management; introduction to economics; introduction to marketing; principles of selling; retail merchandising; supervision; textiles; visual merchandising.

Suggested High School Courses

Algebra; applied communications; bookkeeping; business/applied math; distributive education; home economics; office computer applications; social science. **Dept. of Education School-to-Work Cluster:** Retail and Wholesale Sales and Service.

Essential Knowledge and Skills

Active listening; customer and personal service; English language; sales and marketing; speaking. **Values/Work Environment:** Autonomy; indoors, environmentally controlled.

Other Information Sources

Many career and education information sources use the standard cross-referencing systems noted below. You can use the codes to obtain substantial additional information on the program (via CIP code) and related occupations (via GOE code). The O*NET codes on the opposite page refer to another major career information system. See the Introduction for details on obtaining additional information.

Classification of Instructional Programs (CIP) code(s): 521902 Fashion Merchandising

Guide for Occupational Exploration (GOE) code(s): 10.03 General Sales; 13.02 Management Support

Fire Science/Firefighting

Program/Training Duration: One month to a year or more

Location: Workplace

Career Snapshot

Firefighters respond quickly to fires and other emergencies, using appropriate equipment to put out fires, remove hazardous materials, and perform various kinds of rescue and lifesaving operations. Some specialize in inspecting buildings and making recommendations for how to prevent fires and reduce the potential for loss of property or life. Others specialize in containing and putting out forest fires. Despite the long hours and dangers of firefighting jobs, competition for job openings is expected to be keen.

Related Specialties and Careers

Fire safety inspection, fire scene investigation, forest firefighting, hazardous materials, urban firefighting.

Related Job Titles, Educational Requirements, Projected Growth, and Earnings			
Job Title	Educational Requirements	Projected Growth	Average Earnings
Fire Fighters (O*NET code 33-2011.00)	Long-term on-the-job training	Little or none	$34,680
Fire Inspectors (O*NET code 33-2021.01)	Moderate-term on-the-job training	Average	$42,870
Fire Inspectors and Investigators (O*NET code 33-2021.00)	Moderate-term on-the-job training	Average	$42,870
Forest Fire Fighters (O*NET code 33-2011.02)	Long-term on-the-job training	Little or none	$34,680
Forest Fire Inspectors and Prevention Specialists (O*NET code 33-2022.00)	Moderate-term on-the-job training	Average	$35,120
Municipal Fire Fighters (O*NET code 33-2011.01)	Long-term on-the-job training	Little or none	$34,680

Typical Postsecondary Courses

Construction codes and material rating; fire investigation; fire prevention methods; firefighting strategy and tactics; hazardous materials; introduction to computer science; introduction to fire protection; management of municipal fire protection; principles of chemistry; workplace communications; workplace math.

Suggested High School Courses

Applied communications; business/applied math; chemistry; physics/principles of technology. **Dept. of Education School-to-Work Cluster:** Law and Public Safety.

Essential Knowledge and Skills

Geography; medicine and dentistry; public safety and security; service orientation. **Values/Work Environment:** Achievement; outdoors, exposed to weather; security; social status.

Other Information Sources

Many career and education information sources use the standard cross-referencing systems noted below. You can use the codes to obtain substantial additional information on the program (via CIP code) and related occupations (via GOE code). The O*NET codes on the opposite page refer to another major career information system. See the Introduction for details on obtaining additional information.

Classification of Instructional Programs (CIP) code(s): 430203 Fire Science/Firefighting

Guide for Occupational Exploration (GOE) code(s): 04.03 Law Enforcement; 04.04 Public Safety

---

Flight Attendant Training

Program/Training Duration: More than one year

Location: Workplace

Career Snapshot

Flight attendants make the experience of airplane travel comfortable and safe for passengers. They attend to passengers' needs for food, drink, and other comforts; make sure that safety procedures are followed; and have the skills to provide first aid and other assistance in emergencies. Job outlook appears good, especially for those with some college and experience working with the public.

Related Specialties and Careers

Cabin attendant, purser.

Related Job Titles, Educational Requirements, Projected Growth, and Earnings			
Job Title	Educational Requirements	Projected Growth	Average Earnings
Flight Attendants (O*NET code 39-6031.00)	Long-term on-the-job training	Average	$40,600

Typical Postsecondary Courses

Airline company policies for flight attendants; airline passenger relations; flight attendant emergency procedures; flight regulations and duties; personal grooming.

Suggested High School Courses

Applied communications; foreign language; public speaking; social science. **Dept. of Education School-to-Work Cluster:** Transportation, Distribution, and Logistics.

Essential Knowledge and Skills

Customer and personal service; public safety and security; service orientation; social perceptiveness. **Values/Work Environment:** Co-workers; indoors, environmentally controlled; social service; spend time standing; spend time walking and running; supervision, technical.

Other Information Sources

Many career and education information sources use the standard cross-referencing systems noted below. You can use the codes to obtain substantial additional information on the program (via CIP code) and related occupations (via GOE code). The O*NET codes on the opposite page refer to another major career information system. See the Introduction for details on obtaining additional information.

Classification of Instructional Programs (CIP) code(s): 490106 Airline Flight Attendant

Guide for Occupational Exploration (GOE) code(s): 11.03 Transportation and Lodging Services

 # Food Service Management

Program/Training Duration: Several years

Location: Workplace, perhaps vocational classroom

Career Snapshot

Food service managers work at restaurants and cafeterias. They plan menus, oversee purchasing of food and beverage supplies, and supervise cooks and serving staff. They maintain financial records and ensure that facilities meet local sanitation codes. A two-year degree program may provide sufficient credentials for a trainee job. Work experience in the industry is important and often is part of the academic program. Job opportunities are expected to be good as people increasingly eat away from home.

Related Specialties and Careers

Catering, clinical food service, dining room management, food preparation, industrial food service, menu planning, restaurant food service.

Related Job Titles, Educational Requirements, Projected Growth, and Earnings			
Job Title	Educational Requirements	Projected Growth	Average Earnings
Food Service Managers (O*NET code 11-9051.00)	Work experience in a related occupation	Average	$33,630

Typical Postsecondary Courses

Accounting; business reports and communication; food and beverage cost control; food and beverage production and management; food and beverage purchasing; food service operational management; food service sanitation and safety; introduction to nutrition; menu design and analysis.

Suggested High School Courses

Applied communications; biology; bookkeeping; business/applied math; distributive education; home economics. **Dept. of Education School-to-Work Cluster:** Hospitality and Tourism.

Essential Knowledge and Skills

Administration and management; coordination; customer and personal service; economics and accounting; management of personnel resources; monitoring.

Values/Work Environment: Authority; autonomy; indoors, environmentally controlled; security.

Other Information Sources

Many career and education information sources use the standard cross-referencing systems noted below. You can use the codes to obtain substantial additional information on the program (via CIP code) and related occupations (via GOE code). The O*NET codes on the opposite page refer to another major career information system. See the Introduction for details on obtaining additional information.

Classification of Instructional Programs (CIP) code(s): 520905 Restaurant/Food Services Management

Guide for Occupational Exploration (GOE) code(s): 11.01 Managerial Work in Recreation, Travel, and Other Personal Services

---

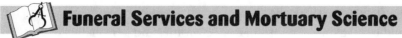

Funeral Services and Mortuary Science

Program/Training Duration: Two years or more

Location: College classroom, followed by workplace

Career Snapshot

Funeral directors need especially good people skills for comforting diverse clients in stressful circumstances. Embalmers, who prepare the body for the funeral, may see considerably less of the public, but the trend is toward combining the two job functions. All states except Colorado require funeral directors to be licensed, and all states require embalmers to be licensed. (In some states, one license covers both.) Typically those who sit for the licensing exam must have completed two years of college, at least partially in mortuary science, plus an apprenticeship of at least a year. Employment opportunities are expected to be good, especially for those who are willing to relocate.

Related Specialties and Careers

Embalmer, funeral director, grief counselor.

Related Job Titles, Educational Requirements, Projected Growth, and Earnings			
Job Title	Educational Requirements	Projected Growth	Average Earnings
Embalmers (O*NET code 39-4011.00)	Postsecondary vocational training	Declining	$33,030
Funeral Attendants (O*NET code 39-4021.00)	Short-term on-the-job training	Average	$17,630
Funeral Directors (O*NET code 11-9061.00)	Associate degree	Little or none	$42,020

Typical Postsecondary Courses

Basic counseling skills; business information processing; embalming; Federal Trade Commission funeral regulations; funeral arranging; funeral directing; funeral home management; funeral merchandising; general chemistry; history of funeral service; human anatomy; introduction to accounting; introduction to business management; legal environment of business; microbiology; pathology; professional ethics; psychology of grief; restorative art; sociology of funeral service.

Suggested High School Courses

Algebra; applied communications; art; biology; bookkeeping; chemistry; office computer applications; public speaking; social science. **Dept. of Education School-to-Work Cluster:** Health Science; Retail and Wholesale Sales and Service.

Essential Knowledge and Skills

Customer and personal service; psychology; social perceptiveness. **Values/Work Environment:** Indoors, environmentally controlled; security.

Other Information Sources

Many career and education information sources use the standard cross-referencing systems noted below. You can use the codes to obtain substantial additional information on the program (via CIP code) and related occupations (via GOE code). The O*NET codes on the opposite page refer to another major career information system. See the Introduction for details on obtaining additional information.

Classification of Instructional Programs (CIP) code(s): 120301 Funeral Service and Mortuary Science, General

Guide for Occupational Exploration (GOE) code(s): 11.08 Other Personal Services; 13.01 General Management Work and Management of Support Functions

---

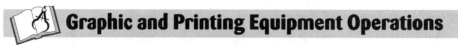

Graphic and Printing Equipment Operations

Program/Training Duration: One month to more than one year

Location: Workplace, perhaps vocational classroom

Career Snapshot

Most printing press operators and prepress technicians learn their skills through informal on-the-job training, but some learn through apprenticeships or through programs at technical or community colleges. Training may take from a few months to several years, depending on the specialization. Since prepress operations are becoming increasingly computerized and workers need to keep pace with changing technology, the best opportunities in that field are expected to be for graduates of postsecondary programs. Similarly, printing press operators with formal training probably will have the best job prospects.

Related Specialties and Careers

Dot etching, film stripping, flexography, gravure, letterpress, lithography, screen printing.

Related Job Titles, Educational Requirements, Projected Growth, and Earnings			
Job Title	**Educational Requirements**	**Projected Growth**	**Average Earnings**
Camera Operators (O*NET code 51-5022.04)	Long-term on-the-job training	Declining	$30,790
Data Entry Keyers (O*NET code 43-9021.00)	Moderate-term on-the-job training	Little or none	$21,960
Design Printing Machine Setters and Set-Up Operators (O*NET code 51-5023.04)	Postsecondary vocational training	Little or none	$29,010
Dot Etchers (O*NET code 51-5022.08)	Long-term on-the-job training	Declining	$30,790
Electronic Masking System Operators (O*NET code 51-5022.09)	Long-term on-the-job training	Declining	$30,790
Electrotypers and Stereotypers (O*NET code 51-5022.10)	Long-term on-the-job training	Declining	$30,790
Embossing Machine Set-Up Operators (O*NET code 51-5023.07)	Postsecondary vocational training	Little or none	$29,010

Job Title	Educational Requirements	Projected Growth	Average Earnings
Engraver Set-Up Operators (O*NET code 51-5023.08)	Long-term on-the-job training	Little or none	$29,010
Hand Compositors and Typesetters (O*NET code 51-5022.01)	Long-term on-the-job training	Declining	$30,790
Job Printers (O*NET code 51-5021.00)	Long-term on-the-job training	Little or none	$29,220
Letterpress Setters and Set-Up Operators (O*NET code 51-5023.03)	Moderate-term on-the-job training	Little or none	$29,010
Marking and Identification Printing Machine Setters and Set-Up Operators (O*NET code 51-5023.05)	Short-term on-the-job training	Little or none	$29,010

Typical Postsecondary Courses

Business information processing; computer-aided publishing; digital image preparation; English composition; field experience/internship; introduction to graphic arts; photo-offset lithography; printing estimating; printing management; printing production practices; reproduction photography.

Suggested High School Courses

Business/applied math; English; industrial arts; office computer applications; photography; physics/principles of technology. **Dept. of Education School-to-Work Cluster:** Arts, A/V Technology, and Communication.

Essential Knowledge and Skills

Operation and control; production and processing. **Values/Work Environment:** Independence; indoors, environmentally controlled; moral values.

Other Information Sources

Many career and education information sources use the standard cross-referencing systems noted below. You can use the codes to obtain substantial additional information on the program (via CIP code) and related occupations (via GOE code). The O*NET codes on the opposite page refer to another major career information system. See the Introduction for details on obtaining additional information.

Classification of Instructional Programs (CIP) code(s): 100308 Computer Typography and Composition Equipment Operator; 100305 Graphic and Printing Equipment Operator, General Production; 100306 Platemaker/Imager; 100307 Printing Press Operator

Guide for Occupational Exploration (GOE) code(s): 01.07 Graphic Arts; 08.02 Production Technology; 08.03 Production Work; 09.07 Records Processing; 09.09 Clerical Machine Operation

Graphic Design, Commercial Art, and Illustration

Program/Training Duration: At least one year, often two or more
Location: College/vocational classroom or workplace

Career Snapshot

Many consumer goods, such as books, magazines, and Web pages, consist primarily of graphic elements—illustrations and text. Other goods, such as cereal boxes, use graphic elements conspicuously. Graphic design teaches how to represent ideas graphically and give maximum visual appeal to text and pictures. The program involves considerable studio time, and an important goal is creating a good portfolio of work. Ability to work with computers is becoming vital in this field. Graduates with an associate or bachelor's degree work for publishers and design firms. Some freelance.

Related Specialties and Careers

Cartooning, illustration, letterform, typography, Web page design.

Related Job Titles, Educational Requirements, Projected Growth, and Earnings			
Job Title	**Educational Requirements**	**Projected Growth**	**Average Earnings**
Art Directors (O*NET code 27-1011.00)	Work experience plus degree	Faster than average	$59,800
Artists and Related Workers, All Other (O*NET code 27-1019.99)	Long-term on-the-job training	Average	No salary data available
Camera Operators (O*NET code 51-5022.04)	Long-term on-the-job training	Declining	$30,790
Designers, All Other (O*NET code 27-1029.99)	No data available	Faster than average	No salary data available
Dot Etchers (O*NET code 51-5022.08)	Long-term on-the-job training	Declining	$30,790
Electronic Masking System Operators (O*NET code 51-5022.09)	Long-term on-the-job training	Declining	$30,790
Electrotypers and Stereotypers (O*NET code 51-5022.10)	Long-term on-the-job training	Declining	$30,790
Hand Compositors and Typesetters (O*NET code 51-5022.01)	Long-term on-the-job training	Declining	$30,790

Job Title	Educational Requirements	Projected Growth	Average Earnings
Painting, Coating, and Decorating Workers (O*NET code 51-9123.00)	Short-term on-the-job training	Average	$20,560
Paste-Up Workers (O*NET code 51-5022.02)	Long-term on-the-job training	Declining	$30,790
Photoengravers (O*NET code 51-5022.03)	Long-term on-the-job training	Declining	$30,790
Photoengraving and Lithographing Machine Operators and Tenders (O*NET code 51-5022.13)	Moderate-term on-the-job training	Declining	$30,790

Typical Postsecondary Courses

Art history: Prehistoric to Renaissance; art history: Renaissance to modern; basic drawing; college algebra; computer applications in graphic design; English composition; history of graphic design; introduction to graphic design; letterform; oral communication; presentation graphics; senior design project; three-dimensional design; two-dimensional design; typography; visual communication; visual thinking and problem solving.

Suggested High School Courses

Algebra; art; computer science; English; geometry; mechanical drawing; photography; pre-calculus; public speaking; trigonometry. **Dept. of Education School-to-Work Cluster:** Arts, A/V Technology, and Communication.

Essential Knowledge and Skills

Fine arts; operation and control; production and processing. **Values/Work Environment:** Independence; indoors, environmentally controlled; moral values.

Other Information Sources

Many career and education information sources use the standard cross-referencing systems noted below. You can use the codes to obtain substantial additional information on the program (via CIP code) and related occupations (via GOE code). The O*NET codes on the opposite page refer to another major career information system. See the Introduction for details on obtaining additional information.

Classification of Instructional Programs (CIP) code(s): 500402 Commercial and Advertising Art; 500409 Graphic Design; 500410 Illustration

Guide for Occupational Exploration (GOE) code(s): 01.01 Managerial Work in Arts, Entertainment, and Media; 01.04 Visual Arts; 01.07 Graphic Arts; 08.03 Production Work; 09.09 Clerical Machine Operation; 12.03 Educational Services

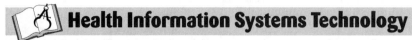

Health Information Systems Technology

Program/Training Duration: Two years

Location: College/vocational classroom

Career Snapshot

Health information systems are needed for much more than billing patients or their HMOs. Many medical discoveries have been made when researchers have examined large collections of health information. Therefore, health information systems technicians (sometimes called medical record technicians) must know about the health care system, about various kinds of diseases and vital statistics, about the latest database technologies, and about how researchers compile data to test hypotheses. This is one of the fastest-growing occupations. Although most jobs will continue to be in hospitals, the settings with greatest job growth will be physicians' offices, nursing homes, and home health agencies.

Related Specialties and Careers

Data analysis, health information coding, tumor registry.

Related Job Titles, Educational Requirements, Projected Growth, and Earnings			
Job Title	Educational Requirements	Projected Growth	Average Earnings
Medical Records and Health Information Technicians (O*NET code 29-2071.00)	Associate degree	Much faster than average	$23,530

Typical Postsecondary Courses

Clinical classification systems; clinical experience in health information; college algebra; English composition; fundamentals of medical science; human anatomy and physiology; introduction to health records; introduction to medical terminology; introduction to probability; legal aspects of health information; statistics.

Suggested High School Courses

Algebra; biology; chemistry; computer science; English; keyboarding; public speaking. **Dept. of Education School-to-Work Cluster:** Health Science.

Essential Knowledge and Skills

Clerical; computers and electronics; mathematics; reading comprehension. **Values/ Work Environment:** Indoors, environmentally controlled; moral values; spend time sitting.

Other Information Sources

Many career and education information sources use the standard cross-referencing systems noted below. You can use the codes to obtain substantial additional information on the program (via CIP code) and related occupations (via GOE code). The O*NET codes on the opposite page refer to another major career information system. See the Introduction for details on obtaining additional information.

Classification of Instructional Programs (CIP) code(s): 510707 Health Information/Medical Records Technology/ Technician

Guide for Occupational Exploration (GOE) code(s): 09.07 Records Processing

---

Heating, Ventilation, A/C Technology

Program/Training Duration: More than one year

Location: Workplace, perhaps vocational classroom

Career Snapshot

Heating, air conditioning, and refrigeration mechanics and installers make it possible for us to live and work in conditions with comfortable temperatures and humidity, even in Phoenix in July or Nome in January. They also install and maintain the equipment that refrigerates our food and other perishables. The fundamental processes that produce heat and refrigeration are not undergoing much change, but the electronic control systems are changing rapidly. Job opportunities are expected to be very good for workers with technical school or formal apprenticeship training.

Related Specialties and Careers

Air conditioning mechanic, heating equipment technician, refrigeration mechanic.

Related Job Titles, Educational Requirements, Projected Growth, and Earnings			
Job Title	**Educational Requirements**	**Projected Growth**	**Average Earnings**
Heating and Air Conditioning Mechanics (O*NET code 49-9021.01)	Long-term on-the-job training	Faster than average	$34,020
Heating, Air Conditioning, and Refrigeration Mechanics and Installers (O*NET code 49-9021.00)	Long-term on-the-job training	Faster than average	$34,020
Refrigeration Mechanics (O*NET code 49-9021.02)	Long-term on-the-job training	Faster than average	$34,020

Typical Postsecondary Courses

Air conditioning systems; commercial refrigeration; controls for heating and air conditioning; domestic refrigeration; duct fabrication; fossil fuel heating; heat load calculation; heat pumps; hydronics and zoning; physical principles of heating and refrigeration; workplace communications; workplace math.

Suggested High School Courses

Applied communications; business/applied math; electronics shop; mechanical drawing; metal shop; physics/principles of technology. **Dept. of Education School-to-Work Cluster:** Architecture and Construction.

Essential Knowledge and Skills

Design; engineering and technology; installation; mechanical devices; repairing; troubleshooting. **Values/Work Environment:** Indoors, environmentally controlled; moral values.

Other Information Sources

Many career and education information sources use the standard cross-referencing systems noted below. You can use the codes to obtain substantial additional information on the program (via CIP code) and related occupations (via GOE code). The O*NET codes on the opposite page refer to another major career information system. See the Introduction for details on obtaining additional information.

Classification of Instructional Programs (CIP) code(s): 150501 Heating, Air Conditioning and Refrigeration Technology/Technician (ACH/ACR/ACHR/HRAC/HVAC); 470201 Heating, Air Conditioning, Ventilation and Refrigeration Maintenance Technology/Technician

Guide for Occupational Exploration (GOE) code(s): 05.03 Mechanical Work

---

Home Appliance Repair

Program/Training Duration: A few weeks to a year or more

Location: Workplace or vocational classroom

Career Snapshot

Home appliance repairers (or service technicians) often specialize in electrical, gas, heating, or refrigeration appliances or in installation or repair. Those servicing small appliances may work in a shop; others may need to do on-site servicing in the home. Some technicians learn on the job or in classes offered by a manufacturer or chain store. For more complex appliances, employers prefer those who have received formal training (perhaps one or two years) in a vocational school or a community or technical college. Some technicians get certification by passing an exam. Employment is expected to be steady, with best opportunities in larger shops and for those who are skilled with electronics.

Related Specialties and Careers

Electrical appliances, gas appliances.

Related Job Titles, Educational Requirements, Projected Growth, and Earnings			
Job Title	Educational Requirements	Projected Growth	Average Earnings
Gas Appliance Repairers (O*NET code 49-9031.02)	Long-term on-the-job training	Little or none	$29,570
Home Appliance Installers (O*NET code 49-9031.01)	Long-term on-the-job training	Little or none	$29,570
Home Appliance Repairers (O*NET code 49-9031.00)	Postsecondary vocational training	Little or none	$29,570

Typical Postsecondary Courses

Air conditioning systems; appliance service shop; commercial refrigeration; control systems; electric motors; heating systems; physical principles of heating and refrigeration; principles of electricity; workplace communications.

Suggested High School Courses

Algebra; applied communications; electronics shop; industrial arts; office computer applications; physics/principles of technology. **Dept. of Education School-to-Work Cluster:** Manufacturing.

Essential Knowledge and Skills

Building and construction; installation; mechanical devices; repairing; trouble-shooting. **Values/Work Environment:** Indoors, environmentally controlled; moral values.

Other Information Sources

Many career and education information sources use the standard cross-referencing systems noted below. You can use the codes to obtain substantial additional information on the program (via CIP code) and related occupations (via GOE code). The O*NET codes on the opposite page refer to another major career information system. See the Introduction for details on obtaining additional information.

Classification of Instructional Programs (CIP) code(s): 470106 Appliance Installation and Repair Technology/Technician

Guide for Occupational Exploration (GOE) code(s): 05.02 Electrical and Electronic Systems; 05.03 Mechanical Work

---

Home Health Aide Training

Program/Training Duration: One month or less

Location: Workplace

Career Snapshot

Home health aides care for people who are elderly, disabled, or recovering and are well enough to live at home but need help with hygiene and basic health-related procedures. Aides follow the directions of a nurse or doctor and help patients with activities such as bathing, taking oral medications, performing simple exercises, or putting on artificial limbs. They also may take the patient's pulse, temperature, and respiration rate. The need to keep down health costs and the aging of the population have created a growing need for home health aides. To work for an employer that receives Medicare reimbursement, an aide must pass a competency test. Hospitals, health management companies, community colleges, and technical schools offer a training program that typically takes only a few weeks.

Related Specialties and Careers

Rehabilitation, senior care.

Related Job Titles, Educational Requirements, Projected Growth, and Earnings			
Job Title	Educational Requirements	Projected Growth	Average Earnings
Home Health Aides (O*NET code 31-1011.00)	Short-term on-the-job training	Much faster than average	$17,590

Typical Postsecondary Courses

Basic infection control procedures; communications skills; documentation of patient status and care; emergency procedures; evaluating characteristics of patients; introduction to nutrition; maintenance of a healthy environment; normal range of motion and positioning; personal hygiene and grooming; reading and recording vital signs; safe transfer techniques.

Suggested High School Courses

Applied communications; biology; social science. **Dept. of Education School-to-Work Cluster:** Health Science.

Essential Knowledge and Skills

Customer and personal service; medicine and dentistry; psychology; service orientation. **Values/Work Environment:** Indoors, environmentally controlled; social service.

Other Information Sources

Many career and education information sources use the standard cross-referencing systems noted below. You can use the codes to obtain substantial additional information on the program (via CIP code) and related occupations (via GOE code). The O*NET codes on the opposite page refer to another major career information system. See the Introduction for details on obtaining additional information.

Classification of Instructional Programs (CIP) code(s): 512602 Home Health Aide/Home Attendant

Guide for Occupational Exploration (GOE) code(s): 14.07 Patient Care and Assistance

---

Hotel/Motel and Restaurant Management

Program/Training Duration: Two to several years

Location: College/vocational classroom or workplace

Career Snapshot

Students of hotel/motel and restaurant management learn many skills required in any management program—economics, accounting, human resources, finance—plus the specialized skills needed for the hospitality industry. Some enter the field with an associate degree, but opportunities are better with a bachelor's degree. Usually new hires enter an on-the-job training program, where they learn all aspects of the business. The outlook for employment is mostly good, especially in restaurants.

Related Specialties and Careers

Hotels/motels, resorts and theme parks, restaurants.

Related Job Titles, Educational Requirements, Projected Growth, and Earnings			
Job Title	Educational Requirements	Projected Growth	Average Earnings
Food Service Managers (O*NET code 11-9051.00)	Work experience in a related occupation	Average	$33,630
Lodging Managers (O*NET code 11-9081.00)	Work experience in a related occupation	Little or none	$32,860

Typical Postsecondary Courses

Business finance; business writing; calculus for business and social sciences; English composition; field experience/internship; food and beverage production and management; food service and lodging operations; hospitality human resource management; hospitality technology applications; hotel financial management; introduction to accounting; introduction to management information systems; introduction to marketing; introduction to psychology; introduction to the hospitality industry; law and the hospitality industry; legal environment of business; marketing hospitality and leisure services; operations management; principles of macroeconomics; principles of management and organization; principles of microeconomics; statistics for business and social sciences; strategic management.

Suggested High School Courses

Algebra; bookkeeping; computer science; English; foreign language; geometry; public speaking; science; trigonometry. **Dept. of Education School-to-Work Cluster:** Hospitality and Tourism.

Essential Knowledge and Skills

Administration and management; coordination; customer and personal service; management of personnel resources; personnel and human resources. **Values/Work Environment:** Authority; autonomy; indoors, environmentally controlled.

Other Information Sources

Many career and education information sources use the standard cross-referencing systems noted below. You can use the codes to obtain substantial additional information on the program (via CIP code) and related occupations (via GOE code). The O*NET codes on the opposite page refer to another major career information system. See the Introduction for details on obtaining additional information.

Classification of Instructional Programs (CIP) code(s): 520904 Hotel/Motel Administration/Management; 520905 Restaurant/Food Services Management

Guide for Occupational Exploration (GOE) code(s): 11.01 Managerial Work in Recreation, Travel, and Other Personal Services; 12.02 Social Services

---

Human Services

Program/Training Duration: One month to a year or more

Location: Workplace or college/vocational classroom

Career Snapshot

Social service assistants work in government agencies, health care facilities, group homes, and other settings. They assist professionals such as social workers, psychologists, and therapists. Different localities have differing educational requirements for social service assistants. Some require a bachelor's degree and some require only a high school diploma, but an associate degree in human services is often sufficient preparation to be hired and to be given more than a minimal amount of responsibility. Volunteer work in the field is often helpful as an adjunct to education. Employment opportunities are expected to be excellent, especially in rural areas.

Related Specialties and Careers

Case assistant, counseling paraprofessional, gerontology assistant, medical social service aide.

Related Job Titles, Educational Requirements, Projected Growth, and Earnings			
Job Title	Educational Requirements	Projected Growth	Average Earnings
Social and Human Service Assistants (O*NET code 21-1093.00)	Moderate-term on-the-job training	Much faster than average	$23,070

Typical Postsecondary Courses

Basic counseling skills; English composition; field experience/internship; human growth and development; introduction to human services; introduction to psychology; introduction to sociology; introduction to speech communication; personal and social adjustment.

Suggested High School Courses

Applied communications; business/applied math; foreign language; office computer applications; social science. **Dept. of Education School-to-Work Cluster:** Human Service.

Essential Knowledge and Skills

Active listening; customer and personal service; education and training; service orientation; social perceptiveness; therapy and counseling. **Values/Work Environment:** Indoors, environmentally controlled; social service.

Other Information Sources

Many career and education information sources use the standard cross-referencing systems noted below. You can use the codes to obtain substantial additional information on the program (via CIP code) and related occupations (via GOE code). The O*NET codes on the opposite page refer to another major career information system. See the Introduction for details on obtaining additional information.

Classification of Instructional Programs (CIP) code(s): 440000 Human Services, General

Guide for Occupational Exploration (GOE) code(s): 12.01 Managerial Work in Education and Social Service

---

Instrumentation Technology

Program/Training Duration: One to two years

Location: Workplace or college/vocational classroom

Career Snapshot

Electronic instruments measure and control many processes and conditions that are vital to manufacturing, transportation, health care, pollution control, and scientific research. Instrumentation technologists work in all of these industries to develop, install, calibrate, test, and repair these instruments. Best opportunities will be for graduates of two-year programs at community colleges and technical schools. Continuous training is necessary to stay abreast of new technology.

Related Specialties and Careers

Calibration and repair, design, manufacture, sales.

Related Job Titles, Educational Requirements, Projected Growth, and Earnings			
Job Title	Educational Requirements	Projected Growth	Average Earnings
Precision Instrument and Equipment Repairers, All Other (O*NET code 49-9069.99)	Long-term on-the-job training	Little or none	No salary data available

Typical Postsecondary Courses

AC/DC circuit analysis; digital process control systems; electrical automation theory; electronic devices and circuits; electronic devices in instrumentation; instrument testing, calibration, and repair; pneumatic and mechanical measurements; technical mathematics; technical writing.

Suggested High School Courses

Algebra; applied communications; computer science; electronics shop; geometry; physics/principles of technology; pre-calculus; trigonometry. **Dept. of Education School-to-Work Cluster:** Scientific Research/Engineering; Manufacturing.

Essential Knowledge and Skills

No data available. **Values/Work Environment:** No data available.

Other Information Sources

Many career and education information sources use the standard cross-referencing systems noted below. You can use the codes to obtain substantial additional information on the program (via CIP code) and related occupations (via GOE code). The O*NET codes on the opposite page refer to another major career information system. See the Introduction for details on obtaining additional information.

Classification of Instructional Programs (CIP) code(s): 150404 Instrumentation Technology/Technician

Guide for Occupational Exploration (GOE) code(s): 05.03 Mechanical Work

 **Interior Design**

Program/Training Duration: At least two years, usually four

Location: College classroom

Career Snapshot

Interior designers need a mixture of artistic creativity, mastery of furnishing and decorating materials, business sense, and knowledge of construction codes and methods. Most employers of interior designers prefer new hires to have a bachelor's degree, but it is possible to enter this career as an assistant designer with an associate degree. Licensure or registration is necessary in 19 states, and a combination of education and experience is required to sit for the licensing exam. Competition for jobs is expected to be keen.

Related Specialties and Careers

Commercial, furnishings, residential.

Related Job Titles, Educational Requirements, Projected Growth, and Earnings			
Job Title	**Educational Requirements**	**Projected Growth**	**Average Earnings**
Interior Designers (O*NET code 27-1025.00)	Bachelor's degree	Average	$39,580

Typical Postsecondary Courses

Advanced rendering and presentation; architectural drafting; business procedures for interior design; college algebra; commercial interior design; computer-aided drafting (CAD); English composition; introduction to interior design; introduction to speech communication; lighting and furnishings; residential interior design; textiles for interior design; three-dimensional design; three-dimensional drawing and rendering.

Suggested High School Courses

Algebra; applied communications; art; drafting; English; geometry; home economics; office computer applications; public speaking; social science. **Dept. of Education School-to-Work Cluster:** Retail and Wholesale Sales and Service.

Essential Knowledge and Skills

Active listening; administration and management; coordination; design; operations analysis. Values/Work Environment: Ability utilization; achievement; creativity; indoors, environmentally controlled.

Other Information Sources

Many career and education information sources use the standard cross-referencing systems noted below. You can use the codes to obtain substantial additional information on the program (via CIP code) and related occupations (via GOE code). The O*NET codes on the opposite page refer to another major career information system. See the Introduction for details on obtaining additional information.

Classification of Instructional Programs (CIP) code(s): 500408 Interior Design

Guide for Occupational Exploration (GOE) code(s): 01.04 Visual Arts; 12.03 Educational Services

---

 **Investigative Services**

Program/Training Duration: One year or more

Location: Workplace, perhaps vocational classroom

Career Snapshot

Private investigators have been the subject of many novels, movies, and TV shows. The reality (odd hours, perhaps tedium or stress) is not as glamorous, but the demand for workers is growing as our society becomes more security-conscious and involved in lawsuits. Those who want to enter the field can expect a lot of competition, often from people who are moving from a career in law enforcement, the military, or insurance. Most states require a license, and some mandate specific training programs. A degree in law enforcement can be a help, and some specialized schools offer training programs. Employers may also be looking for skills that applicants have developed in a previous job, such as doing database searches, interpreting financial documents, or operating photographic or electronic surveillance equipment.

Related Specialties and Careers

Corporate investigation, financial investigation, legal investigation, loss prevention.

Related Job Titles, Educational Requirements, Projected Growth, and Earnings			
Job Title	Educational Requirements	Projected Growth	Average Earnings
Animal Control Workers (O*NET code 33-9011.00)	Moderate-term on-the-job training	Average	$24,250
Crossing Guards (O*NET code 33-9091.00)	Short-term on-the-job training	Little or none	$17,780
First-Line Supervisors/Managers, Protective Service Workers, All Other (O*NET code 33-1099.99)	Work experience in a related occupation	Faster than average	No salary data available
Lifeguards, Ski Patrol, and Other Recreational Protective Service Workers (O*NET code 33-9092.00)	Short-term on-the-job training	Faster than average	No salary data available

Job Title	Educational Requirements	Projected Growth	Average Earnings
Parking Enforcement Workers (O*NET code 33-3041.00)	Short-term on-the-job training	Average	$26,820
Protective Service Workers, All Other (O*NET code 33-9099.99)	No data available	Faster than average	No salary data available
Transit and Railroad Police (O*NET code 33-3052.00)	Long-term on-the-job training	Average	$43,110

Typical Postsecondary Courses

Court system; covert techniques; investigative agency office operations; investigative information sources; investigative report writing methods; overt operation methods; surveillance methods.

Suggested High School Courses

Applied communications; business/applied math; computer science; photography; public speaking; social science. **Dept. of Education School-to-Work Cluster:** Law and Public Safety.

Essential Knowledge and Skills

Critical thinking; public safety and security. **Values/Work Environment:** Moral values; outdoors, exposed to weather.

Other Information Sources

Many career and education information sources use the standard cross-referencing systems noted below. You can use the codes to obtain substantial additional information on the program (via CIP code) and related occupations (via GOE code). The O*NET codes on the opposite page refer to another major career information system. See the Introduction for details on obtaining additional information.

Classification of Instructional Programs (CIP) code(s): 439999 Security and Protective Services, Other

Guide for Occupational Exploration (GOE) code(s): 04.01 Managerial Work in Law, Law Enforcement, and Public Safety; 04.03 Law Enforcement

---

Law Enforcement

Program/Training Duration: Two to five years

Location: College classroom plus police academy or workplace

Career Snapshot

We live in a society that is governed by laws at the municipal, state, and federal levels. These laws are enforced by people who understand the laws themselves; the workings of the agencies that are empowered to enforce them; and the techniques for detecting violation of the laws, arresting violators, and processing them through the court system. Public concern about crime has created many job opportunities in this field, especially at the local level. A college degree is increasingly being required for entry to a police academy, but some law enforcement jobs are learned on the job.

Related Specialties and Careers

Police administration, police work, security.

Related Job Titles, Educational Requirements, Projected Growth, and Earnings			
Job Title	Educational Requirements	Projected Growth	Average Earnings
Bailiffs (O*NET code 33-3011.00)	Moderate-term on-the-job training	Average	$31,390
Child Support, Missing Persons, and Unemployment Insurance Fraud Investigators (O*NET code 33-3021.04)	Work experience in a related occupation	Average	$50,960
Criminal Investigators and Special Agents (O*NET code 33-3021.03)	Work experience in a related occupation	Average	$50,960
Detectives and Criminal Investigators (O*NET code 33-3021.00)	Work experience in a related occupation	Average	$50,960
Highway Patrol Pilots (O*NET code 33-3051.02)	Long-term on-the-job training	Faster than average	$40,970
Immigration and Customs Inspectors (O*NET code 33-3021.05)	Work experience in a related occupation	Average	$50,960

Job Title	Educational Requirements	Projected Growth	Average Earnings
Police and Sheriff's Patrol Officers (O*NET code 33-3051.00)	Long-term on-the-job training	Faster than average	$40,970
Police Detectives (O*NET code 33-3021.01)	Work experience in a related occupation	Average	$50,960
Police Identification and Records Officers (O*NET code 33-3021.02)	Work experience in a related occupation	Average	$50,960
Police Patrol Officers (O*NET code 33-3051.01)	Long-term on-the-job training	Faster than average	$40,970
Private Detectives and Investigators (O*NET code 33-9021.00)	Work experience in a related occupation	Faster than average	$28,380
Sheriffs and Deputy Sheriffs (O*NET code 33-3051.03)	Long-term on-the-job training	Faster than average	$40,970

Typical Postsecondary Courses

Criminal investigation; criminal law; criminal procedures; emergency life support procedures; ethics, diversity, and conflict; introduction to criminal justice; introduction to psychology; law enforcement weaponry; police organization and administration; police-community relations; seminar (reporting on research); technical writing; traffic control and accident investigation.

Suggested High School Courses

English; public speaking; social science. **Dept. of Education School-to-Work Cluster:** Law and Public Safety.

Essential Knowledge and Skills

Active listening; law and government; public safety and security. **Values/Work Environment:** Indoors, environmentally controlled; security; supervision, human relations.

Other Information Sources

Many career and education information sources use the standard cross-referencing systems noted below. You can use the codes to obtain substantial additional information on the program (via CIP code) and related occupations (via GOE code). The O*NET codes on the opposite page refer to another major career information system. See the Introduction for details on obtaining additional information.

Classification of Instructional Programs (CIP) code(s): 430107 Criminal Justice/Police Science

Guide for Occupational Exploration (GOE) code(s): 04.03 Law Enforcement; 12.03 Educational Services

Library Technology

Program/Training Duration: One month or less

Location: Workplace

Career Snapshot

Much of the work that is done in libraries—acquiring and organizing materials, helping users find information, checking out materials—is done by technicians. Some library technicians are trained on the job, but opportunities are probably better for those with formal training. Since libraries and information services are increasingly automated, experience working with computers and especially databases is helpful. Job opportunities are uncertain; libraries strapped for funds may cut back on hiring, but they may also hire more technicians in place of professionals.

Related Specialties and Careers

Audiovisual services, circulation, reference, special libraries.

Related Job Titles, Educational Requirements, Projected Growth, and Earnings			
Job Title	**Educational Requirements**	**Projected Growth**	**Average Earnings**
Library Assistants, Clerical (O*NET code 43-4121.00)	Short-term on-the-job training	Average	$18,580
Library Technicians (O*NET code 25-4031.00)	Short-term on-the-job training	Average	$23,790

Typical Postsecondary Courses

Acquisitions; audiovisual services; circulation services; English composition; field experience/internship; introduction to libraries; management of libraries and information services; public services; reference services and resources; technical services; technology in the library.

Suggested High School Courses

Applied communications; business/applied math; computer science; foreign language; keyboarding; office computer applications; public speaking. **Dept. of Education School-to-Work Cluster:** Education and Training.

Essential Knowledge and Skills

Clerical; customer and personal service; reading comprehension. **Values/Work Environment:** Indoors, environmentally controlled; moral values; good working conditions.

Other Information Sources

Many career and education information sources use the standard cross-referencing systems noted below. You can use the codes to obtain substantial additional information on the program (via CIP code) and related occupations (via GOE code). The O*NET codes on the opposite page refer to another major career information system. See the Introduction for details on obtaining additional information.

Classification of Instructional Programs (CIP) code(s): 250301 Library Assistant/Technician

Guide for Occupational Exploration (GOE) code(s): 12.03 Educational Services

---

 **Machinist Training**

Program/Training Duration: One month to more than a year
Location: Workplace, perhaps vocational classroom

Career Snapshot

Machinists use power equipment to produce metal parts that meet specifications. Training is obtained through an apprenticeship, vocational school, or technical college. Prior work experience as a machine setter, tender, or operator is helpful. Computer-controlled machines help machinists to work more productively, eliminating some jobs. However, employment opportunities for machinists are expected to be excellent.

Related Specialties and Careers

CNC programming, maintenance, production.

Related Job Titles, Educational Requirements, Projected Growth, and Earnings			
Job Title	**Educational Requirements**	**Projected Growth**	**Average Earnings**
Buffing and Polishing Set-Up Operators (O*NET code 51-4033.02)	Moderate-term on-the-job training	Little or none	$25,530
Combination Machine Tool Operators and Tenders, Metal and Plastic (O*NET code 51-4081.02)	Moderate-term on-the-job training	Average	$27,910
Combination Machine Tool Setters and Set-Up Operators, Metal and Plastic (O*NET code 51-4081.01)	Moderate-term on-the-job training	Average	$27,910
Cutting, Punching, and Press Machine Setters, Operators, and Tenders, Metal and Plastic (O*NET code 51-4031.00)	Moderate-term on-the-job training	Declining	$24,080
Drilling and Boring Machine Tool Setters, Operators, and Tenders, Metal and Plastic (O*NET code 51-4032.00)	Moderate-term on-the-job training	Declining	$26,670
Extruding and Drawing Machine Setters, Operators, and Tenders, Metal and Plastic (O*NET code 51-4021.00)	Moderate-term on-the-job training	Average	$25,170
Forging Machine Setters, Operators, and Tenders, Metal and Plastic (O*NET code 51-4022.00)	Moderate-term on-the-job training	Little or none	$25,880

Job Title	Educational Requirements	Projected Growth	Average Earnings
Grinding, Honing, Lapping, and Deburring Machine Set-Up Operators (O*NET code 51-4033.01)	Moderate-term on-the-job training	Little or none	$25,530
Grinding, Lapping, Polishing, and Buffing Machine Tool Setters, Operators, and Tenders, (O*NET code 51-4033.00)	Moderate-term on-the-job training	Little or none	$25,530
Heat Treating Equipment Setters, Operators, and Tenders, Metal and Plastic (O*NET code 51-4191.00)	Moderate-term on-the-job training	Average	$27,540
Heat Treating, Annealing, and Tempering Machine Operators and Tenders, Metal and Plastic (O*NET code 51-4191.02)	Moderate-term on-the-job training	Average	$27,540
Heaters, Metal and Plastic (O*NET code 51-4191.03)	Moderate-term on-the-job training	Average	$27,540

Typical Postsecondary Courses

Blueprint reading; drill press operations; introduction to machine tools; lathe operations; mathematics for machine trades; mill operations; surface grinding operations.

Suggested High School Courses

Algebra; computer science; geometry; industrial arts; mechanical drawing; metal shop; physics/principles of technology; trigonometry. **Dept. of Education School-to-Work Cluster:** Manufacturing.

Essential Knowledge and Skills

Mechanical devices; operation and control; operation monitoring; production and processing. **Values/Work Environment:** Exposed to hazardous equipment; indoors, environmentally controlled; moral values; spend time standing.

Other Information Sources

Many career and education information sources use the standard cross-referencing systems noted below. You can use the codes to obtain substantial additional information on the program (via CIP code) and related occupations (via GOE code). The O*NET codes on the opposite page refer to another major career information system. See the Introduction for details on obtaining additional information.

Classification of Instructional Programs (CIP) code(s): 480501 Machine Tool Technology/Machinist

Guide for Occupational Exploration (GOE) code(s): 08.02 Production Technology; 08.03 Production Work; 08.04 Metal and Plastics Machining Technology

---

Marine Transportation Operations

Program/Training Duration: At least one year

Location: Vocational classroom

Career Snapshot

Jobs in the water transportation industry range from captain to sailor. Ships' officers and operators are licensed by the Coast Guard, and candidates for the licensing exam must have appropriate education or experience at sea. Those who do not get training and experience in the military may attend a specialized technical school or maritime college. Some get training at a union-operated school and gain a few years' experience as an unlicensed deckhand or engineer. Almost 75 percent of deep-sea mariners are union members and are hired through hiring halls in major seaports. Competition for jobs is keen, and although a job may last for many months, a mariner may be unemployed for weeks or months afterward.

Related Specialties and Careers

Cargo stowage, marine engineering, navigation, piloting.

Related Job Titles, Educational Requirements, Projected Growth, and Earnings			
Job Title	Educational Requirements	Projected Growth	Average Earnings
Captains, Mates, and Pilots of Water Vessels (O*NET code 53-5021.00)	Long-term on-the-job training	Little or none	$48,680
Mates—Ship, Boat, and Barge (O*NET code 53-5021.02)	Work experience in a related occupation	Little or none	$48,680
Pilots, Ship (O*NET code 53-5021.03)	Work experience plus degree	Little or none	$48,680
Ship and Boat Captains (O*NET code 53-5021.01)	Long-term on-the-job training	Little or none	$48,680

Typical Postsecondary Courses

Basic piloting and navigation; celestial navigation; dry cargo stowage; electronic navigation; English composition; introduction to marine engineering; leadership and management; liquid cargo stowage; marine mathematics; marine meteorology;

marine safety; maritime law; naval architecture; principles of marine mechanics; ship handling; ship information systems; vessel maintenance; water survival.

Suggested High School Courses

Algebra; computer science; English; geography; geometry; physics/principles of technology; trigonometry. **Dept. of Education School-to-Work Cluster:** Transportation, Distribution, and Logistics.

Essential Knowledge and Skills

Coordination; geography; judgment and decision making; operation and control; transportation. **Values/Work Environment:** Authority; autonomy; outdoors, exposed to weather; responsibility.

Other Information Sources

Many career and education information sources use the standard cross-referencing systems noted below. You can use the codes to obtain substantial additional information on the program (via CIP code) and related occupations (via GOE code). The O*NET codes on the opposite page refer to another major career information system. See the Introduction for details on obtaining additional information.

Classification of Instructional Programs (CIP) code(s): 490309 Marine Science/Merchant Marine Officer

Guide for Occupational Exploration (GOE) code(s): 07.04 Water Vehicle Operation

---

 **Marketing**

Program/Training Duration: More than two years

Location: College classroom plus work

Career Snapshot

Marketing is the study of how buyers and sellers of goods and services find one another, how businesses can tailor their offerings to meet demand, and how businesses can anticipate and influence demand. It uses the findings of economics, psychology, and sociology in a business context. An associate degree may lead to a position as management trainee, but a bachelor's degree is the best preparation for a job in marketing research. Usually some experience in this field is required before a person can move into a marketing management position. Job outlook varies, with some industries looking more favorable than others.

Related Specialties and Careers

Marketing management, marketing research.

Related Job Titles, Educational Requirements, Projected Growth, and Earnings			
Job Title	Educational Requirements	Projected Growth	Average Earnings
Advertising and Promotions Managers (O*NET code 11-2011.00)	Work experience plus degree	Faster than average	$55,940
Marketing Managers (O*NET code 11-2021.00)	Work experience plus degree	Faster than average	$74,370
Sales Managers (O*NET code 11-2022.00)	Work experience plus degree	Faster than average	$71,620

Typical Postsecondary Courses

Business finance; business writing; buyer behavior; calculus for business and social sciences; decision support systems for management; English composition; introduction to accounting; introduction to management information systems; introduction to marketing; introduction to psychology; legal environment of business; marketing research; marketing strategy; operations management; principles of macroeconomics; principles of management and organization; principles of microeconomics; statistics for business and social sciences; strategic management.

Suggested High School Courses

Algebra; bookkeeping; computer science; English; foreign language; geometry; science; trigonometry. **Dept. of Education School-to-Work Cluster:** Retail and Wholesale Sales and Service.

Essential Knowledge and Skills

Administration and management; coordination; customer and personal service; judgment and decision making; sales and marketing; speaking. **Values/Work Environment:** Compensation; creativity; indoors, environmentally controlled; spend time sitting; good working conditions.

Other Information Sources

Many career and education information sources use the standard cross-referencing systems noted below. You can use the codes to obtain substantial additional information on the program (via CIP code) and related occupations (via GOE code). The O*NET codes on the opposite page refer to another major career information system. See the Introduction for details on obtaining additional information.

Classification of Instructional Programs (CIP) code(s): 521401 Marketing/Marketing Management, General

Guide for Occupational Exploration (GOE) code(s): 10.01 Managerial Work in Sales and Marketing; 12.03 Educational Services

---

 **Masonry**

Program/Training Duration: At least one year

Location: Workplace

Career Snapshot

Brickmasons and blockmasons build and repair walls, chimneys, floors, and partitions by using bricks, concrete blocks, and other masonry materials. Stonemasons do similar work with stone blocks but usually work on nonresidential buildings. Cement masons and concrete finishers prepare the forms that receive concrete, pour the concrete into place, and finish its surface. The work is physically demanding and usually done outdoors. Most masons learn on the job, either in formal apprenticeships or by working as helpers. Some programs are also available at trade and technical schools and community colleges. Job opportunities are expected to be excellent.

Related Specialties and Careers

Brick masonry, cement masonry, concrete block masonry, stone masonry.

Related Job Titles, Educational Requirements, Projected Growth, and Earnings			
Job Title	**Educational Requirements**	**Projected Growth**	**Average Earnings**
Brickmasons and Blockmasons (O*NET code 47-2021.00)	Long-term on-the-job training	Average	$41,590
First-Line Supervisors and Manager/Supervisors—Construction Trades Workers (O*NET code 47-1011.01)	Work experience in a related occupation	Average	$46,570
First-Line Supervisors/ Managers of Construction Trades and Extraction Workers (O*NET code 47-1011.00)	Work experience in a related occupation	Average	$46,570
Helpers—Brickmasons, Blockmasons, Stonemasons, and Tile and Marble Setters (O*NET code 47-3011.00)	Short-term on-the-job training	Average	$23,620
Stonemasons (O*NET code 47-2022.00)	Long-term on-the-job training	Faster than average	$32,470

Typical Postsecondary Courses

Blueprint reading; brick arches; brick masonry; cement masonry; concrete block masonry; construction math and estimating; construction safety and materials; finish masonry; fireplace construction; masonry fundamentals; stone masonry; technical writing.

Suggested High School Courses

Applied communications; business/applied math; industrial arts; mechanical drawing; physics/principles of technology. **Dept. of Education School-to-Work Cluster:** Architecture and Construction.

Essential Knowledge and Skills

Building and construction; equipment selection. **Values/Work Environment:** Moral values; outdoors, exposed to weather.

Other Information Sources

Many career and education information sources use the standard cross-referencing systems noted below. You can use the codes to obtain substantial additional information on the program (via CIP code) and related occupations (via GOE code). The O*NET codes on the opposite page refer to another major career information system. See the Introduction for details on obtaining additional information.

Classification of Instructional Programs (CIP) code(s): 460101 Mason/Masonry

Guide for Occupational Exploration (GOE) code(s): 06.01 Managerial Work in Construction, Mining, and Drilling; 06.02 Construction; 06.04 Hands-on Work in Construction, Extraction, and Maintenance

---

 **Massage Therapy**

Program/Training Duration: A few weeks to more than a year

Location: Vocational classroom

Career Snapshot

Half the states now regulate massage therapists, and the standard for entry to the field has become a minimum of 500 hours of training, often followed by a certifying exam. Those considering training may benefit from previous education in health care, psychology, or business and should take care to find a training program that is approved by a reputable national accreditation agency. Employment opportunities are expected to be good because of the general interest in health and well-being and the increasing acceptance of massage therapy by the public and by health insurers.

Related Specialties and Careers

Sports massage, therapeutic massage.

Related Job Titles, Educational Requirements, Projected Growth, and Earnings			
Job Title	Educational Requirements	Projected Growth	Average Earnings
Massage Therapists (O*NET code 31-9011.00)	Postsecondary vocational training	Faster than average	$28,050

Typical Postsecondary Courses

Human anatomy and physiology; introduction to medical terminology; kinesiology; massage techniques; pathology; sports massage; supervised clinical practice.

Suggested High School Courses

Applied communications; biology; business/applied math; chemistry; physics/principles of technology; public speaking. **Dept. of Education School-to-Work Cluster:** Health Science.

Essential Knowledge and Skills

No data available. **Values/Work Environment:** No data available.

Other Information Sources

Many career and education information sources use the standard cross-referencing systems noted below. You can use the codes to obtain substantial additional information on the program (via CIP code) and related occupations (via GOE code). The O*NET codes on the opposite page refer to another major career information system. See the Introduction for details on obtaining additional information.

Classification of Instructional Programs (CIP) code(s): 513502 Asian Bodywork Therapy; 513501 Massage Therapy/Therapeutic Massage; 513503 Somatic Bodywork; 513599 Somatic Bodywork and Related Therapeutic Services, Other

Guide for Occupational Exploration (GOE) code(s): 12.03 Educational Services; 14.06 Medical Therapy

Mechanical Engineering Technology

Program/Training Duration: Two years

Location: College classroom

Career Snapshot

Mechanical engineering technologists help engineers solve problems in the design, testing, and manufacture of mechanical devices used in industry, in transportation, and as consumer goods. They often prepare computerized graphics that represent a mechanical part or system and control how it is manufactured. Job prospects are better for graduates of programs (typically lasting two years) approved by the Technology Accreditation Commission of the Accreditation Board for Engineering and Technology (TAC/ABET).

Related Specialties and Careers

Computer-aided design (CAD), design, manufacture, testing.

Related Job Titles, Educational Requirements, Projected Growth, and Earnings			
Job Title	Educational Requirements	Projected Growth	Average Earnings
Mechanical Engineering Technicians (O*NET code 17-3027.00)	Associate degree	Average	$40,910

Typical Postsecondary Courses

Computer applications in engineering; computer-aided drafting (CAD); descriptive geometry; engineering circuit analysis; engineering graphics; general physics; machine design; manufacturing processes; mechanics; mechanics of materials; technical mathematics; technical writing.

Suggested High School Courses

Algebra; applied communications; computer science; geometry; mechanical drawing; physics/principles of technology; trigonometry. **Dept. of Education School-to-Work Cluster:** Manufacturing.

Essential Knowledge and Skills

Design; engineering and technology; mathematics; mechanical devices; operation and control; technology design. **Values/Work Environment:** Exposed to hazardous equipment; indoors, environmentally controlled; moral values.

Other Information Sources

Many career and education information sources use the standard cross-referencing systems noted below. You can use the codes to obtain substantial additional information on the program (via CIP code) and related occupations (via GOE code). The O*NET codes on the opposite page refer to another major career information system. See the Introduction for details on obtaining additional information.

Classification of Instructional Programs (CIP) code(s): 150805 Mechanical Engineering/Mechanical Technology/Technician

Guide for Occupational Exploration (GOE) code(s): 02.08 Engineering Technology

---

 Medical Assistant Training

Program/Training Duration: One month to a year

Location: Workplace

Career Snapshot

Medical assistants perform routine administrative and clinical tasks in the offices of health practitioners (e.g., doctors, optometrists, chiropractors). They direct patients to examination rooms, retrieve patients' medical charts, arrange for laboratory work and HMO billing, and schedule appointments. Depending on the state where they work and the procedures of their office, they may take a patient's blood pressure and temperature, draw blood, sterilize medical instruments, perform laboratory tests on specimens, or instruct patients about diet and exercise. Some specialize, and others are generalists who can perform many of these functions. This is one of the fastest-growing occupations, and job prospects are expected to be very good.

Related Specialties and Careers

Administrative assistant, generalist, ophthalmic medical assistant, podiatric medical assistant.

Related Job Titles, Educational Requirements, Projected Growth, and Earnings			
Job Title	Educational Requirements	Projected Growth	Average Earnings
Medical Assistants (O*NET code 31-9092.00)	Moderate-term on-the-job training	Much faster than average	$23,610
Medical Equipment Preparers (O*NET code 31-9093.00)	Short-term on-the-job training	Average	$22,490

Typical Postsecondary Courses

Clinical experience in medical assisting; computer applications in the medical office; human anatomy and physiology; introduction to health records; introduction to medical assisting; introduction to medical terminology; introduction to psychology.

Suggested High School Courses

Algebra; biology; bookkeeping; chemistry; computer science; English; keyboarding; office computer applications; public speaking. **Dept. of Education School-to-Work Cluster:** Health Science.

Essential Knowledge and Skills

Clerical; medicine and dentistry; reading comprehension. **Values/Work Environment:** Exposed to disease or infections; indoors, environmentally controlled; moral values.

Other Information Sources

Many career and education information sources use the standard cross-referencing systems noted below. You can use the codes to obtain substantial additional information on the program (via CIP code) and related occupations (via GOE code). The O*NET codes on the opposite page refer to another major career information system. See the Introduction for details on obtaining additional information.

Classification of Instructional Programs (CIP) code(s): 510801 Medical/Clinical Assistant

Guide for Occupational Exploration (GOE) code(s): 14.02 Medicine and Surgery; 14.05 Medical Technology

---

Medical Laboratory Technology

Program/Training Duration: Two years

Location: College/vocational classroom

Career Snapshot

The detection, diagnosis, and prevention of disease depend heavily on various kinds of medical tests—of blood, urine, tissue samples, etc. Medical (or clinical) laboratory technicians perform a variety of laboratory tests under the supervision of a clinical laboratory scientist (also called a medical technologist). Job opportunities are unclear, because at the same time that the number of medical tests is increasing, automation is playing a growing role.

Related Specialties and Careers

Histology technician, phlebotomist.

Related Job Titles, Educational Requirements, Projected Growth, and Earnings			
Job Title	Educational Requirements	Projected Growth	Average Earnings
Medical and Clinical Laboratory Technicians (O*NET code 29-2012.00)	Associate degree	Average	$28,810

Typical Postsecondary Courses

Body fluid analysis; clinical chemistry; clinical experience in medical lab technology; clinical microbiology; English composition; general chemistry; hematology and coagulation; human anatomy and physiology; immunohematology; introduction to organic chemistry and biochemistry; microbiology.

Suggested High School Courses

Algebra; biology; chemistry; English; physics/principles of technology. **Dept. of Education School-to-Work Cluster:** Health Science.

Essential Knowledge and Skills

Biology; chemistry; medicine and dentistry; science. **Values/Work Environment:** Ability utilization; exposed to disease or infections; indoors, environmentally controlled.

Other Information Sources

Many career and education information sources use the standard cross-referencing systems noted below. You can use the codes to obtain substantial additional information on the program (via CIP code) and related occupations (via GOE code). The O*NET codes on the opposite page refer to another major career information system. See the Introduction for details on obtaining additional information.

Classification of Instructional Programs (CIP) code(s): 510802 Clinical/Medical Laboratory Assistant

Guide for Occupational Exploration (GOE) code(s): 12.03 Educational Services; 14.05 Medical Technology

 ## Medical Transcription

Program/Training Duration: Two years

Location: College/vocational classroom

Career Snapshot

As the health care industry moves steadily toward keeping all health records in electronic form, medical transcriptionists are needed to key in medical information about patients. The work requires more than just keyboard ability and mastery of the technology; transcriptionists must understand the medical terminology and be able to use a variety of reference materials to ensure that records are entered correctly. Sometimes they have to check with a health care professional when information seems contradictory. The work can readily be done at home, but it requires investment in equipment and reference materials, and prior experience in an office setting is helpful. Employment opportunities are expected to be best for those who get an associate degree and/or certification from the American Association for Medical Transcription.

Related Specialties and Careers

Transcription, transcription business management.

Related Job Titles, Educational Requirements, Projected Growth, and Earnings			
Job Title	Educational Requirements	Projected Growth	Average Earnings
Medical Transcriptionists (O*NET code 31-9094.00)	Associate degree	Faster than average	$26,460

Typical Postsecondary Courses

Disease processes; English grammar and punctuation; field experience/internship; human anatomy and physiology; introduction to health records; introduction to medical terminology; medical transcription practice; medicolegal issues, confidentiality, and ethics; pharmacology and laboratory medicine; transcription technology.

Suggested High School Courses

Biology; business/applied math; chemistry; English; keyboarding; office computer applications. **Dept. of Education School-to-Work Cluster:** Health Science.

Essential Knowledge and Skills

No data available. **Values/Work Environment:** No data available.

Other Information Sources

Many career and education information sources use the standard cross-referencing systems noted below. You can use the codes to obtain substantial additional information on the program (via CIP code) and related occupations (via GOE code). The O*NET codes on the opposite page refer to another major career information system. See the Introduction for details on obtaining additional information.

Classification of Instructional Programs (CIP) code(s): 510708 Medical Transcription/Transcriptionist

Guide for Occupational Exploration (GOE) code(s): 09.07 Records Processing

---

Multimedia Design and Production

Program/Training Duration: At least one year

Location: Workplace or college/vocational classroom

Career Snapshot

So many industries use multimedia technology—from education to advertising to entertainment—that job opportunities should be good for people with skills in this field. The work requires a combination of artistic and technical skills, although workers may lean more toward one of these aspects. Because the technology is constantly evolving, workers need to get regular training in the latest applications to stay employable.

Related Specialties and Careers

Audio production, broadcast and cable television, corporate communications, educational media development, multimedia production, presentation support, video production.

Related Job Titles, Educational Requirements, Projected Growth, and Earnings			
Job Title	Educational Requirements	Projected Growth	Average Earnings
Art Directors (O*NET code 27-1011.00)	Work experience plus degree	Faster than average	$59,800
Cartoonists (O*NET code 27-1013.03)	Long-term on-the-job training	Average	$32,870
Fine Artists, Including Painters, Sculptors, and Illustrators (O*NET code 27-1013.00)	Long-term on-the-job training	Average	$32,870

Typical Postsecondary Courses

Art history; audio production; computer graphics; digital photography; English composition; introduction to multimedia; introduction to visual design; oral communication; video production; Web site design.

Suggested High School Courses

Algebra; applied communications; art; computer science; photography; public speaking. **Dept. of Education School-to-Work Cluster:** Arts, A/V Technology, and Communication.

Essential Knowledge and Skills

Active listening; communications and media; design; fine arts. **Values/Work Environment:** Ability utilization; autonomy; creativity; indoors, environmentally controlled; spend time sitting.

Other Information Sources

Many career and education information sources use the standard cross-referencing systems noted below. You can use the codes to obtain substantial additional information on the program (via CIP code) and related occupations (via GOE code). The O*NET codes on the opposite page refer to another major career information system. See the Introduction for details on obtaining additional information.

Classification of Instructional Programs (CIP) code(s): 500706 Intermedia/Multimedia

Guide for Occupational Exploration (GOE) code(s): 01.01 Managerial Work in Arts, Entertainment, and Media; 01.04 Visual Arts; 12.03 Educational Services

---

Network and Telecommunications Technology

Program/Training Duration: Two years

Location: College/vocational classroom

Career Snapshot

The information-based economy demands that computers be networked to each other, often over long distances. The telephone system now serves computers and faxes as well as talkative people. These advances in technology have created a growing demand for technicians who can set up, manage, and troubleshoot computer networks and systems for voice communications. This field is changing so rapidly that entry requirements are not yet well defined. Some workers prepare by taking a one- or two-year program at a trade or technical school. Others prepare in the Armed Forces. Continuous learning is a must in this field, and employers often pay for workers to get certified in a particular technology.

Related Specialties and Careers

Call center management, communications technology, Internet solutions consulting, network administration, network analysis and design, sales, system installation/maintenance.

Related Job Titles, Educational Requirements, Projected Growth, and Earnings			
Job Title	Educational Requirements	Projected Growth	Average Earnings
Calibration and Instrumentation Technicians (O*NET code 17-3023.02)	Associate degree	Average	$42,130
Electrical and Electronic Engineering Technicians (O*NET code 17-3023.00)	Associate degree	Average	$42,130
Electrical Engineering Technicians (O*NET code 17-3023.03)	Associate degree	Average	$42,130
Electronics Engineering Technicians (O*NET code 17-3023.01)	Associate degree	Average	$42,130

Typical Postsecondary Courses

Advanced topics in telecommunications; analog and digital telephony; computer applications in telecommunications; data communications systems; local and wide networks; programming in a language (e.g., C, PASCAL, COBOL); technical mathematics; technical writing; telecommunications protocols.

Suggested High School Courses

Algebra; applied communications; computer science; electronics shop; geometry; physics/principles of technology; trigonometry. **Dept. of Education School-to-Work Cluster:** Manufacturing.

Essential Knowledge and Skills

Active learning; computers and electronics; design; engineering and technology; technology design. **Values/Work Environment:** Indoors, environmentally controlled; moral values.

Other Information Sources

Many career and education information sources use the standard cross-referencing systems noted below. You can use the codes to obtain substantial additional information on the program (via CIP code) and related occupations (via GOE code). The O*NET codes on the opposite page refer to another major career information system. See the Introduction for details on obtaining additional information.

Classification of Instructional Programs (CIP) code(s): 150305 Telecommunications Technology/Technician

Guide for Occupational Exploration (GOE) code(s): 02.08 Engineering Technology

---

Nuclear Medicine Technology

Program/Training Duration: Two years

Location: College/vocational classroom

Career Snapshot

Nuclear medicine technologists use radioactive materials for the diagnosis and treatment of disease. They administer radioactive compounds to patients and then use a specialized camera or scanner to record the behavior of the compound in the body. They need to know safe procedures for storing and handling radioactive materials. This is a small occupation, so there are not many openings, all the more so because many hospitals are merging their nuclear medicine department with their radiography department. Best job prospects will be for those who also have knowledge of radiologic technology.

Related Specialties and Careers

Imaging, radioimmunoassay studies.

Related Job Titles, Educational Requirements, Projected Growth, and Earnings			
Job Title	Educational Requirements	Projected Growth	Average Earnings
Nuclear Medicine Technologists (O*NET code 29-2033.00)	Associate degree	Faster than average	$47,400

Typical Postsecondary Courses

Clinical experience in nuclear medicine; college algebra; computers in nuclear medicine; English composition; general chemistry; general physics; health physics for nuclear medicine; human anatomy and physiology; introduction to nuclear medicine; non-imaging procedures in nuclear medicine; nuclear medicine imaging; nuclear medicine instrumentation; oral communication.

Suggested High School Courses

Algebra; biology; chemistry; English; physics/principles of technology. **Dept. of Education School-to-Work Cluster:** Health Science.

Essential Knowledge and Skills

Biology; computers and electronics; mathematics; medicine and dentistry; reading comprehension; science. **Values/Work Environment:** Ability utilization; exposed to disease or infections; exposed to radiation; indoors, environmentally controlled.

Other Information Sources

Many career and education information sources use the standard cross-referencing systems noted below. You can use the codes to obtain substantial additional information on the program (via CIP code) and related occupations (via GOE code). The O*NET codes on the opposite page refer to another major career information system. See the Introduction for details on obtaining additional information.

Classification of Instructional Programs (CIP) code(s): 510905 Nuclear Medical Technology/Technologist

Guide for Occupational Exploration (GOE) code(s): 12.03 Educational Services; 14.05 Medical Technology

---

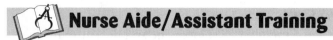 Nurse Aide/Assistant Training

Program/Training Duration: One month or less

Location: Workplace

Career Snapshot

Nursing aides, also known as nursing assistants, perform routine clinical tasks under the supervision of medical and nursing staff. They bring patients food, make beds, help with personal hygiene, answer call bells, help patients out of bed, take their temperature and pulse rate, report on signs of illness, and escort patients to examination or operating rooms. Job opportunity is expected to be good, especially in long-term health care facilities.

Related Specialties and Careers

Geriatric aide, hospital attendant, nursing assistant, psychiatric aide.

Related Job Titles, Educational Requirements, Projected Growth, and Earnings			
Job Title	**Educational Requirements**	**Projected Growth**	**Average Earnings**
Nursing Aides, Orderlies, and Attendants (O*NET code 31-1012.00)	Short-term on-the-job training	Faster than average	$19,290

Typical Postsecondary Courses

Clinical nursing experience; human growth and development; nursing assistant.

Suggested High School Courses

Algebra; biology; chemistry; English. **Dept. of Education School-to-Work Cluster:** Health Science.

Essential Knowledge and Skills

Chemistry; customer and personal service; medicine and dentistry; social perceptiveness. **Values/Work Environment:** Exposed to disease or infections; indoors, environmentally controlled; social service; spend time standing.

Other Information Sources

Many career and education information sources use the standard cross-referencing systems noted below. You can use the codes to obtain substantial additional information on the program (via CIP code) and related occupations (via GOE code). The O*NET codes on the opposite page refer to another major career information system. See the Introduction for details on obtaining additional information.

Classification of Instructional Programs (CIP) code(s): 511614 Nurse/Nursing Assistant/Aide and Patient Care Assistant

Guide for Occupational Exploration (GOE) code(s): 14.07 Patient Care and Assistance

Occupational Therapy Assisting

Program/Training Duration: Two years

Location: College/vocational classroom

Career Snapshot

Occupational therapy helps people with various kinds of disabilities—developmental, emotional, etc.—overcome them or compensate for them and thus lead more productive and enjoyable lives. Occupational therapy assistants work under the supervision of occupational therapists to provide appropriate rehabilitative services and evaluate the patients' progress. Cuts in federal coverage of therapeutic services have limited the growth of occupational therapy for the short run, but the long-run outlook for jobs is good.

Related Specialties and Careers

Occupational therapist aide, occupational therapist assistant.

Related Job Titles, Educational Requirements, Projected Growth, and Earnings			
Job Title	Educational Requirements	Projected Growth	Average Earnings
Occupational Therapist Aides (O*NET code 31-2012.00)	Short-term on-the-job training	Much faster than average	$21,570
Occupational Therapist Assistants (O*NET code 31-2011.00)	Associate degree	Much faster than average	$35,840

Typical Postsecondary Courses

Abnormal psychology; analysis of movement; clinical experience in occupational therapy assisting; English composition; human anatomy and physiology; human growth and development; introduction to medical terminology; introduction to psychology; occupational therapy for developmental problems; occupational therapy for physiological diagnoses; occupational therapy for psychosocial diagnoses.

Suggested High School Courses

Algebra; biology; chemistry; English; public speaking; social science. **Dept. of Education School-to-Work Cluster:** Health Science.

Essential Knowledge and Skills

Education and training; medicine and dentistry; social perceptiveness; therapy and counseling. **Values/Work Environment:** Indoors, environmentally controlled; security; social service.

Other Information Sources

Many career and education information sources use the standard cross-referencing systems noted below. You can use the codes to obtain substantial additional information on the program (via CIP code) and related occupations (via GOE code). The O*NET codes on the opposite page refer to another major career information system. See the Introduction for details on obtaining additional information.

Classification of Instructional Programs (CIP) code(s): 510803 Occupational Therapist Assistant

Guide for Occupational Exploration (GOE) code(s): 12.03 Educational Services; 14.06 Medical Therapy

---

# Office Technology

Program/Training Duration: One month to a year

Location: Workplace

Career Snapshot

As business offices have become high-tech, office technology has replaced the old program called secretarial science. Technology has encouraged professionals to do more typing and manage their own phone calls, and it has also made secretaries and administrative assistants more productive. As a result, job growth for secretaries and administrative assistants has slowed down. Nevertheless, this is such a huge field that a large number of jobs will open as people retire or change jobs. Workers need to take classes periodically to stay up to date with the latest technology.

Related Specialties and Careers

Accounting, database management, document production, multimedia presentation.

Related Job Titles, Educational Requirements, Projected Growth, and Earnings			
Job Title	Educational Requirements	Projected Growth	Average Earnings
Data Entry Keyers (O*NET code 43-9021.00)	Moderate-term on-the-job training	Little or none	$21,960

Typical Postsecondary Courses

Business math; business writing; computer fundamentals; computer spreadsheet; database management systems; document production; general office procedures; Internet basics; introduction to accounting; keyboarding; office communications; office technology externship; presentation graphics; word processing.

Suggested High School Courses

Applied communications; bookkeeping; business/applied math; keyboarding; office computer applications. **Dept. of Education School-to-Work Cluster:** Business and Administration.

Essential Knowledge and Skills

Clerical; computers and electronics; reading comprehension. **Values/Work Environment:** Independence; indoors, environmentally controlled; moral values; spend time making repetitive motions; spend time sitting.

Other Information Sources

Many career and education information sources use the standard cross-referencing systems noted below. You can use the codes to obtain substantial additional information on the program (via CIP code) and related occupations (via GOE code). The O*NET codes on the opposite page refer to another major career information system. See the Introduction for details on obtaining additional information.

Classification of Instructional Programs (CIP) code(s): 520407 Business/Office Automation/Technology/Data Entry

Guide for Occupational Exploration (GOE) code(s): 09.09 Clerical Machine Operation

---

Optical Laboratory Technology

Program/Training Duration: One month to a year

Location: Workplace

Career Snapshot

Although some optical laboratory technicians work on telescopes and binoculars, most make prescription eyeglasses and contact lenses. Working in labs and following written specifications, they cut, grind, edge, and finish lenses and may mount them in eyeglass frames. The work is increasingly done by automated equipment, which means that although the demand for eyeglasses is increasing as the population ages, the need for workers is growing only slowly. Almost all workers learn on the job, moving from simple to more complex tasks over the course of perhaps six months.

Related Specialties and Careers

Contact lenses, eyeglass lenses, laboratory management, mounting lenses, scientific instruments.

Related Job Titles, Educational Requirements, Projected Growth, and Earnings			
Job Title	Educational Requirements	Projected Growth	Average Earnings
Ophthalmic Laboratory Technicians (O*NET code 51-9083.00)	Moderate-term on-the-job training	Little or none	$21,350
Optical Instrument Assemblers (O*NET code 51-9083.02)	Moderate-term on-the-job training	Little or none	$21,350
Precision Lens Grinders and Polishers (O*NET code 51-9083.01)	Moderate-term on-the-job training	Little or none	$21,350

Typical Postsecondary Courses

Algebra and trigonometry; anatomy and physiology of the eye; business writing; contact lenses; eyewear lens selection and dispensing; field experience/internship; frame selection and dispensing; optical business management; optical dispensing; optical laboratory techniques; optical theory.

Suggested High School Courses

Algebra; geometry; office computer applications; photography; physics/principles of technology; trigonometry. **Dept. of Education School-to-Work Cluster:** Manufacturing.

Essential Knowledge and Skills

Equipment selection; mechanical devices; physics. **Values/Work Environment:** Independence; indoors, environmentally controlled; moral values.

Other Information Sources

Many career and education information sources use the standard cross-referencing systems noted below. You can use the codes to obtain substantial additional information on the program (via CIP code) and related occupations (via GOE code). The O*NET codes on the opposite page refer to another major career information system. See the Introduction for details on obtaining additional information.

Classification of Instructional Programs (CIP) code(s): 511006 Ophthalmic Laboratory Technology/Technician

Guide for Occupational Exploration (GOE) code(s): 05.03 Mechanical Work; 08.02 Production Technology

---

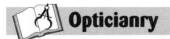 **Opticianry**

Program/Training Duration: More than one year

Location: Workplace

Career Snapshot

Dispensing opticians help fit patients with glasses and contact lenses. They place orders with optical labs and sometimes assemble lenses and frames. They may work in retail settings or in the offices of optometrists or ophthalmologists. Most are trained on the job; large employers may offer a structured apprenticeship program. Some complete formal programs at a community or technical college. Certification may be helpful for employment. The occupation is expected to grow at about the average rate, but it does not employ a large work force and is sensitive to economic downturns.

Related Specialties and Careers

Fitting contact lenses, fitting eyeglasses, lens grinding.

Related Job Titles, Educational Requirements, Projected Growth, and Earnings			
Job Title	Educational Requirements	Projected Growth	Average Earnings
Opticians, Dispensing (O*NET code 29-2081.00)	Long-term on-the-job training	Average	$26,100

Typical Postsecondary Courses

Anatomy and physiology of the eye; anatomy, physiology, and pathology of the eye; applied optic principles; college algebra; communications skills; contact lenses; internship in opticianry; introduction to computer applications; introduction to health care; introduction to psychology; ophthalmic dispensing; ophthalmic materials; optical business management; optical theory; opticianry sales and business management.

Suggested High School Courses

Algebra; applied communications; biology; bookkeeping; distributive education; geometry; office computer applications; physics/principles of technology; public speaking; trigonometry. **Dept. of Education School-to-Work Cluster:** Health Science.

Essential Knowledge and Skills

Administration and management; customer and personal service; reading comprehension; sales and marketing. **Values/Work Environment:** Achievement; indoors, environmentally controlled; social service; social status; spend time sitting.

Other Information Sources

Many career and education information sources use the standard cross-referencing systems noted below. You can use the codes to obtain substantial additional information on the program (via CIP code) and related occupations (via GOE code). The O*NET codes on the opposite page refer to another major career information system. See the Introduction for details on obtaining additional information.

Classification of Instructional Programs (CIP) code(s): 511801 Opticianry/Ophthalmic Dispensing Optician

Guide for Occupational Exploration (GOE) code(s): 14.04 Health Specialties

---

Ornamental Horticulture

Program/Training Duration: At least one year, perhaps several

Location: Workplace or vocational classroom

Career Snapshot

Graduates of ornamental horticulture programs are employed by greenhouses and nurseries, landscaping and horticultural services, amusement parks and golf courses, and local parks and recreation departments. Workers enjoy many of the same pleasures as in farming—working with growing things and the soil—but also need to be cautious about some of the same dangers from power equipment and toxic chemicals. Employment opportunities are probably best in the Sunbelt, where there is a longer season for outdoor recreation and the growing of ornamental plants.

Related Specialties and Careers

Greenhouse management, landscaping, nursery management.

Related Job Titles, Educational Requirements, Projected Growth, and Earnings			
Job Title	Educational Requirements	Projected Growth	Average Earnings
Agricultural Crop Farm Managers (O*NET code 11-9011.02)	Work experience in a related occupation	Little or none	$42,170
Farm, Ranch, and Other Agricultural Managers (O*NET code 11-9011.00)	Work experience in a related occupation	Little or none	$42,170
Farmers and Ranchers (O*NET code 11-9012.00)	Long-term on-the-job training	Declining	$42,170
First-Line Supervisors and Manager/Supervisors—Landscaping Workers (O*NET code 37-1012.02)	Work experience in a related occupation	Average	$32,100
First-Line Supervisors/Managers of Landscaping, Lawn Service, and Groundskeeping Workers (O*NET code 37-1012.00)	Work experience in a related occupation	Average	$32,100

Job Title	Educational Requirements	Projected Growth	Average Earnings
Lawn Service Managers (O*NET code 37-1012.01)	Work experience in a related occupation	Average	$32,100
Nursery and Greenhouse Managers (O*NET code 11-9011.01)	Work experience in a related occupation	Little or none	$42,170

Typical Postsecondary Courses

Annual and perennial flowers; botany; computers in agriculture; English composition; general biology; general entomology; greenhouse management; herbaceous/exotic plants; horticulture practicum; indoor plants; introduction to horticulture; introduction to landscape design; introduction to ornamental horticulture; introduction to soil science; landscape management; pest management; plant pathology; plant propagation; small business management; technical writing; woody ornamentals.

Suggested High School Courses

Applied communications; biology; bookkeeping; business/applied math; chemistry; office computer applications; physics/principles of technology. **Dept. of Education School-to-Work Cluster:** Agriculture/Natural Resources.

Essential Knowledge and Skills

Administration and management; coordination; food production; management of personnel resources; personnel and human resources. **Values/Work Environment:** Authority; autonomy; outdoors, exposed to weather; responsibility.

Other Information Sources

Many career and education information sources use the standard cross-referencing systems noted below. You can use the codes to obtain substantial additional information on the program (via CIP code) and related occupations (via GOE code). The O*NET codes on the opposite page refer to another major career information system. See the Introduction for details on obtaining additional information.

Classification of Instructional Programs (CIP) code(s): 010603 Ornamental Horticulture

Guide for Occupational Exploration (GOE) code(s): 03.01 Managerial Work in Plants and Animals; 12.03 Educational Services; 13.01 General Management Work and Management of Support Functions

Paralegal Services

Program/Training Duration: At least two years

Location: College classroom, followed by workplace

Career Snapshot

Paralegals (or legal assistants) help lawyers with such tasks as interviewing clients and witnesses, drafting legal documents, and doing legal research. Although some paralegals get on-the-job training, the trend is toward hiring graduates of two- and even four-year programs or college graduates from other fields who have completed a certificate program in paralegal studies. For example, someone with a background in nursing might work as a paralegal in the field of medical-related litigation. Competition for jobs is expected to be intense.

Related Specialties and Careers

Law office management, legal research.

Related Job Titles, Educational Requirements, Projected Growth, and Earnings			
Job Title	**Educational Requirements**	**Projected Growth**	**Average Earnings**
Legal Support Workers, All Other (O*NET code 23-2099.99)	No data available	Average	No salary data available
Paralegals and Legal Assistants (O*NET code 23-2011.00)	Associate degree	Faster than average	$36,670
Title Examiners and Abstractors (O*NET code 23-2093.02)	Long-term on-the-job training	Little or none	$31,770
Title Examiners, Abstractors, and Searchers (O*NET code 23-2093.00)	Moderate-term on-the-job training	Little or none	$31,770
Title Searchers (O*NET code 23-2093.01)	Moderate-term on-the-job training	Little or none	$31,770

Typical Postsecondary Courses

Business law; civil procedure and litigation; computer applications in the law office; criminal law and procedure; family law; introduction to legal assisting; law office management; legal assistant internship; legal research and writing; probate practices and procedures; real estate law; tort law; wills, trusts, and estate administration.

Suggested High School Courses

Business/applied math; English; keyboarding; office computer applications; public speaking; social science. **Dept. of Education School-to-Work Cluster:** Law and Public Safety.

Essential Knowledge and Skills

Clerical; critical thinking; English language; law and government; reading comprehension; writing. **Values/Work Environment:** Company policies and practices; indoors, environmentally controlled; spend time sitting.

Other Information Sources

Many career and education information sources use the standard cross-referencing systems noted below. You can use the codes to obtain substantial additional information on the program (via CIP code) and related occupations (via GOE code). The O*NET codes on the opposite page refer to another major career information system. See the Introduction for details on obtaining additional information.

Classification of Instructional Programs (CIP) code(s): 220302 Legal Assistant/Paralegal

Guide for Occupational Exploration (GOE) code(s): 04.02 Law

 **Personal Trainer**

Program/Training Duration: A year or more

Location: Vocational classroom

Career Snapshot

Personal trainers work one-on-one with clients, who may be sedentary people who want to get in shape or very fit people who want to stay in top condition. Probably most are self-employed. The key to being hired is to have certification from an organization such as the American College of Sports Medicine, the American Council on Exercise, or the National Strength and Conditioning Association. Training courses are offered by some of these organizations and by specialized schools.

Related Specialties and Careers

Rehabilitation, senior fitness.

Related Job Titles, Educational Requirements, Projected Growth, and Earnings			
Job Title	Educational Requirements	Projected Growth	Average Earnings
Fitness Trainers and Aerobics Instructors (O*NET code 39-9031.00)	Postsecondary vocational training	Much faster than average	$23,340

Typical Postsecondary Courses

Body composition; cardiovascular fitness; fitness assessments; flexibility training; human anatomy and physiology; nutrition; resistance training.

Suggested High School Courses

Biology; business/applied math; physics/principles of technology; public speaking.
Dept. of Education School-to-Work Cluster: Education and Training.

Essential Knowledge and Skills

Coordination; customer and personal service; education and training; instructing; learning strategies; psychology. **Values/Work Environment:** Authority; creativity; outdoors, exposed to weather; responsibility; spend time standing.

Other Information Sources

Many career and education information sources use the standard cross-referencing systems noted below. You can use the codes to obtain substantial additional information on the program (via CIP code) and related occupations (via GOE code). The O*NET codes on the opposite page refer to another major career information system. See the Introduction for details on obtaining additional information.

Classification of Instructional Programs (CIP) code(s): 319999 Parks, Recreation, Leisure, and Fitness Studies, Other

Guide for Occupational Exploration (GOE) code(s): 11.02 Recreational Services

 Pet Grooming

Program/Training Duration: A few weeks to several months

Location: Vocational classroom or workplace

Career Snapshot

Americans love pets, and many of the most popular breeds require periodic grooming to keep them clean, comfortable, and good looking. Groomers need an artistic eye, a great amount of patience, and physical stamina. They should not be allergic to pets or be squeamish. The workplace is often hot and noisy. Some groomers learn by working for an established business, often starting out washing pets. Many get initial training at a specialized trade school and then perfect their skills on the job. This career offers many opportunities for self-employment or for arrangements to work as an independent contractor for a pet business. So far there has been very little governmental movement toward licensure or regulation.

Related Specialties and Careers

Cat grooming, dog grooming, pet care management.

Related Job Titles, Educational Requirements, Projected Growth, and Earnings			
Job Title	Educational Requirements	Projected Growth	Average Earnings
Nonfarm Animal Caretakers (O*NET code 39-2021.00)	Short-term on-the-job training	Faster than average	$16,570

Typical Postsecondary Courses

Anatomy of the dog and cat; breed recognition and trims; brushing, combing, and dematting; clipper and scissoring techniques; customer relations; grooming tools: use and care; introduction to grooming; pet diseases and parasites; pet first aid; pet nutrition; pet psychology and handling; shop management.

Suggested High School Courses

Biology; business/applied math; distributive education; office computer applications. **Dept. of Education School-to-Work Cluster:** Agriculture/Natural Resources.

Essential Knowledge and Skills

Active listening; biology; building and construction; medicine and dentistry. **Values/ Work Environment:** Exposed to contaminants; moral values; outdoors, exposed to weather; spend time standing.

Other Information Sources

Many career and education information sources use the standard cross-referencing systems noted below. You can use the codes to obtain substantial additional information on the program (via CIP code) and related occupations (via GOE code). The O*NET codes on the opposite page refer to another major career information system. See the Introduction for details on obtaining additional information.

Classification of Instructional Programs (CIP) code(s): 010504 Dog/Pet/Animal Grooming

Guide for Occupational Exploration (GOE) code(s): 03.02 Animal Care and Training

---

Pharmacy Technology

Program/Training Duration: One month to a year

Location: Workplace

Career Snapshot

Pharmacy technicians work mostly in retail and hospital pharmacies, where they help licensed pharmacists with many tasks associated with filling prescriptions. Most technicians are trained informally on the job, but some get training in the military, a hospital, or a technical or community college. Certification is not required but may improve job prospects. The job outlook is expected to be good.

Related Specialties and Careers

Hospital pharmacy, retail pharmacy.

Related Job Titles, Educational Requirements, Projected Growth, and Earnings			
Job Title	Educational Requirements	Projected Growth	Average Earnings
Pharmacy Aides (O*NET code 31-9095.00)	Moderate-term on-the-job training	Average	$18,010
Pharmacy Technicians (O*NET code 29-2052.00)	Moderate-term on-the-job training	Much faster than average	$21,630

Typical Postsecondary Courses

Dispensing and compounding prescriptions; dosage forms and routes of administration; drug information sources; general biology; general chemistry; hospital clinical pharmacy; introduction to pharmacy technology; pharmaceutical calculations; pharmacology for pharmacy technicians; prescribers of drugs; retail clinical pharmacy; sterile products.

Suggested High School Courses

Algebra; biology; bookkeeping; chemistry; office computer applications; physics/principles of technology. **Dept. of Education School-to-Work Cluster:** Health Science.

Essential Knowledge and Skills

Clerical; computers and electronics; medicine and dentistry; reading comprehension.
Values/Work Environment: Co-workers; indoors, environmentally controlled; good working conditions.

Other Information Sources

Many career and education information sources use the standard cross-referencing systems noted below. You can use the codes to obtain substantial additional information on the program (via CIP code) and related occupations (via GOE code). The O*NET codes on the opposite page refer to another major career information system. See the Introduction for details on obtaining additional information.

Classification of Instructional Programs (CIP) code(s): 510805 Pharmacy Technician/Assistant

Guide for Occupational Exploration (GOE) code(s): 12.03 Educational Services; 14.02 Medicine and Surgery

 # Photography

Program/Training Duration: More than one year

Location: Workplace

Career Snapshot

Photography is a highly competitive field, and for certain specializations—such as photojournalism and industrial and scientific photography—at least an associate degree is needed. Vocational or on-the-job training may suffice for jobs in freelance or portrait photography. Opportunities for self-employment are particularly good in this field. The spread of digital photography is expected to slow down job growth somewhat, partly because it will increase the productivity of photographers and partly because many users of photographs will be able to find appropriate existing images in collections rather than hire photographers to create new images.

Related Specialties and Careers

Digital, photojournalism, portrait.

Related Job Titles, Educational Requirements, Projected Growth, and Earnings			
Job Title	Educational Requirements	Projected Growth	Average Earnings
Photographers (O*NET code 27-4021.00)	Long-term on-the-job training	Average	$23,040
Photographers, Scientific (O*NET code 27-4021.02)	Long-term on-the-job training	Average	$23,040
Professional Photographers (O*NET code 27-4021.01)	Long-term on-the-job training	Average	$23,040

Typical Postsecondary Courses

Advanced black-and-white photography; color photography; digital photography; intermediate photography; introduction to photography; photographic portraiture.

Suggested High School Courses

Algebra; applied communications; art; chemistry; computer science; geometry; office computer applications; photography; physics/principles of technology; trigonometry. **Dept. of Education School-to-Work Cluster:** Arts, A/V Technology, and Communication.

Essential Knowledge and Skills

Chemistry; communications and media; equipment selection; fine arts. **Values/Work Environment:** Ability utilization; achievement; creativity; spend time standing.

Other Information Sources

Many career and education information sources use the standard cross-referencing systems noted below. You can use the codes to obtain substantial additional information on the program (via CIP code) and related occupations (via GOE code). The O*NET codes on the opposite page refer to another major career information system. See the Introduction for details on obtaining additional information.

Classification of Instructional Programs (CIP) code(s): 500605 Photography

Guide for Occupational Exploration (GOE) code(s): 01.08 Media Technology; 02.05 Laboratory Technology; 12.03 Educational Services

---

Physical Therapist Assisting

Program/Training Duration: Two years

Location: College/vocational classroom

Career Snapshot

Physical therapist assistants perform various tasks under the supervision of a physical therapist, helping patients overcome or limit disability from disease or injury, improve mobility, and reduce pain. For example, they may assist patients with exercises; apply heat, cold, or electrical stimulation; or use ultrasound. In the short run, the growth of physical therapy services has been held back by cuts in federal medical coverage, but in the long run the job outlook is expected to be very good.

Related Specialties and Careers

Electrical stimulation, exercise therapy, massage, ultrasound.

Related Job Titles, Educational Requirements, Projected Growth, and Earnings			
Job Title	Educational Requirements	Projected Growth	Average Earnings
Physical Therapist Aides (O*NET code 31-2022.00)	Associate degree	Much faster than average	$20,300
Physical Therapist Assistants (O*NET code 31-2021.00)	Associate degree	Much faster than average	$35,280

Typical Postsecondary Courses

English composition; fundamentals of medical science; human anatomy and physiology; introduction to medical terminology; introduction to psychology; kinesiology; physical therapist assistant practicum; principles of physical therapist assisting; procedures for physical therapist assistant; therapeutic exercise techniques.

Suggested High School Courses

Algebra; biology; chemistry; English; physics/principles of technology; public speaking; social science. **Dept. of Education School-to-Work Cluster:** Health Science.

Essential Knowledge and Skills

Customer and personal service; education and training; learning strategies; reading comprehension; service orientation; therapy and counseling. **Values/Work Environment:** Indoors, environmentally controlled; security; social service; spend time standing.

Other Information Sources

Many career and education information sources use the standard cross-referencing systems noted below. You can use the codes to obtain substantial additional information on the program (via CIP code) and related occupations (via GOE code). The O*NET codes on the opposite page refer to another major career information system. See the Introduction for details on obtaining additional information.

Classification of Instructional Programs (CIP) code(s): 510806 Physical Therapist Assistant

Guide for Occupational Exploration (GOE) code(s): 12.03 Educational Services; 14.06 Medical Therapy

---

Pilot Training

Program/Training Duration: A few weeks to a year or more

Location: Vocational classroom

Career Snapshot

All pilots need to pass an exam to be licensed or certified by the Federal Aviation Administration. They also must have a certain amount of flight experience; instruction in an FAA-approved flight school can partially offset this requirement. Traditionally, most pilots have received their training in the military, but increasingly they are learning their skills at private flight schools or in pilot training programs offered by community colleges. A college degree may even be required by some employers, especially airlines. Competition for jobs is expected to be keen, and demand is sensitive to upswings and downswings in the economy.

Related Specialties and Careers

Airplane pilot, balloon pilot, crop duster, flight instructor, helicopter pilot.

Related Job Titles, Educational Requirements, Projected Growth, and Earnings			
Job Title	Educational Requirements	Projected Growth	Average Earnings
Commercial Pilots (O*NET code 53-2012.00)	Postsecondary vocational training	Faster than average	$47,420

Typical Postsecondary Courses

Flight instruction; ground instruction; simulator training.

Suggested High School Courses

Algebra; geometry; office computer applications; physics/principles of technology.
Dept. of Education School-to-Work Cluster: Transportation, Distribution, and Logistics.

Essential Knowledge and Skills

Geography; instructing; operation and control; operation monitoring; physics; transportation. **Values/Work Environment:** Ability utilization; company policies and practices; compensation; exposed to high places; spend time sitting.

Other Information Sources

Many career and education information sources use the standard cross-referencing systems noted below. You can use the codes to obtain substantial additional information on the program (via CIP code) and related occupations (via GOE code). The O*NET codes on the opposite page refer to another major career information system. See the Introduction for details on obtaining additional information.

Classification of Instructional Programs (CIP) code(s): 490102 Airline/Commercial/Professional Pilot and Flight Crew

Guide for Occupational Exploration (GOE) code(s): 07.03 Air Vehicle Operation

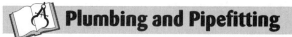 **Plumbing and Pipefitting**

Program/Training Duration: One month to more than a year

Location: Workplace

Career Snapshot

Pipes are used not only in the home, but also in industry, in agriculture, in fire suppression systems, and in many other settings. Plumbers, pipefitters, and steamfitters are needed to install and maintain these systems. Most of these workers learn their skills through formal apprenticeships. Training in the armed forces or in a certificate program may sometimes be sufficient or may help meet some of the requirements of an apprenticeship. Local governments usually require plumbers to pass a licensing exam. Job opportunities are expected to be excellent because comparatively few young people are entering this field. The field is also less sensitive to economic cycles than are most other construction trades.

Related Specialties and Careers

Pipelaying, pipefitting, plumbing, steamfitting.

Related Job Titles, Educational Requirements, Projected Growth, and Earnings			
Job Title	**Educational Requirements**	**Projected Growth**	**Average Earnings**
First-Line Supervisors and Manager/Supervisors—Construction Trades Workers (O*NET code 47-1011.01)	Work experience in a related occupation	Average	$46,570
First-Line Supervisors/Managers of Construction Trades and Extraction Workers (O*NET code 47-1011.00)	Work experience in a related occupation	Average	$46,570
Helpers—Pipelayers, Plumbers, Pipefitters, and Steamfitters (O*NET code 47-3015.00)	Short-term on-the-job training	Average	$21,830
Pipe Fitters (O*NET code 47-2152.01)	Long-term on-the-job training	Average	$38,710
Pipelayers (O*NET code 47-2151.00)	Moderate-term on-the-job training	Average	$28,190

Job Title	Educational Requirements	Projected Growth	Average Earnings
Pipelaying Fitters (O*NET code 47-2152.03)	Moderate-term on-the-job training	Average	$38,710
Plumbers (O*NET code 47-2152.02)	Long-term on-the-job training	Average	$38,710
Plumbers, Pipefitters, and Steamfitters (O*NET code 47-2152.00)	Long-term on-the-job training	Average	$38,710
Septic Tank Servicers and Sewer Pipe Cleaners (O*NET code 47-4071.00)	Moderate-term on-the-job training	Average	$27,260

Typical Postsecondary Courses

Basic welding; blueprint reading; commercial/industrial plumbing; construction math and estimating; construction safety; plumbing codes; residential plumbing.

Suggested High School Courses

Algebra; applied communications; business/applied math; drafting; industrial arts; metal shop; physics/principles of technology. **Dept. of Education School-to-Work Cluster:** Architecture and Construction.

Essential Knowledge and Skills

Building and construction; installation; mechanical devices. **Values/Work Environment:** Moral values; outdoors, exposed to weather; spend time bending or twisting the body; spend time standing.

Other Information Sources

Many career and education information sources use the standard cross-referencing systems noted below. You can use the codes to obtain substantial additional information on the program (via CIP code) and related occupations (via GOE code). The O*NET codes on the opposite page refer to another major career information system. See the Introduction for details on obtaining additional information.

Classification of Instructional Programs (CIP) code(s): 460502 Pipefitting/Pipefitter and Sprinkler Fitter; 460503 Plumbing Technology/Plumber

Guide for Occupational Exploration (GOE) code(s): 06.01 Managerial Work in Construction, Mining, and Drilling; 06.02 Construction; 06.04 Hands-on Work in Construction, Extraction, and Maintenance

Practical Nursing (L.P.N. Training)

Program/Training Duration: A few weeks to more than a year

Location: Vocational classroom

Career Snapshot

Licensed practical nurses take care of patients under the direction of doctors and registered nurses. (They are called licensed vocational nurses in California and Texas.) They provide basic bedside care, such as taking vital signs, applying dressings, helping with personal hygiene, giving massages, reporting signs of illness, and providing emotional support. State laws vary on whether they can administer prescribed medicines or start intravenous fluids. Job growth will be about average overall, with the best opportunities in nursing homes and home health care services.

Related Specialties and Careers

Adult care, child care, geriatric care, infant care, nursing home care, private home care.

Related Job Titles, Educational Requirements, Projected Growth, and Earnings			
Job Title	Educational Requirements	Projected Growth	Average Earnings
Licensed Practical and Licensed Vocational Nurses (O*NET code 29-2061.00)	Postsecondary vocational training	Average	$30,670

Typical Postsecondary Courses

Adult health nursing; clinical nursing experience; English composition; human anatomy and physiology; introduction to medical terminology; introduction to psychology; medical-surgical nursing; mental health nursing; microbiology; oral communication; pediatric nursing; reproductive health nursing.

Suggested High School Courses

Algebra; biology; chemistry; English; public speaking. **Dept. of Education School-to-Work Cluster:** Health Science.

Essential Knowledge and Skills

Biology; customer and personal service; medicine and dentistry; service orientation.

Values/Work Environment: Achievement; co-workers; indoors, environmentally controlled; social service.

Other Information Sources

Many career and education information sources use the standard cross-referencing systems noted below. You can use the codes to obtain substantial additional information on the program (via CIP code) and related occupations (via GOE code). The O*NET codes on the opposite page refer to another major career information system. See the Introduction for details on obtaining additional information.

Classification of Instructional Programs (CIP) code(s): 511613 Licensed Practical /Vocational Nurse Training (LPN, LVN, Cert, Dipl, AAS)

Guide for Occupational Exploration (GOE) code(s): 14.07 Patient Care and Assistance

---

Property Management

Program/Training Duration: Several years

Location: Workplace

Career Snapshot

Property and real estate managers oversee commercial and residential properties on behalf of the owners. Besides collecting rents and paying bills, they deal with issues of marketing, security, safety, maintenance, and construction. Almost half are self-employed. A degree in business is useful, and opportunities will be best for those with a bachelor's. Nevertheless, it is possible to enter the job as an assistant after completing a certification program or after working in a related job such as security guard or real estate agent. The job outlook is generally good.

Related Specialties and Careers

Asset property management, commercial property, real estate asset management, residential property.

Related Job Titles, Educational Requirements, Projected Growth, and Earnings			
Job Title	Educational Requirements	Projected Growth	Average Earnings
First-Line Supervisors and Manager/Supervisors—Construction Trades Workers (O*NET code 47-1011.01)	Work experience in a related occupation	Average	$46,570
First-Line Supervisors/Managers of Construction Trades and Extraction Workers (O*NET code 47-1011.00)	Work experience in a related occupation	Average	$46,570

Typical Postsecondary Courses

Economics of property management; introduction to property management; leases; legal issues in property management; maintaining the premises; managing commercial property; managing residential property; managing safety and environmental issues; property management reports; real estate marketing; tenant relations.

Suggested High School Courses

Algebra; applied communications; bookkeeping; distributive education; office computer applications; public speaking; social science. **Dept. of Education School-to-Work Cluster:** Architecture and Construction.

Essential Knowledge and Skills

Administration and management; building and construction; coordination; management of personnel resources; personnel and human resources; time management. **Values/Work Environment:** Authority; autonomy; exposed to hazardous equipment; outdoors, exposed to weather; responsibility; spend time standing.

Other Information Sources

Many career and education information sources use the standard cross-referencing systems noted below. You can use the codes to obtain substantial additional information on the program (via CIP code) and related occupations (via GOE code). The O*NET codes on the opposite page refer to another major career information system. See the Introduction for details on obtaining additional information.

Classification of Instructional Programs (CIP) code(s): 460401 Building/Property Maintenance and Management

Guide for Occupational Exploration (GOE) code(s): 06.01 Managerial Work in Construction, Mining, and Drilling

---

Radiologic Technology

Program/Training Duration: Two years

Location: College/vocational classroom

Career Snapshot

Radiographers make X-ray images of the human body for use in the diagnosis of medical problems. They prepare and position patients, apply lead shielding for protection, position the equipment and set it for the kind of exposure needed, position the film to be exposed, and then remove and develop the film after it has been exposed. Best job opportunities are expected for those who are also trained in sonography, computerized tomography (CAT), MRI (magnetic resonance imaging), or nuclear medical technology.

Related Specialties and Careers

CAT technology, MRI technology, radiography.

Related Job Titles, Educational Requirements, Projected Growth, and Earnings			
Job Title	Educational Requirements	Projected Growth	Average Earnings
Radiation Therapists (O*NET code 29-1124.00)	Associate degree	Faster than average	$49,050
Radiologic Technicians (O*NET code 29-2034.02)	Associate degree	Faster than average	$37,680
Radiologic Technologists (O*NET code 29-2034.01)	Associate degree	Faster than average	$37,680
Radiologic Technologists and Technicians (O*NET code 29-2034.00)	Associate degree	Faster than average	$37,680

Typical Postsecondary Courses

Clinical experience in radiology; English composition; human anatomy and physiology; introduction to medical terminology; introduction to radiology; oral communication; radiation protection; radiologic imaging; radiologic positioning.

Suggested High School Courses

Algebra; biology; chemistry; English; physics/principles of technology; public speaking. **Dept. of Education School-to-Work Cluster:** Health Science.

Essential Knowledge and Skills

Biology; computers and electronics; medicine and dentistry; operation and control; reading comprehension. **Values/Work Environment:** Exposed to radiation; indoors, environmentally controlled; moral values.

Other Information Sources

Many career and education information sources use the standard cross-referencing systems noted below. You can use the codes to obtain substantial additional information on the program (via CIP code) and related occupations (via GOE code). The O*NET codes on the opposite page refer to another major career information system. See the Introduction for details on obtaining additional information.

Classification of Instructional Programs (CIP) code(s): 510907 Medical Radiologic Technology/Science—Radiation Therapist

Guide for Occupational Exploration (GOE) code(s): 12.03 Educational Services; 14.05 Medical Technology; 14.06 Medical Therapy

---

 **Real Estate**

Program/Training Duration: A few weeks to more than a year

Location: Vocational classroom

Career Snapshot

Real estate agents usually face a lot of competition for listings and for buyers, and many agents drop out of the career after a couple of years. Those who succeed have a love of selling, a lot of drive, and the willingness to work on evenings and weekends. All states require a license, and many require 30 to 90 hours of instruction as preparation for the licensing exam, which covers the procedures and laws related to real estate. Courses are offered by community colleges, real estate firms, and night schools; it is also possible to get an associate degree in real estate.

Related Specialties and Careers

Asset management, commercial property, corporate real estate management, leasing agency, property management, residential property.

Related Job Titles, Educational Requirements, Projected Growth, and Earnings			
Job Title	**Educational Requirements**	**Projected Growth**	**Average Earnings**
Appraisers and Assessors of Real Estate (O*NET code 13-2021.00)	Postsecondary vocational training	Average	$38,950
Appraisers, Real Estate (O*NET code 13-2021.02)	Postsecondary vocational training	Average	$38,950
Assessors (O*NET code 13-2021.01)	Postsecondary vocational training	Average	$38,950
Real Estate Brokers (O*NET code 41-9021.00)	Work experience in a related occupation	Average	$51,370
Real Estate Sales Agents (O*NET code 41-9022.00)	Postsecondary vocational training	Little or none	$28,570

Typical Postsecondary Courses

Introduction to real estate; real estate and taxation; real estate finance; real estate law; real estate marketing; real estate ownership; real estate valuation; transferring real estate.

Suggested High School Courses

Applied communications; bookkeeping; business/applied math; distributive education; office computer applications; public speaking; social science. **Dept. of Education School-to-Work Cluster:** Retail and Wholesale Sales and Service.

Essential Knowledge and Skills

Economics and accounting; mathematics; reading comprehension. **Values/Work Environment:** Responsibility; spend time sitting.

Other Information Sources

Many career and education information sources use the standard cross-referencing systems noted below. You can use the codes to obtain substantial additional information on the program (via CIP code) and related occupations (via GOE code). The O*NET codes on the opposite page refer to another major career information system. See the Introduction for details on obtaining additional information.

Classification of Instructional Programs (CIP) code(s): 521501 Real Estate

Guide for Occupational Exploration (GOE) code(s): 10.03 General Sales; 13.01 General Management Work and Management of Support Functions; 13.02 Management Support

---

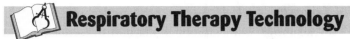

Respiratory Therapy Technology

Program/Training Duration: A few weeks to two years

Location: Workplace or college/vocational classroom

Career Snapshot

Respiratory therapists help people with breathing problems. They evaluate patients' lung capacity, the inward and outward flow of air, and the efficiency with which the blood acquires oxygen and sheds carbon dioxide. They use equipment such as oxygen masks and ventilator tubes. They administer medications as aerosols. Job opportunities are expected to be good, especially for those with skill at cardiopulmonary and infant care.

Related Specialties and Careers

Chest physiotherapy, emergency care, stress testing.

Related Job Titles, Educational Requirements, Projected Growth, and Earnings			
Job Title	Educational Requirements	Projected Growth	Average Earnings
Respiratory Therapists (O*NET code 29-1126.00)	Associate degree	Faster than average	$39,370
Respiratory Therapy Technicians (O*NET code 29-2054.00)	Postsecondary vocational training	Faster than average	$33,840

Typical Postsecondary Courses

Cardiopulmonary anatomy and physiology; cardiopulmonary diagnostics; clinical experience in respiratory therapy; English composition; fundamentals of medical science; general chemistry; human anatomy and physiology; introduction to medical terminology; neonatal and pediatric respiratory procedures; oral communication; pharmacology for respiratory care; respiratory care procedures.

Suggested High School Courses

Algebra; biology; chemistry; English; physics/principles of technology; public speaking. **Dept. of Education School-to-Work Cluster:** Health Science.

Essential Knowledge and Skills

Active listening; biology; medicine and dentistry; reading comprehension; service orientation; therapy and counseling. **Values/Work Environment:** Achievement; co-workers; indoors, environmentally controlled; social service.

Other Information Sources

Many career and education information sources use the standard cross-referencing systems noted below. You can use the codes to obtain substantial additional information on the program (via CIP code) and related occupations (via GOE code). The O*NET codes on the opposite page refer to another major career information system. See the Introduction for details on obtaining additional information.

Classification of Instructional Programs (CIP) code(s): 510908 Respiratory Care Therapy/Therapist

Guide for Occupational Exploration (GOE) code(s): 12.03 Educational Services; 14.06 Medical Therapy

---

 Surgical Technology

Program/Training Duration: A year or more

Location: Vocational classroom

Career Snapshot

Surgical technologists are important members of the operating room team. They learn their skills either in certification programs that take about one year to complete or in associate degree programs; for either kind of program, look for accreditation by the Commission on Accreditation of Allied Health Education Programs. Employers generally prefer technologists who have passed a national certifying exam. Continuing education or reexamination is required to maintain certification. The job outlook is expected to be good, because as the population ages and new operating room technologies are developed, the number of surgical operations will increase.

Related Specialties and Careers

Circulating technologist, surgical specialization.

Related Job Titles, Educational Requirements, Projected Growth, and Earnings			
Job Title	Educational Requirements	Projected Growth	Average Earnings
Surgical Technologists (O*NET code 29-2055.00)	Postsecondary vocational training	Faster than average	$30,090

Typical Postsecondary Courses

Clinical experience in surgical technology; English composition; human anatomy and physiology; microbiology; operating room orientation; patient care; pharmacology for surgical technology; surgical asepsis; surgical instruments, supplies, and equipment; surgical lab procedures; surgical procedures.

Suggested High School Courses

Algebra; biology; chemistry; English; physics/principles of technology. **Dept. of Education School-to-Work Cluster:** Health Science.

Essential Knowledge and Skills

Biology; medicine and dentistry; reading comprehension. **Values/Work Environment:** Exposed to disease or infections; indoors, environmentally controlled; moral values; security; social service; spend time standing.

Other Information Sources

Many career and education information sources use the standard cross-referencing systems noted below. You can use the codes to obtain substantial additional information on the program (via CIP code) and related occupations (via GOE code). The O*NET codes on the opposite page refer to another major career information system. See the Introduction for details on obtaining additional information.

Classification of Instructional Programs (CIP) code(s): 510909 Surgical Technology/Technologist

Guide for Occupational Exploration (GOE) code(s): 12.03 Educational Services; 14.02 Medicine and Surgery

---

Surveying Technology

Program/Training Duration: One to several years

Location: College/vocational classroom, perhaps workplace

Career Snapshot

Surveying is changing rapidly with the advent of technologies such as global positioning systems (GPS) and geographic information systems (GIS). These trends are increasingly making the four-year degree the standard entry route for licensed land surveyors. Therefore, those who want to go into this field with less education usually work as unlicensed surveying technicians, gathering information under the direction of a licensed surveyor. In some states, after a certain amount of experience, they may qualify to take the licensing exam. Job opportunities are expected to be good for technicians who keep their skills current with the advancing technologies.

Related Specialties and Careers

Geodetic surveying, geographic information, geophysical prospecting surveying, land surveying, mapping, marine surveying.

Related Job Titles, Educational Requirements, Projected Growth, and Earnings			
Job Title	Educational Requirements	Projected Growth	Average Earnings
Mapping Technicians (O*NET code 17-3031.02)	Moderate-term on-the-job training	Faster than average	$28,210
Surveying and Mapping Technicians (O*NET code 17-3031.00)	Moderate-term on-the-job training	Faster than average	$28,210
Surveying Technicians (O*NET code 17-3031.01)	Long-term on-the-job training	Faster than average	$28,210

Typical Postsecondary Courses

Advanced survey instrumentation; boundary surveying; college algebra; computer-aided drafting (CAD); construction and layout surveying; control surveying; drainage and geology; elementary surveying; general physics; introduction to computer programming concepts; pre-calculus; route surveying; survey drafting applications; technical writing.

Suggested High School Courses

Algebra; applied communications; computer science; drafting; geometry; office computer applications; physics/principles of technology; pre-calculus; trigonometry. **Dept. of Education School-to-Work Cluster:** Scientific Research/Engineering.

Essential Knowledge and Skills

Design; engineering and technology; mathematics. **Values/Work Environment:** Indoors, environmentally controlled; moral values.

Other Information Sources

Many career and education information sources use the standard cross-referencing systems noted below. You can use the codes to obtain substantial additional information on the program (via CIP code) and related occupations (via GOE code). The O*NET codes on the opposite page refer to another major career information system. See the Introduction for details on obtaining additional information.

Classification of Instructional Programs (CIP) code(s): 151102 Surveying Technology/Surveying

Guide for Occupational Exploration (GOE) code(s): 02.08 Engineering Technology

---

 Taxidermy

Program/Training Duration: A month to a year

Location: Vocational classroom or workplace

Career Snapshot

Taxidermy is the art of preparing the skins of animals so they can be displayed in a lifelike fashion as trophies, museum exhibits, or rugs. Some taxidermists learn on the job, while others take classes in taxidermy at a vocational school, adult education program, or specialized trade school. Most taxidermists are self-employed and run small businesses in communities where hunting or fishing are popular. Taxidermists are licensed in some states, and a federal license is needed to work with federally protected species.

Related Specialties and Careers

Birds, fish, mammals, museum exhibits.

Related Job Titles, Educational Requirements, Projected Growth, and Earnings			
Job Title	Educational Requirements	Projected Growth	Average Earnings
Craft Artists (O*NET code 27-1012.00)	Associate degree	Average	No salary data available

Typical Postsecondary Courses

Bird taxidermy; fish taxidermy; mammal taxidermy; principles of taxidermy; small business management.

Suggested High School Courses

Art; biology; business/applied math; chemistry; distributive education. **Dept. of Education School-to-Work Cluster:** Arts, A/V Technology, and Communication.

Essential Knowledge and Skills

No data available. **Values/Work Environment:** No data available.

Other Information Sources

Many career and education information sources use the standard cross-referencing systems noted below. You can use the codes to obtain substantial additional information on the program (via CIP code) and related occupations (via GOE code). The O*NET codes on the opposite page refer to another major career information system. See the Introduction for details on obtaining additional information.

Classification of Instructional Programs (CIP) code(s): 010508 Taxidermy/Taxidermist

Guide for Occupational Exploration (GOE) code(s): 01.06 Craft Arts

Teacher Aide Training

Program/Training Duration: One month to two years

Location: Workplace and/or college classroom

Career Snapshot

Teacher aides, also known as paraeducators, assist teachers with instructional tasks. Sometimes they may help with non-instructional tasks, such as monitoring the cafeteria. They may do clerical tasks such as grading tests or may help provide individualized instruction for students. Most teacher aides are trained on the job (perhaps in an apprenticeship program), but some are graduates of two-year or certificate programs. The legislative trend is toward requiring teacher aides to pass a licensing exam. The overall job outlook is expected to be good, especially in fast-growing parts of the country. Ability to speak a foreign language is very helpful.

Related Specialties and Careers

Bilingual teacher aide, computer lab assistant, special education assistant.

Related Job Titles, Educational Requirements, Projected Growth, and Earnings			
Job Title	Educational Requirements	Projected Growth	Average Earnings
Teacher Assistants (O*NET code 25-9041.00)	Short-term on-the-job training	Faster than average	$18,070

Typical Postsecondary Courses

Child guidance; curriculum planning; educational alternatives for exceptional students; educational psychology; field experience/internship; history and philosophy of education; human growth and development; introduction to psychology; preschool administration.

Suggested High School Courses

Algebra; English; history; public speaking; science; social science. **Dept. of Education School-to-Work Cluster:** Education and Training.

Essential Knowledge and Skills

Active listening; education and training; English language; learning strategies; speaking. **Values/Work Environment:** Co-workers; indoors, environmentally controlled; social service.

Other Information Sources

Many career and education information sources use the standard cross-referencing systems noted below. You can use the codes to obtain substantial additional information on the program (via CIP code) and related occupations (via GOE code). The O*NET codes on the opposite page refer to another major career information system. See the Introduction for details on obtaining additional information.

Classification of Instructional Programs (CIP) code(s): 131501 Teacher Assistant/Aide

Guide for Occupational Exploration (GOE) code(s): 12.03 Educational Services

---

 Tool and Die Maker Training

Program/Training Duration: More than one year

Location: Workplace

Career Snapshot

Precise metal components are needed in manufacturing processes, such as dies that stamp out metal parts, molds that shape plastics and other substances, and fixtures that hold components while they are being drilled or stamped. Tool and die makers are trained to machine these parts, and they generally learn their skills in formal apprenticeships, sometimes after working as machinists or in other machine shop jobs. Although the number of jobs is not expanding, employment opportunities are expected to be excellent.

Related Specialties and Careers

CNC programming, diemaking, moldmaking, toolmaking.

Related Job Titles, Educational Requirements, Projected Growth, and Earnings			
Job Title	Educational Requirements	Projected Growth	Average Earnings
Tool and Die Makers (O*NET code 51-4111.00)	Long-term on-the-job training	Little or none	$41,620

Typical Postsecondary Courses

Blueprint reading; CNC programming and planning; cutting tools; die design; jigs and fixtures; machine technology; materials and metallurgy for machine trades; mathematics for machine trades; metrology; tool and die theory; tool design.

Suggested High School Courses

Algebra; computer science; geometry; industrial arts; mechanical drawing; metal shop; physics/principles of technology; trigonometry. **Dept. of Education School-to-Work Cluster:** Manufacturing.

Essential Knowledge and Skills

Building and construction; equipment selection; mechanical devices; operation and control; production and processing; repairing. **Values/Work Environment:** Exposed to hazardous equipment; indoors, environmentally controlled; moral values.

Other Information Sources

Many career and education information sources use the standard cross-referencing systems noted below. You can use the codes to obtain substantial additional information on the program (via CIP code) and related occupations (via GOE code). The O*NET codes on the opposite page refer to another major career information system. See the Introduction for details on obtaining additional information.

Classification of Instructional Programs (CIP) code(s): 480507 Tool and Die Technology/Technician

Guide for Occupational Exploration (GOE) code(s): 08.04 Metal and Plastics Machining Technology

Travel Services Marketing Operations

Program/Training Duration: One month to a year or more

Location: Workplace or vocational classroom

Career Snapshot

Much of the routine work of travel agents—researching schedules and fares, issuing tickets—is now being done by Internet sites. This is expected to limit the growth of this occupation, and it also means that the best opportunities will be for workers who enjoy providing personalized attention or who are good at selling to groups. Because of increased competition for jobs and the impact of technology, formal academic training is becoming more important for job entry. Many vocational schools, night schools, and community colleges offer specialized travel agent training.

Related Specialties and Careers

Airline reservations, corporate travel, cruise line reservations, leisure travel, tour companies.

Related Job Titles, Educational Requirements, Projected Growth, and Earnings			
Job Title	Educational Requirements	Projected Growth	Average Earnings
Reservation and Transportation Ticket Agents (O*NET code 43-4181.02)	Short-term on-the-job training	Average	$24,090
Reservation and Transportation Ticket Agents and Travel Clerks (O*NET code 43-4181.00)	Short-term on-the-job training	Average	$24,090
Travel Agents (O*NET code 41-3041.00)	Postsecondary vocational training	Little or none	$25,580
Travel Clerks (O*NET code 43-4181.01)	Short-term on-the-job training	Average	$24,090

Typical Postsecondary Courses

Air reservations; car rental and hotel accommodations; computer reservation systems; customer service relations; touristic geography; travel sales and marketing.

Suggested High School Courses

Applied communications; bookkeeping; business/applied math; distributive education; foreign language; geography; keyboarding; office computer applications; public speaking; social science. **Dept. of Education School-to-Work Cluster:** Hospitality and Tourism.

Essential Knowledge and Skills

Customer and personal service; geography; service orientation; transportation. **Values/Work Environment:** Indoors, environmentally controlled; spend time sitting; good working conditions.

Other Information Sources

Many career and education information sources use the standard cross-referencing systems noted below. You can use the codes to obtain substantial additional information on the program (via CIP code) and related occupations (via GOE code). The O*NET codes on the opposite page refer to another major career information system. See the Introduction for details on obtaining additional information.

Classification of Instructional Programs (CIP) code(s): 521905 Tourism and Travel Services Marketing Operations

Guide for Occupational Exploration (GOE) code(s): 09.05 Customer Service; 10.03 General Sales; 11.03 Transportation and Lodging Services

---

Truck, Bus, and Other Commercial Vehicle Driving

Program/Training Duration: One month to a year or more
Location: Workplace

Career Snapshot

Many truck drivers, especially of smaller trucks, learn on the job or through working as a driver's helper. Others get training in the military. Driving tractor-trailers requires considerably more skill and often is learned through specialized schools; before enrolling in such a school, you should make sure that local employers approve of the curriculum. Bus drivers who work for intercity carriers or local transportation agencies often get a few weeks of training from their employer, partly in the classroom and partly behind the wheel. Rail vehicle operators are trained in similar programs. Truck and bus drivers need a commercial driver's license, must have a clean driving record, must meet certain physical requirements, and must pass drug testing. The employment outlook is expected to be good for both truck and bus drivers. Truck drivers can expect a lot of competition for the more desirable jobs, however, and opportunities are sensitive to the state of the economy. Bus drivers may experience seasonal ups and downs. Rail vehicle operators can expect keen competition for a limited number of jobs.

Related Specialties and Careers

Bus driver, light truck driver, tractor-trailer driver.

Related Job Titles, Educational Requirements, Projected Growth, and Earnings			
Job Title	**Educational Requirements**	**Projected Growth**	**Average Earnings**
Bus Drivers, School (O*NET code 53-3022.00)	Short-term on-the-job training	Average	$21,990
Bus Drivers, Transit and Intercity (O*NET code 53-3021.00)	Moderate-term on-the-job training	Average	$28,060
Rail Transportation Workers, All Other (O*NET code 53-4099.99)	No data available	Declining	No salary data available
Rail Yard Engineers, Dinkey Operators, and Hostlers (O*NET code 53-4013.00)	Work experience in a related occupation	Declining	$38,110
Railroad Brake, Signal, and Switch Operators (O*NET code 53-4021.00)	Moderate-term on-the-job training	Declining	$44,920

Job Title	Educational Requirements	Projected Growth	Average Earnings
Railroad Conductors and Yardmasters (O*NET code 53-4031.00)	Work experience in a related occupation	Declining	$42,840
Railroad Yard Workers (O*NET code 53-4021.02)	Work experience in a related occupation	Declining	$44,920
Subway and Streetcar Operators (O*NET code 53-4041.00)	Moderate-term on-the-job training	Declining	No salary data available
Taxi Drivers and Chauffeurs (O*NET code 53-3041.00)	Short-term on-the-job training	Faster than average	$17,920
Tractor-Trailer Truck Drivers (O*NET code 53-3032.02)	Moderate-term on-the-job training	Average	$32,580
Train Crew Members (O*NET code 53-4021.01)	Work experience in a related occupation	Declining	$44,920
Truck Drivers, Heavy (O*NET code 53-3032.01)	Short-term on-the-job training	Average	$32,580

Typical Postsecondary Courses

Backing and shifting techniques; coupling and uncoupling; defensive driving; preventive maintenance and servicing; regulations on trucks and buses; trip planning and map reading; troubleshooting and emergency repairs; vehicle systems.

Suggested High School Courses

Applied communications; auto shop; business/applied math; driver education. **Dept. of Education School-to-Work Cluster:** Transportation, Distribution, and Logistics.

Essential Knowledge and Skills

Operation and control; transportation. **Values/Work Environment:** Outdoors, exposed to weather; supervision, human relations.

Other Information Sources

Many career and education information sources use the standard cross-referencing systems noted below. You can use the codes to obtain substantial additional information on the program (via CIP code) and related occupations (via GOE code). The O*NET codes on the opposite page refer to another major career information system. See the Introduction for details on obtaining additional information.

Classification of Instructional Programs (CIP) code(s): 490205 Truck and Bus Driver/Commercial Vehicle Operation

Guide for Occupational Exploration (GOE) code(s): 07.01 Managerial Work in Transportation; 07.02 Vehicle Expediting and Coordinating; 07.05 Truck Driving; 07.06 Rail Vehicle Operation; 07.07 Other Services Requiring Driving; 07.08 Support Work

---

Veterinary Technology

Program/Training Duration: Two years

Location: College classroom

Career Snapshot

Veterinary technicians do for veterinarians the tasks that nurses, anesthesiologists, laboratory technicians, and radiographers do for physicians. They get their training in associate degree programs that include clinical experience. (Four-year degrees in veterinary technology are also available.) States vary on licensing, registration, and certification requirements; an exam is often required, as is graduation from an approved program. Job prospects are expected to be excellent, with many more openings than qualified applicants.

Related Specialties and Careers

Large animals, small animals, veterinary nurse, veterinary radiographer, veterinary surgical assistant.

Related Job Titles, Educational Requirements, Projected Growth, and Earnings			
Job Title	Educational Requirements	Projected Growth	Average Earnings
Veterinary Assistants and Laboratory Animal Caretakers (O*NET code 31-9096.00)	Short-term on-the-job training	Much faster than average	$17,470
Veterinary Technologists and Technicians (O*NET code 29-2056.00)	Associate degree	Much faster than average	$22,430

Typical Postsecondary Courses

Animal anatomy and physiology; animal care experience; English composition; general chemistry; introduction to computer applications; introduction to speech communication; parasitology; pharmacology for veterinary technicians; veterinary anesthesiology; veterinary microbiology; veterinary nursing procedures; veterinary pathology; veterinary radiology.

Suggested High School Courses

Algebra; biology; chemistry; English; geometry; office computer applications; public speaking. **Dept. of Education School-to-Work Cluster:** Health Science.

Essential Knowledge and Skills

Biology; medicine and dentistry; reading comprehension; therapy and counseling. **Values/Work Environment:** Indoors, environmentally controlled; moral values.

Other Information Sources

Many career and education information sources use the standard cross-referencing systems noted below. You can use the codes to obtain substantial additional information on the program (via CIP code) and related occupations (via GOE code). The O*NET codes on the opposite page refer to another major career information system. See the Introduction for details on obtaining additional information.

Classification of Instructional Programs (CIP) code(s): 510808 Veterinary/Animal Health Technology/Technician and Veterinary Assistant

Guide for Occupational Exploration (GOE) code(s): 03.02 Animal Care and Training; 12.03 Educational Services

---

Watchmaking and Jewelrymaking

Program/Training Duration: A few weeks to more than a year

Location: Vocational classroom or workplace

Career Snapshot

Because inexpensive timepieces are easier to replace than repair, watch and clock repairers work almost exclusively on expensive timepieces, especially antiques and other timepieces with old-fashioned mechanical innards. Some worn parts cannot be replaced with off-the-shelf components and must be machined to order. Jewelry repairers also do fine work with metals, and because both jewelry repair and watch repair are often done in jewelry stores, there is some overlap between the training for the two specializations, especially when the training is acquired on the job. Formal training programs offered by specialized schools tend to focus more exclusively on either timepieces or jewelry. Employment opportunities are expected to be good because a large proportion of the workers in this field are approaching retirement age.

Related Specialties and Careers

Clock repair, jewelry fabrication, jewelry repair, watch repair.

Related Job Titles, Educational Requirements, Projected Growth, and Earnings			
Job Title	Educational Requirements	Projected Growth	Average Earnings
Bench Workers, Jewelry (O*NET code 51-9071.04)	Long-term on-the-job training	Little or none	$27,210
Gem and Diamond Workers (O*NET code 51-9071.06)	Moderate-term on-the-job training	Little or none	$27,210
Jewelers (O*NET code 51-9071.01)	Postsecondary vocational training	Little or none	$27,210
Jewelers and Precious Stone and Metal Workers (O*NET code 51-9071.00)	Long-term on-the-job training	Little or none	$27,210
Model and Mold Makers, Jewelry (O*NET code 51-9071.03)	Long-term on-the-job training	Little or none	$27,210

Job Title	Educational Requirements	Projected Growth	Average Earnings
Pewter Casters and Finishers (O*NET code 51-9071.05)	Postsecondary vocational training	Little or none	$27,210
Silversmiths (O*NET code 51-9071.02)	Long-term on-the-job training	Little or none	$27,210
Timing Device Assemblers, Adjusters, and Calibrators (O*NET code 51-2093.00)	Moderate-term on-the-job training	Little or none	$23,550
Watch Repairers (O*NET code 49-9064.00)	Long-term on-the-job training	Little or none	$25,930

Typical Postsecondary Courses

Antique and European clock repair; battery watches; chime clock repair; escapements; gem identification; hairsprings; horological lathes; introduction to clock repair; introduction to watch repair; jewelry appraisal; jewelry casting; jewelry design and rendering; jewelry repair/fabrication; jewelry techniques; making watch and clock parts; repair problems; stonesetting.

Suggested High School Courses

Algebra; art; industrial arts; metal shop; physics/principles of technology. **Dept. of Education School-to-Work Cluster:** Manufacturing or Retail and Wholesale Sales and Service.

Essential Knowledge and Skills

Equipment selection; mechanical devices. **Values/Work Environment:** Independence; indoors, environmentally controlled.

Other Information Sources

Many career and education information sources use the standard cross-referencing systems noted below. You can use the codes to obtain substantial additional information on the program (via CIP code) and related occupations (via GOE code). The O*NET codes on the opposite page refer to another major career information system. See the Introduction for details on obtaining additional information.

Classification of Instructional Programs (CIP) code(s): 470408 Watchmaking and Jewelrymaking

Guide for Occupational Exploration (GOE) code(s): 05.03 Mechanical Work; 08.02 Production Technology

Water/Wastewater Treatment Technology

Program/Training Duration: One to two years

Location: Workplace or college/vocational classroom

Career Snapshot

Water/wastewater treatment plant operators work for municipalities or for large commercial or industrial facilities that maintain their own supplies of water and treat their own wastewater output. As the technology of pollution control gets more complex, employers are looking increasingly for graduates of one-year certificate programs or two-year associate degree programs. Certification is often required by law, and job applicants may also need to take a civil service exam. Job opportunities are expected to be good. This field is one of the few in which a person without a four-year degree can work each day to help the natural environment.

Related Specialties and Careers

Wastewater treatment plant operations, water distribution operations, water treatment plant operations.

Related Job Titles, Educational Requirements, Projected Growth, and Earnings			
Job Title	Educational Requirements	Projected Growth	Average Earnings
Water and Liquid Waste Treatment Plant and System Operators (O*NET code 51-8031.00)	Long-term on-the-job training	Average	$32,560

Typical Postsecondary Courses

Environmental regulations; wastewater collection systems; wastewater treatment plant operations; water distribution systems; water hydraulics; water treatment plant operations; workplace communications; workplace math.

Suggested High School Courses

Applied communications; biology; business/applied math; chemistry. **Dept. of Education School-to-Work Cluster:** Agriculture/Natural Resources.

Essential Knowledge and Skills

Chemistry; mechanical devices; operation and control; operation monitoring; production and processing; science. **Values/Work Environment:** Exposed to contaminants; moral values.

Other Information Sources

Many career and education information sources use the standard cross-referencing systems noted below. You can use the codes to obtain substantial additional information on the program (via CIP code) and related occupations (via GOE code). The O*NET codes on the opposite page refer to another major career information system. See the Introduction for details on obtaining additional information.

Classification of Instructional Programs (CIP) code(s): 150506 Water Quality and Wastewater Treatment Management and Recycling Technology/Technician

Guide for Occupational Exploration (GOE) code(s): 08.06 Systems Operation

Welding Technology

Program/Training Duration: One month to more than a year

Location: Workplace or vocational classroom

Career Snapshot

Welders may be trained on the job, in the military, or in formal training programs at vocational-technical schools, community and technical colleges, and specialized welding schools. Some welders get certification for their ability to perform specific welding tasks according to industry standards. Although robot welders are replacing certain low-skill jobs, technology is creating many job opportunities for welders with up-to-date skills, so the overall outlook is very good.

Related Specialties and Careers

Arc welding, brazing, flamecutting, MIG/TIG welding, underwater welding.

Related Job Titles, Educational Requirements, Projected Growth, and Earnings			
Job Title	**Educational Requirements**	**Projected Growth**	**Average Earnings**
Brazers (O*NET code 51-4121.05)	Short-term on-the-job training	Average	$28,490
Solderers (O*NET code 51-4121.04)	Short-term on-the-job training	Average	$28,490
Soldering and Brazing Machine Operators and Tenders (O*NET code 51-4122.04)	Short-term on-the-job training	Average	$28,220
Soldering and Brazing Machine Setters and Set-Up Operators (O*NET code 51-4122.03)	Moderate-term on-the-job training	Average	$28,220
Welder-Fitters (O*NET code 51-4121.03)	Long-term on-the-job training	Average	$28,490
Welders and Cutters (O*NET code 51-4121.02)	Long-term on-the-job training	Average	$28,490
Welders, Cutters, Solderers, and Brazers (O*NET code 51-4121.00)	Long-term on-the-job training	Average	$28,490

Job Title	Educational Requirements	Projected Growth	Average Earnings
Welders, Production (O*NET code 51-4121.01)	Short-term on-the-job training	Average	$28,490
Welding Machine Operators and Tenders (O*NET code 51-4122.02)	Moderate-term on-the-job training	Average	$28,220
Welding Machine Setters and Set-Up Operators (O*NET code 51-4122.01)	Postsecondary vocational training	Average	$28,220
Welding, Soldering, and Brazing Machine Setters, Operators, and Tenders (O*NET code 51-4122.00)	Moderate-term on-the-job training	Average	$28,220

Typical Postsecondary Courses

Basic arc welding; blueprint reading; flux core arc welding; gas metal arc welding; gas tungsten arc welding; layout and fabrication techniques; metallurgy fundamentals; pipe welding; shop safety; workplace communications; workplace math.

Suggested High School Courses

Algebra; drafting; geometry; industrial arts; mechanical drawing; metal shop; physics/principles of technology. **Dept. of Education School-to-Work Cluster:** Manufacturing.

Essential Knowledge and Skills

Building and construction; mechanical devices; operation and control; production and processing. **Values/Work Environment:** Indoors, environmentally controlled; moral values.

Other Information Sources

Many career and education information sources use the standard cross-referencing systems noted below. You can use the codes to obtain substantial additional information on the program (via CIP code) and related occupations (via GOE code). The O*NET codes on the opposite page refer to another major career information system. See the Introduction for details on obtaining additional information.

Classification of Instructional Programs (CIP) code(s): 480508 Welding Technology/Welder

Guide for Occupational Exploration (GOE) code(s): 08.02 Production Technology; 08.03 Production Work

---

 **Winemaking**

Program/Training Duration: At least one year

Location: College/vocational classroom and workplace

Career Snapshot

Wine production is increasing and spreading to new places. People who oversee winemaking usually get specialized training at a university in California or at a wine school in Europe or Australia. It is helpful for them to have prior coursework in chemistry, biology, and business. After they complete their formal schooling, they usually acquire additional skills by working as an assistant, sometimes in a foreign wine region.

Related Specialties and Careers

Cellar management, cooperage, distribution, fermentation, import/export, quality control, sales.

Related Job Titles, Educational Requirements, Projected Growth, and Earnings			
Job Title	**Educational Requirements**	**Projected Growth**	**Average Earnings**
Food and Tobacco Roasting, Baking, and Drying Machine Operators and Tenders (O*NET code 51-3091.00)	Short-term on-the-job training	Declining	$23,210
Food Batchmakers (O*NET code 51-3092.00)	Short-term on-the-job training	Little or none	$21,690
Food Cooking Machine Operators and Tenders (O*NET code 51-3093.00)	Short-term on-the-job training	Little or none	$21,420
Mixing and Blending Machine Setters, Operators, and Tenders (O*NET code 51-9023.00)	Moderate-term on-the-job training	Little or none	$26,860

Typical Postsecondary Courses

College algebra; general chemistry; introduction to computer science; introduction to viticulture; sensory evaluation of wine; wine analysis; wine chemistry; wine microbiology; wine production; winery operations; wines of the world.

Suggested High School Courses

Algebra; biology; chemistry; computer science; French; geography; geometry; trigonometry. **Dept. of Education School-to-Work Cluster:** Agriculture/Natural Resources; Manufacturing.

Essential Knowledge and Skills

Operation and control; production and processing. **Values/Work Environment:** Indoors, environmentally controlled; moral values; spend time making repetitive motions; spend time standing.

Other Information Sources

Many career and education information sources use the standard cross-referencing systems noted below. You can use the codes to obtain substantial additional information on the program (via CIP code) and related occupations (via GOE code). The O*NET codes on the opposite page refer to another major career information system. See the Introduction for details on obtaining additional information.

Classification of Instructional Programs (CIP) code(s): 010401 Agricultural and Food Products Processing

Guide for Occupational Exploration (GOE) code(s): 08.03 Production Work; 12.03 Educational Services

Index

Interest Areas Index

Job Titles Index

A

B

C

D

Related Specialties and Careers Index

Skills Index

Work Groups Index